THIS TEAM IS
RUINING
MY LIFE

(BUT I LOVE THEM)

THIS TEAM IS
RUINING
MY LIFE

(BUT I LOVE THEM)

HOW I BECAME A
PROFESSIONAL HOCKEY FAN

STEVE "DANGLE" GLYNN

FOREWORD BY JEFF MAREK

Copyright © Steve Glynn, 2019

Published by ECW Press
665 Gerrard Street East
Toronto, Ontario, Canada M4M 1Y2
416-694-3348 / info@ecwpress.com

Editor for the Press: Michael Holmes
Cover design: Troy Cunningham
Cover photo: © Jen Squires /
www.jensquiresphotographer.com

To the best of his abilities, the author has
related experiences, places, people, and
organizations from his memories of them.

LIBRARY AND ARCHIVES CANADA
CATALOGUING IN PUBLICATION

Glynn, Steve, author
    This team is ruining my life (but I love
them) : how I became a professional
hockey fan / Steve "Dangle" Glynn.

Issued in print and electronic formats.
ISBN 978-1-77041-444-0 (softcover)
ISBN 978-1-77305-306-6 (PDF)
ISBN 978-1-77305-305-9 (EPUB)

1. Glynn, Steve. 2. Bloggers—
Canada—Biography. 3. Sportscasters—
Canada—Biography. 4. Sportswriters—
Canada—Biography. 5. Hockey
fans—Canada—Biography. I. Title.

GV742.42.G59A3 2019   070.4'49796962092
C2018-905291-0   C2018-905292-9

The publication of *This Team Is Ruining My Life (But I Love Them)* is funded in part by the Government
of Canada. *Ce livre est financé en partie par le gouvernement du Canada*. We acknowledge the contribution
of the Government of Ontario through the Ontario Book Publishing Tax Credit, and through Ontario
Creates for the marketing of this book.

PRINTED AND BOUND IN CANADA   PRINTING: FRIESENS   5   4   3   2   1

MIX
Paper from
responsible sources
FSC® C016245

For my grandparents, Ernest, Joy, Raffaele, and Rocchina,
for your sacrifice and being the foundation of our family.

For my parents, Tina and Gary, and my sister, Rachel.
Thank you for reading to me, and sorry for all the yelling.
Hockey was on.

For my wife, Sarah-Louise, my favourite person.
Thank you — for everything.

John Tavares is a Leaf.

CONTENTS

FOREWORD BY JEFF MAREK

It's November 20, 2018, and I'm sitting in the Lotus room at the Sportsnet hockey studios, on the 10th floor of the CBC building in downtown Toronto. This is where we watch games while we work and throw it around about hockey: the rumours, the gossip, who's getting traded or punted — all of it grist for the mill in the Lotus. But best of all, this is where we share stories — most not suitable for broadcast.

Everybody has either a story or, at the very least, a thought about Dangle. It's impossible to hear his name and just shrug. When people ask me about Steve, the conversation usually goes something like this: *Steve Dangle? Yeah, I know him. He's a nice bunch of guys.*

Tonight, I'm working with NHLer turned beloved hockey analyst Colby Armstrong. He remembers Dangle from his playing days with the Toronto Maple Leafs.

I first saw him on one of his now-famous LFRs (I don't even know that that means) when I was playing with the Leafs. I loved to surf the net, especially YouTube. I'd go down massive rabbit holes, and one night I came across this video.

Why not give it a click?

This kid popped up in his decked-out Leafs bedroom, going absolutely bananas over how embarrassing it was that we got beat by Nashville. I was laying on the couch, watching this kid as he just ripped us apart, losing it Leafs super-fan style.

I yelled to my wife, "Hey, you gotta check out this Leafs fan," as I was dying laughing. "This guy's an animal."

When I got past how crazy and hardcore of a Leafs fan he was, I was actually pretty amazed at the style of video. I had never seen a style like that before. It was so good. I learned later it's called jump cuts. I wasn't even mad he was destroying us; I was impressed at how good the video was.

But when I first met him, he was quieter than I thought he'd be — maybe I was expecting the guy from the video. Now I work with Steve at Sportsnet. How funny is that?

Like many of you, I first "met" Steve on YouTube; although, "saw" is a better way to put it. Actually, to say I first "experienced" Steve on YouTube might be even better. It was 2008, and one of his videos was linked on Greg Wyshynski's highly popular and influential *Puck Daddy* blog on Yahoo Sports. I hadn't seen anything like it before.

Part of me was stunned.

What is this?

And who is this guy?

Steve is a fan talking — and at times screaming — to himself and his alter ego, Hat Guy, call and response style. But these are more than just fan videos, and Steve is more than just a fan.

These are open letters to hockey fans about how Steve feels about his team. Part of it even seems like therapy. Steve is the fan who has to get it all out.

I love it.

There's a rule in our industry: no cheering in the press box. But there's no rule about cheering on from your bedroom. Steve was, and still is, the epitome of the "fan journalist." To many people in the broadcast and print world, those two words form a dichotomy, but in the new era of media currency, it's become more and more accepted and commonplace. It represents a refreshing change in many ways: being honest about your bias.

More than anyone else, I point to Steve when I talk to young people who want to break into hockey media. His is the way you do it.

When I started at the Fan 590 in 1995, the only way to get in was to catch a break. Somebody had to hire you and, generally, you had to go to small-town Canada to learn how to work in broadcasting. Maybe you came back, but you probably didn't. This industry gives you a reason and opportunity to quit just about every day. But today, you don't need to wait for someone to wave a magic wand over your head and hire you. You can just do it yourself. That's what Steve did.

Sure, he had some internships and caught some breaks along the way, but Steve got in because he used everything around him. Every bit of technology and every marketing platform — he was on it, and he stayed on it, consistently cranking out videos and keeping his name in the mix. Steve was consistent. He started and never stopped.

Want to be a broadcaster? Start a podcast, start making videos, write a blog. This has been my message to people looking for a way in. Build a body of work, and they will find you. They found Steve.

Steve tapped on the hockey world's shoulder for years, and when it turned around, he knew what to say.

Jeff Marek, 2018

MY FIRST SCAR

Do you have hockey scars? I have only one, though I don't recall getting it.

I was about three and playing ball hockey in the driveway with the neighbour kids. As my mom remembers it, I ran inside crying and bleeding from the corner of my left eye. The game must have gotten crazy, or maybe it was just because I was a motor-mouthed hyperactive kid who hadn't developed proper balancing skills yet: I had apparently ran into the brick corner of our garage.

My mom patched me up, the tears soon stopped, and I started to run back outside.

"Where are you going?" my mom asked.

I yelled back, "I gotta finish the game!"

It's what Don Cherry would call a "Good Ol' Canadian Boy" moment — but sadly, I don't have one that relates to actual ice.

Why?

I never played the game.

Although I did fantasize about scoring the Stanley Cup–winning goal (and I still do), it never *really* bothered me that I didn't play "real" hockey because deep down, I knew I wasn't destined to be a star athlete. I wanted something different.

In *Anchorman*, there's a scene where Ron Burgundy comes on the TV at a bar, and a biker shouts, "Hey, everybody! Shut

1

the hell up! Ron Burgundy's on!" That is exactly the way Don Cherry and Ron MacLean were treated at my house during my childhood. I remember watching "Coach's Corner" as a kid — whether it was with my parents, aunts, uncles, and other family members, the reaction was the same.

Ron and Don would appear on the TV during the first intermission and yell and scream at each other. There's no way I understood what the hell they were talking about; what I was paying attention to, even at the age of four or five, was how the adults reacted.

From one rant to another, my family would go from laughing *at* Ron and Don to laughing *with* them. That was fascinating to me. Every Saturday, Ron and Don had the attention of millions around the country. More importantly from my little perspective, they had the attention of every adult in my house. As a kid, all you want is for adults to pay attention to you and take you seriously. So to me, that was just as incredible as any Doug Gilmour goal, any Wendel Clark hit, or any Felix Potvin flashy glove save.

Fast forward about a quarter of a century to spring 2017, and I'm sitting in a restaurant in Whitby, Ontario, with three friends. I look up and Ron and Don are talking about Jarome Iginla on "Coach's Corner." At least that's what I assumed they were talking about because the sound was off.

A few minutes later, I looked down at my phone. I had text messages from 17 different people, missed calls, voicemails, and a bunch of notifications.

I'm not even kidding when I say my first thought was that somebody had died.

"OMG CALL ME RIGHT NOW!" my wife messaged me. About a dozen messages from others were some variation of "HOLY SHIT!!!"

Ron MacLean had said my name on "Coach's Corner" live on *Hockey Night in Canada*. Apparently, he had seen a video that I had made for Sportsnet about how Jarome Iginla should have been named one of the NHL's top 100 players of all time.

"We've never met Steve Dangle, but he said he should have been one of the 100," Ron said.

"Who?" Don interrupted.

"Steve Dangle. He's on *Hockey Central* every weeknight," Ron explained.

Don then went off about how ludicrous it was that Evgeni Malkin wasn't one of the top 100 either, but I had got what I needed.

So how the hell did it happen?

Whether you're a fan of mine, you can't stand me, or you have no idea who the hell I am, I want to give you my sincerest thanks for picking up this book. Time is precious and every single day there are new ways for us to spend it. The fact that you would choose to spend some time reading this book or listening to my manic hockey rants is truly an honour.

I love reading books or hearing stories from hockey broad-casters about how they got to where they are. Most of them, however, tend to be older — in their 50s, 60s, 70s — and are accomplished individuals who have led interesting lives.

While I don't have the profile of those guys, and I haven't been on national television for three decades, and, in fact, I only started writing this book at the ripe age of 29, just three short years after moving out of my parents' house, I'm in the thick of it right now, trying to establish myself in sports media — an industry that appears to be shrinking by the day.

If you are looking to pursue a career in sports, broadcast-ing, or anything else for that matter, my hope is that you will find the stories of me desperately trying over and over again to get my foot in the sports broadcasting door relatable and proof that you should never give up. I'll also tell you all of the dumb mistakes I've made while trying to stick said foot in said door. Hopefully you'll read about my silly mistakes and learn from them. If nothing else, hopefully you'll laugh.

And if you're not looking to work in sports media, I hope this gives you an idea of what people are going through right now as they try to establish their own career and identity. You may even relate to many of the stories in this book; even though industries and technology change, humans are still just human . . .

Some of us just yell louder than others.

THE JUMP TO NORTH AMERICA

My family's story begins outside of Canada, which makes it extremely Canadian.

More than 100 years ago, my great-grandfather on my dad's side was an orphan in England. Because we don't know who his parents were, there's a natural mystery about his origin. The rumour within the family is that he's a royal bastard — not a bad-guy bastard, a literal bastard. It goes like this: King Edward VII had a child with a chambermaid and that child is my great-grandfather. Look, I'm just relaying the story my family told me, OK?

Obviously we couldn't prove that. Photos of my grandpa as a young man look quite a bit like King George V's son, King George VI, but that's hardly evidence.

However, my great-grandfather did attend an expensive naval academy, despite growing up in an orphanage. Who paid for that? I was even able to find a record of him on a naval ship in 1911. At 18 years old, he was the youngest member of the crew.

But it doesn't really matter who his parents were. He made a life for himself, married my great-grandmother, and started a family that included my grandpa. That's all that matters.

My grandmother on my dad's side has an interesting story, too. Her family lived on the island of Guernsey. While technically one of the British Channel Islands, it's actually right off

5

the coast of France. In fact, most of the streets have French names. Before she began losing her memory, my grandma also recounted that her family had Norwegian ancestry and potentially a bit of Irish, but she wasn't sure.

Her family had money. My aunt said she heard someone in the family line had invented something to do with milk cartons. My grandmother's father owned a hotel in Guernsey called The Swan. The problem with him, however, was that he was a royal bastard in the bad-guy sense. He was a playboy and a gambler. By the time my grandmother was a young child, her father had racked up such terrible gambling debt that he was left with two options: send his children, including my grandmother, to a workhouse or sell off the hotels. His wife, my great-grandmother, refused to let her children be sent away, so bye-bye, hotel.

He abandoned his family, never to be seen again.

From a very young age, my grandmother proved she was not to be messed with. She was at school one day with a painful ear infection. For some reason, one of her teachers grabbed her harshly by the ear. My grandma hauled off and headbutted this lady right in her chest, like she was Zinedine Zidane at the World Cup.

While some of my distant family was in Guernsey as the Germans occupied the Channel Islands during the Second World War, my great-grandmother had brought her children to mainland England years before. There is a story of my grandmother, in her mid-teens, running around with two large pails of water during the Blitz to help put out countless fires from the bombings. The next day, with her adrenaline gone, she couldn't lift them at all.

My grandpa, proving to be no chicken himself, enlisted in the navy one day in 1942, when he was just 17. In case you're not the biggest history buff, that's smack dab in the middle of the Second World War. Think about what you were doing at 17.

"How old are you?" the man at the office asked.

"Eighteen," my grandpa lied.

"Right, sure you are," said the man, continuing to fill out the paperwork.

Soon after, my grandpa was on a Royal Navy ship bound for the southwest coast of Italy. He was a signalman, first class.

On my grandpa's ship's approach to the beaches of Salerno, it was hit by a depth charge, an anti-ship missile. He was wounded in the back during the attack.

Once he managed to swim and drag himself to shore, Grandpa was rescued by American troops who had already reached the beach.

"We got a limey," the Americans told their medics as they brought my grandpa in to get looked at.

In the shock of the moment, my grandpa thought they said they were going to cut his leg off. He started fighting them as hard as he could. When they managed to wrestle him to the table, they told him they were only going to cut his pants off.

"Oh, OK." I've always loved the way my grandpa tells that story.

To this day, over three-quarters of a century later, my grandpa still has a chunk of metal about the size of a loonie stuck in his back, less than an inch away from his spine. They never removed it because they were too worried about potentially paralyzing him. Decades later, it was the cause of a few awkward conversations at airport security.

After my grandpa was fully healed, he was told to report to Scotland for training for a secret mission. That mission ended up being D-Day, which I'm proud to say my grandpa participated in.

After the war, my grandparents married and decided to move to Canada to live in Scarborough, a suburb just outside of Toronto.

My grandma, a brilliant woman fluent in French, German, and Flemish, worked in communications throughout mainland Europe during the war. She found a job doing similar work for

Bell Canada. My grandpa found a government job with the province. One of the jobs he had was as a television repairman.

Together, they had three children: my dad was born first, followed by my two aunts.

Then there's the Italian side of my family.

My nonni both came from a small Italian town called Monteleone, in the province of Foggia, in the Puglia region. If you can't be bothered to google it, it's right around the Achilles tendon of the boot.

They both came from generations of farmers. My mom's parents were just young children during the Second World War, but my nonna's mom and several other family members were arrested during a riot in 1942.

As the story goes, all the men were off at war. Meanwhile, the women of Monteleone were at home, angry and starving. One day, several women were arrested when they tried to stop an officer who was confiscating a pot of their corn flour. The women were thrown into a warehouse where they discovered large rations of food. The fascist-appointed politicians in charge had been hoarding the food.

The three women set fire to the warehouse and broke free. When the townsfolk, my family included, discovered what happened, they formed an angry mob outside of the Carabinieri's office, armed with clubs and pitchforks. About 180 people were arrested or detained that day.

Years later, with the war over and my nonna and nonno in their late teens, they made their way to a place where a large number of the town's population had immigrated: Toronto. It's not an uncommon story: my grandparents left with very little money but a strong family and community connection in town.

My nonno worked as a machinist for Canada Bread. A job like that comes with perks, like fresh bread for your family each day. My nonna worked as a seamstress in Toronto's garment district on Spadina Avenue. It was piece work, meaning she basically had to fight off her own coworkers for pieces of fabric to sew.

Before my nonno died of cancer when my mom was just 12 years old, my nonni had four children: my three uncles and their little sister, my mom.

My mom's oldest brother, my godfather Lenny, was the athlete of the year at his high school and captain of the wrestling team. The second oldest brother, Rocky, allegedly fought off five guys at once as a teenager. The third brother, Dom, has about half a foot on both of them, and his muscles got him into the *Toronto Sun* as the Sunshine Boy many years ago. (I'd say that he'd be embarrassed that I put this tidbit in a book, but he's had the picture proudly displayed in his house for as long as I can remember.)

When that same uncle was younger, he used to make a backyard ice rink by flooding the tomato garden in the winter. And in the spring, when he left his hockey sticks in the backyard, my nonno would saw off the blades and use them as tomato-plant stakes. It's like they were trying to jam as many Italian-Canadian stereotypes into one situation as possible.

These family tales might not seem important to my weird little hockey story, but they are. Without my grandparents taking the risks they did to move to this country, it's unlikely I would have grown up to be a hockey fan. In fact, I wouldn't have grown up at all because my parents would never have met.

Despite the potentially intimidating trio of brothers, my dad still had the nerve to show up at their house and start dating my mom.

My dad had long rocker hair and played the drums. Now over 60 years of age, he still plays in a metal band and beats those drums like they're the Ottawa Senators in the playoffs and his sticks are Gary Roberts.

One day, Dad went to his best friend Mike's house. When he showed up, Mike's younger sister and her friend, a tall, athletic brunette, were getting ready to go dancing with their fake IDs. Guess who that friend with the fake ID was. That's right — my mom.

The moment they laid eyes on each other, they said, "Let's make a hockey blogger together." True romance.

After a few years of dating, my parents were married in 1985, and they moved to a house in east Scarborough, near the Pickering border. For those of you who can only navigate Toronto using Drake lyrics, that's about a five minute drive east of Morningside.

My mom worked as a secretary at the Yellow Pages not too far west of their new home. Knowing how she drives, however, the drive probably took her somewhere between 45 minutes and five days. My dad worked in Toronto for a company called Cadillac Fairview, which owns several buildings right in the downtown core. He worked as a maintenance operator, fixing fans, air conditioners, and so on.

After three years of peaceful marital bliss, during an ice storm on the night of March 12, 1988, my mom gave birth to a 7 pound, 12 ounce bundle of joy at Scarborough Centenary Hospital. The doctor said I was the first baby he had ever seen born in a Leafs jersey. I'm surprised the doctors weren't more alarmed by that — not because my mom gave birth to a fully clothed baby but because the Leafs sucked in the '80s.

"Are you Steven?" my dad asked, the first time he held me.

Just then, I opened my eyes, and that was that. Thank goodness I did, too. Dad wanted to name me Keith.

My parents say I hardly ever cried, and when I did, you could barely even hear me. I guess I figured I'd save my tears for the lifetime of heartache that comes with Leafs fandom.

My childhood was full of Berenstain Bears stories, Disney books, and more. My parents read to me often and instilled a love of reading, storytelling, and imagination at a very young age. The side effect: I wouldn't shut up.

When I was a toddler, I went to daycare at the YMCA by the Scarborough Town Centre. They put me with kids who were a year older than me because I was yapping circles around the other three-year-olds, who were still learning to talk.

When I was three years old, a monumental event changed my family's lives forever and shaped who I am today.

In the few days prior, Mom told Nonna that she wasn't feeling well. Nonna was concerned because the symptoms my mom described matched the way she felt just before she gave birth. This was especially concerning because it was July and my sister wasn't due to be born until November.

One day, my dad called my mom at work like he always did, but she wasn't there. She had gone into labour and was taken to the hospital. My grandpa drove over to pick my dad up from work and rushed him to the hospital.

With my dad at my mom's bedside, my sister was born at 24 weeks, about four months premature, weighing 1.5 pounds. There's a good chance you have a jar of peanut butter in your house right now that weighs more than my sister did when she was born.

As soon as she came into this world, doctors rushed her away to another room. She was given a 50/50 chance to live.

Rachel spent most of the first four months of her life in an incubator with tubes up her nose. The hospital had tiny diapers specifically made for premature babies, but they had to cut hers in half. Generally speaking, in the event of premature birth, doctors hope that the baby makes it to at least 30 weeks before being born. By then, the organs they need to survive will have been developed enough. Rachel was born about a month and a half earlier than that. She was born with blood on the brain and some brain damage and had a lot of difficulty breathing.

Some of my earliest childhood memories involve visiting Rachel in the hospital. I remember the big bins full of powder blue hospital gowns we all had to wear to get into the ward. I remember my parents being concerned their excitable toddler son would start poking at things or trip over a cord or something.

At the time, I thought everything that was happening was normal. All kids get bedtime stories, all kids love the Ninja

Turtles, and all babies spend the first four months of their lives in the hospital.

After about four months, thanks to the incredible efforts of the doctors at Mount Sinai Hospital and Sick Kids, my sister came home.

The struggle wasn't over, though. I was a quiet baby who slept all night and ate to my heart's content. Rachel was a whole different experience. She came home at just 4.5 pounds and even lost weight in the first couple of weeks she was home.

For the next few years, Rachel did not sleep properly, so neither did my parents. Feeding her was a struggle; it would often take up to an hour and she would sometimes stop breathing in the middle of it.

At about one year old, my sister was diagnosed with cerebral palsy, a neurological disorder that inhibits your motor function. My dad doesn't like admitting it, but he had a hard time accepting this information and angrily rejected what the doctor said at first. Much later, at seven, Rachel was also diagnosed with autism, although the symptoms had always been there.

Time has made me appreciate the gravity of the things I grew up with and accepted as normal. I'm older now than my mom was when my sister was born. I can't imagine the constant anxiety and dread my parents lived with every day, just trying to keep their daughter alive while raising a son at the same time.

Today, Rachel is happy. She still lives at home and will require care for the rest of her life. She can walk around a little bit, but for journeys of any distance longer than car-to-house, she needs a wheelchair. She can't read, she can't write, and her speech is limited. My parents and I can understand what she's trying to say, but others are usually confused.

Rachel can sing as loud as anybody I've ever met; those tiny lungs aren't tiny anymore. She knows the entire script of both *Toy Story* and *The Lion King*, right down to the sound effects. I know because she recites everyone's lines five seconds before they do.

She can spell her name. She can use a spoon and fork. She can smile and laugh. She gives great hugs and knows I'm her brother. She's tough. My parents worked very hard to give Rachel and me the best lives possible.

To add to the stress of my sister's health concerns, my dad was already in constant physical pain. Prior to my sister's birth, my dad picked something up awkwardly and injured his back while at work one day. He was in a great deal of pain and when he woke up the next day, he could barely move.

Well, that sucks, but it happens. Sometimes you wrench your back a bit, right? He'll be better in a jiffy.

Days pass, still not better. Weeks pass, still not better. He went on disability from work. He saw a specialist and they said he was fine. He saw a different specialist months later and they told him he was fine, too.

He finally returned to work, still in agony but able to do a few things. Ironically, returning to work saved him.

The nephew of a co-worker was a kinesiologist and had chiropractic credentials. After well over a year of living in constant agony, my dad was sitting in this man's office explaining his symptoms, with tears in his eyes.

The man stared at Dad for a few seconds.

"Well, I can tell you one part of the problem just by looking at you," he said.

My dad lit up. "What?"

"Your hip's out."

My dad had been misdiagnosed and had been living with his hip out of its socket for the past 15 months. About a week later, with some muscle, a leather wallet, and what I can only imagine was the entire dictionary of curse words, they crudely jammed my dad's hip back into place.

Unfortunately, that was only the beginning of dad's recovery. His back was weak and injured for years afterward — it's probably healthier now in his 60s than it was when he was in his mid-30s. As he often says, one of the worst parts about the whole experience was that he couldn't pick up his toddler son, me.

I've learned you can't put a price on loving parents and you're probably not going to fully appreciate what they have done for you until you're a little older.

When Rachel was born, my mom didn't want her son's entire summer to be spent visiting the hospital. My mom lost a lot of blood during childbirth and despite Nonna's protests, Mom and Dad brought me to the Toronto Zoo while Rachel was still in the hospital — all in an effort to make life seem normal. Needless to say, my mom struggled and didn't have a great time. She didn't have to do that for me, but she wanted to because she cared.

All of this played a part in my upbringing.

The hardships my family endured had lasting effects on me and my development, and they all contributed to the person I am today.

I never felt neglected or unloved as a kid, though my sister definitely required more attention than I did. It's probably normal for older siblings, especially ones who were previously an only child, to get jealous when a newborn baby comes around, and I was no different.

My parents were always home with me, but I often had to entertain myself. I was obsessed with action figures. One Christmas I remember getting Hulk Hogan, Ultimate Warrior, and "Macho Man" Randy Savage action figures from my aunts and uncles. I used to make all of my toys wrestle each other, even the non-wrestling ones. "It's Dr. Peter Venkman of the Ghostbusters versus Raphael from the Ninja Turtles for the World Heavyweight Championship!"

Toys were lots of fun, but they had nothing on attention.

I began school shortly after my sister was born. My friend Adam Rodricks, who has been my friend since kindergarten, swears up and down that one morning in senior kindergarten I pulled my pants down during "O Canada." According to his memory, I didn't wait very long. "O Ca-na—" Bang! Full moon! Right there! Yeah, I probably got into pretty big trouble for that one.

And although attention-seeking would be a theme throughout my school years — "Steven talks a lot in class; Steven is disruptive; Steven needs to pay more attention," they'd say — it didn't stop at school. One time, when a physiotherapist came by the house to work with Rachel's strength and flexibility, I must have felt like I was being ignored. I had this coffee mug–sized roly-poly toy that was made of thick, hard plastic. When I decided I was fed up, I sent the roly-poly flying across the room.

My mom was mortified. "He never does this," she told the physiotherapist truthfully.

The physiotherapist wasn't even phased. They told Mom that they saw this sort of thing all the time. Siblings of newborns crave attention. Siblings of newborns who require even more attention than normal crave it even more.

Mom might have been right that I had never done that with roly-poly toys. But when the Leafs lost? Oh, I would rip the little Leafs jersey off my back and whip it across the room. "This is why we shouldn't let him stay up to watch the end of the game," my mom would say.

I didn't just want any kind of attention, though. Sure, there was the occasional meltdown where I whipped my roly-poly around like I was Doug Flutie, but I knew the difference between good attention and bad attention. One form of good attention: laughter.

Cartoons and kid shows were great as a four- or five-year-old, but what I was interested in was what made my parents laugh.

The creators of kids cartoons are pretty aware that parents get stuck watching them, so they often throw in a little subtle adult humour that most kids don't even understand. *Bugs Bunny* and *Animaniacs* were full of those moments.

The stuff that made my parents laugh was fascinating to me. I wanted their attention, and I'd get it by making them laugh. I would ask why the joke was funny but because it was usually inappropriate, I'd be told, "Ah, you're a little too young for that."

So at school, I would just repeat the stuff that made my parents laugh. Although the kids would straight up say, "I don't get it," I'd get laughs from the teachers, and that was good enough for me. They probably weren't even laughing at the joke — they were laughing at this little five-year-old with a goofy haircut telling jokes he didn't even understand.

Another reason I constantly clowned around was to entertain my sister. She cried a lot as a child. Imagine how frustrating and confusing it would be to not be able to communicate what you wanted or how you felt. That's what she struggled with every day as a kid. Sometimes she would scream and bawl her eyes out when she had to get on and off the school bus in front of our house. Transitions have always been a very upsetting thing for her.

With my parents beat from work and no sleep, I always took on entertaining Rachel and making her happy as my job. It was the one thing I could really contribute to the family back then. She loved when I did pratfalls. Sometimes I would grab her hand and pretend like she was smacking me in the face. I would sing songs with her, play little games with her. There's a photo of her in a baby carrier after I had dumped all of our toys on her and she's laughing her face off. The most foolproof way to make someone stop crying: make them laugh.

Steve, what on earth does this have to do with your stupid video blog?

Look, this is all part of my story.

To this day, my instinct is still: "Hey, everyone! Hey! No! Don't cry! Don't be sad! Look over here! Isn't this funny? Why feel sad when you can watch me jump off this thing and probably hurt myself?" All that childhood practice came in handy for covering the 2014–15 Leafs — but we'll get to that later.

PUCK
HEAD

Apart from playing with toys and craving attention, one thing I've always loved for whatever reason is hockey.

I don't remember exactly how it all started. My parents definitely didn't force hockey on me. All I remember is my dad saying something like, "Our team is the Toronto Maple Leafs," and from day one I was just like, "Yeah! Alright! I'm in! Stanley Cups every year, let's go!"

One of my first-ever hockey memories is the 1993 playoffs: the Leafs versus the L.A. Kings. I had just turned five. I remember being really confused, because to me, the Leafs were the best team in the world, but the Kings had Wayne Gretzky, who was the best player in the world. I distinctly remember thinking this, which means I already knew about Wayne Gretzky, which means I already knew about hockey, which means I was already a fan before that. I've literally been a hockey fan since before I can remember.

My uncles were a big influence on my development as a puck head. They were all big Leafs fans themselves. In fact, two of my mom's brothers were season seat holders during the '80s. Unfortunately they sold their seats just before the Gilmour era, when the Leafs finally got good.

My uncle Lenny is the biggest memorabilia collector in the family. The room I shoot all my YouTube videos in now is just an ongoing effort to rival his office, but I'm still not even close. He has a chair from Maple Leaf Gardens and an old Leafs jersey signed by dozens of former players.

Here's how hardcore he was with his collecting: remember when Kraft Dinner used to have hockey cards that you could cut out from the back of boxes? My uncle hates cheese, but he used to buy the boxes with the cards he still needed, cut out the card, and throw the macaroni and cheese away. I remember hearing that as a kid and thinking, *Dude I want mac and cheese! Give it to me!*

My own collecting exploits started when my dad's sister, Sharon, got married. My new uncle Anthony bought me an enormous box of hockey cards for my birthday. It was probably just a standard box, but to this little kid, it seemed like thousands of cards. From then on, I was hooked.

My parents didn't buy me more giant collectors' boxes of hockey cards, so I hunted down all the other hockey cards I could get my hands on. McDonald's hockey cards were huge. I also ate my weight in fish sticks. Know why? In the '90s, boxes of Captain Highliner fish sticks used to have hockey cards in them. I had Patrick Roy with the Habs, Ron Hextall with the Nordiques — still a thing at the time — and Johnny Bower, who somehow had a card despite having been retired many years before that. Of course, my most treasured card of the bunch was the Leafs goalie at the time: Felix Potvin.

Alright, let's address this.

A lot of people roll their eyes when I tell them Felix Potvin was my favourite Leaf growing up. Most kids at my school idolized Wendel Clark and Doug Gilmour. Look, I loved those players when I was a kid, too. But they weren't Felix Potvin.

First of all, Potvin had the most style out of any goalie in the league. After ditching the boring Dominik Hasek–style bucket and cage he had as a rookie, Potvin switched to an actual goalie mask. And what a goalie mask! Everyone knew the cool Felix Potvin mask. I didn't even know what the design was supposed to look like, I just knew it looked badass. Between that and his big blue goalie pads, I thought he looked like a superhero.

And that's exactly what Potvin was. To me, Doug Gilmour, Wendel Clark, and Dave Andreychuk might score, what, one goal a game, if they're lucky? Maybe two or three? Felix Potvin would be called on to make 30, 35, or 40-plus spectacular saves per game. By the early '90s, goalies had only been actual in-shape athletes for like 10 years, so they were still flailing and flopping around, making desperation saves every shift. Whether it was a two-pad stack or flashing the blue leather, I thought Felix Potvin was the Leafs' MVP.

It's funny because Gilmour's 127-point performance in 1992–93 is arguably the greatest season any Leaf has ever had. But I'm five years old, dude. Don't talk to me about stats; I still wear Velcro shoes.

The first hockey game I ever went to was on February 5, 1994, when I was five. That was actually Don Cherry's 60th birthday, and, as I would find out years later, my future wife's sixth birthday. The Toronto Maple Leafs were hosting the Detroit Red Wings at Maple Leaf Gardens.

My uncle Dom brought me. Mom had to take care of my sister and my dad was working nights at the time. The tickets were $32 each — a huge bargain compared to today's prices, where you might get nosebleeds for triple that.

My dad knew he couldn't go to the game, but he still wanted to contribute, so he helped me make a sign.

It read: "Pluck the Red Wings."

The word pluck wasn't in my vocabulary yet, so I asked what it meant. My dad explained that when you pull out feathers, it's called plucking.

"Oh. OK!" I accepted it.

It wasn't until I was a teenager when I looked at the sign and — *Hey, wait a minute . . .*

I don't remember a whole lot about the game; I vaguely

remember looking down at the ice hoping to see Felix Potvin. My most vivid memory is of two guys sitting in front of my uncle and me. My uncle told them it was my first Leafs game, so they gave me a little commemorative plastic hockey stick that I still have to this day. Maybe they wanted to make my first game special or maybe they thought my "Pluck the Red Wings" sign was hilarious.

Perhaps as foreshadowing for the rest of my life, the Leafs lost that night.

Ray Sheppard scored two goals in the first period to give Detroit the 2–0 lead, but Doug Gilmour brought the Leafs back within one before the intermission.

Kent Manderville took a five-minute checking-from-behind penalty to put the Leafs down a man, and the Red Wings made them pay with a Steve Chiasson power play goal.

Nikolai Borschevsky scored for Toronto, and Gilmour got his second of the game to tie it up at three, but Sergei Fedorov's unassisted second-period goal proved to be the game winner: 4–3, Detroit. Felix Potvin made 34 saves for the Leafs so it wasn't his fault, nor was anything ever.

I fell asleep in Uncle Dom's truck after the game and woke up back at my nonna's house to wait for my dad to pick me up. My nonna's house had the typical Italian setup: nice kitchen upstairs that never got used, busted kitchen downstairs you used for everything. It's a Joe Avati joke, but it's true.

The rest of the basement was filled with old pictures of family and shrines to the Virgin Mary. Being the enormous sports fan that my uncle is, there were also framed newspaper clippings from the Toronto Blue Jays' back-to-back World Series wins. I plan on doing the same for the Leafs one day, just . . . still waiting.

Another person who fostered my love of sports was my neighbour Brian.

One summer day when I was six, a few months after attending my first hockey game, I was playing ball hockey in the driveway by myself. Really I was just taking shots on the little net I had gotten for Christmas.

Across the street, there was this kid I had never seen before just sitting on the edge of his driveway, staring at me. I didn't go say hi because I didn't know if I was allowed. *He's across the street. I can't cross the street. Can I yell across the street? Is that allowed?* I don't know, I'm six.

Finally, he came over and said hi.

Brian was an older, bigger kid, 10 going on 11. His family was from Jamaica, had lived in New York for a while, and had just moved across the street from me in Scarborough.

We took turns trying to shoot a tennis ball past each other. Is it weird that I remember he won 11–10? Looking back, he was definitely letting me score on purpose, but I thought I was the best hockey player West Hill had ever seen.

Hockey, and more directly Brian, even helped me discover my balls.

One day, my dad and Brian were taking shots on me from down the driveway as I flailed around, imitating my best Felix Potvin.

"Big glove save!" I'd declare in my announcer's voice, triumphantly holding up the tennis ball I had just caught in my dad's old baseball glove.

Dad had a better concept of *take it easy on him, he's just a kid* than Brian, who, being a kid himself, didn't quite have that nailed down.

I'm in the net; I'm ready. I look to the left, Dad has the ball. He passes it over to Brian. He shoots!

Bullseye.

Oh, I made the save alright. Right in the Ball-schevskies.

Oh my God. What's happening to me? Am I dying? Am I dead? This must be what dying feels like.

I didn't know that kind of pain even existed. Every bump,

bruise, scrape, or cut I had ever gotten had nothing on this. I would have been crying more if I could actually make the sound leave my chest, but I was paralyzed.

"What happened?" Mom asked after I stumbled inside.

Through shocked tears, I said, "The ball hit me."

"Where?" she asked.

"I . . . I think my stomach," I blubbered. I was six and barely understood what balls were, OK? And I felt like barfing up my vital organs, so I figured it was my stomach. I learned a lot that day.

Brian put up with the little kid across the street and was like an older brother to me. He was always willing to teach me a lesson in driveway hockey and, especially, basketball.

Brian's parents installed a basketball pole and net beside their driveway. I remember watching them install it like it was the event of the season. I had seen basketball nets attached above garage doors and basketball nets with wheels that you could dunk on until it tipped over, but I had never seen a net connected to a metal pole in the front lawn.

Our game of choice was 21. The basic rules are that you take turns, shooting until you miss, until one of you hits 21. Brian was older and really good at basketball, while I was younger and stunk. Although I think my age had little to do with it; if I hopped in a time machine right now and challenged 11-year-old Brian to a game of 21, he'd still destroy me. Most games, I'd just be happy to hit double digits. No wonder I've survived being a Leafs fan for this long; I know what it's like to never give up hope for a constantly losing cause.

And that win finally came. Once. One lousy, little time.

Brian threw up brick after brick; I got red hot and just narrowly beat him. Finally, after years of trying, I had finally beat him at 21. I went nuts, jumping up and down, thrilled, until I saw the look on Brian's face.

I lost the next game 21–0. *Swish, swish, swish*. I don't think I even shot the ball.

He wasn't going to let that little boy beat him ever again.

Another figure in my life who helped nourish my love of sports, especially hockey, was my second grade teacher, Mr. Coady. For reference, I was eight years old in grade two. Over two decades later, I still remember what I learned. You really can't put a price on a good teacher.

Part of the reason why I loved Mr. Coady so much was because he was the first male teacher I ever had. I liked the women who taught me, of course, but at that age, Mr. Coady was my first male authority figure who wasn't my own father. My grandpa was there, as well as my uncles, but not for six hours a day, five days a week.

Mr. Coady was one of the most colourful and animated teachers at St. Brendan Catholic School on Centennial Road in east Scarborough. He had also been there for a long time. So long, in fact, that he was once the teacher and floor hockey coach for a former student named Kris Draper. By the time I had reached second grade, Kris Draper was an up-and-coming centre for the Detroit Red Wings.

Bless Mr. Coady's heart, though — the man was a Montreal Canadiens fan. This was a frequent point of contention for my young self. As it turned out, that was a point of contention for Kris Draper as well.

As Mr. Coady recounted, Draper had a Leafs jacket he would wear to school, which Mr. Coady would make him hang in the hallway because "inappropriate attire was not allowed in the classroom."

Mr. Coady did the same thing with Kris Draper and his classmates that he did with me and my classmates: used hockey as a teaching tool. Now that was how you grabbed the attention of the eight-year-old me. It still works today, actually.

Our class was always covered in hockey memorabilia. I knew when my day came for show-and-tell, I wanted to do something hockey related. April 27, 1996, was my assigned show-and-tell day. Did I remember? You bet I didn't. But I remember the lesson I learned.

When it was my turn to go up, despite having nothing prepared, I defaulted to hockey. I knew that Kris Draper and the Detroit Red Wings had played Game 5 of their first-round series against the Winnipeg Jets the night before. This was a huge deal, not just because of Draper and not just because it was the playoffs, but because if the Jets had lost, it would have been their last game in Winnipeg before moving to Phoenix.

Oh man. *Did the Jets lose last night? Come on, they must have. The Wings are so good and I can't believe the Jets even made the playoffs. Alright cool. I got this.*

I got up in front of the class.

"Last night," I started, "the Detroit Red Wings eliminated the Winnipeg Jets in Game 5 of their . . ."

"No, they didn't," Mr. Coady interrupted.

I was worse off than a deer in headlights. There were deer in the forest who saw me through the window that morning and to this day still use my reaction as a saying. "I thought I heard a wolf and I just froze, you know? I was like a Steve at show-and-tell!" Lesson learned: don't just randomly make up the outcome of hockey games. I would have taken a lower case *l* if I had just admitted that I forgot it was my turn, but, instead, I capitalized it.

One month later on May 29, 1996, something happened to Kris Draper that got the entire class talking.

Almost every student in the class was a Leafs fan, but the Buds, who used to be in the Western Conference — I know, right? — had been eliminated in the first round by the St. Louis Blues.

Because the Leafs were already out, and because Mr. Coady spoke about Kris Draper every time Detroit did something, a lot of students became part-time fans of the Red Wings. It certainly helped that their series with the Colorado Avalanche in the 1996 Western Conference Final was a bloody rivalry for the ages.

In Game 6, Colorado's designated rat, Claude Lemieux, decked Kris Draper from behind, mangling his face and rendering him half-conscious. As Draper recounted in a March 2017 article for *The Player's Tribune*, he had a broken orbital bone, broken cheekbone, broken nose, and broken jaw. He literally had a broken face.

Detroit was eliminated that night, but when everyone got to school the next morning, all we could talk about was the hit. Almost everyone had seen it, either live that night or in the highlights the next morning before the school bus came.

Right away, Mr. Coady had the entire class write get-well letters to Kris Draper, so he could read them while he recovered. In mine, I told Mr. Draper (I think that's what I called him) not to let "Clud" Lemieux get him down. I thought "Clud" was an insult. It sounded like something Bugs Bunny would have called Yosemite Sam. Listen, I was eight.

One day, my parents bought me a pack of hockey cards at the convenience store up the street. I opened it and bang — right there — Kris Draper. I was surprised. Even eight-year-old me was like, *Wow, this guy has a card? He had 10 career goals coming into this season. Whatever — that's awesome!*

I brought the card in to school for a not-made-up-on-the-spot show-and-tell, and Mr. Coady ended up putting it on our school's wall of fame outside the principal's office.

In the dying days of the school year, a commotion arose in the hallway. Mr. Coady stepped out. Kids started looking at each other and whispering. A few moments later, Mr. Coady walked back into the classroom with none other than Kris Draper.

Wow. A real live NHL player! I had never met an actual NHL player before. The biggest celebrities I had ever met were the children's rock band Kideo at one of my dad's work Christmas parties. But this guy? Holy cow! He's a hockey player!

Our school's principal, Mr. Fitzpatrick, asked Mr. Coady something before walking over to me.

What did I do? Am I in trouble? So help me if you stop me from meeting a real live NHL player, I will use every Power Rangers move I've ever seen on your crotch!

Mr. Fitzpatrick stooped down to talk to me.

"Mr. Coady mentioned you had a card," he said.

"Oh!" I said. "Yeah! It's on the wall of fame."

"Great. Thank you!" Mr. Fitzpatrick bolted out of the room.

Kris Draper spoke to all the students from the rocking chair at the front of the classroom. It was basically a media scrum full of seven- and eight-year-olds and he was answering all the questions. I was way too shy to ask anything.

He still had his goatee from the playoffs. I can't imagine it would have been comfortable to shave with a broken face. Looking back at pictures, his jaw still seemed a bit swollen. It's amazing that he came to our class at all, never mind that it was only about one month after the hit.

Mr. Fitzpatrick re-entered the room with a stack of paper. He had taken the card off the wall, photocopied it, neatly cut all the photocopies into individual cards, and handed them out to all the students. He must have printed about a hundred, so that every kid in the second grade could get their very own Kris Draper autograph.

Half of me was over the moon happy that I was finally going to get an autograph from an NHL player. The other half of me was like, *Mr. Fitzpatrick better give me back my card . . .*

Draper came over to my desk and signed my photocopy of the card. I still have the photographic evidence. We were standing in front of a presentation board with a *National Geographic* pamphlet on a bird called the blue-footed booby. It is absolutely a real bird — google it. It's a bird with blue feet called a booby. It exists and that's its name.

For some reason, I was wearing a baseball jersey with a Chicago Bulls logo on it. Why? I have no idea. I'd love to say it was a cheeky nod to Michael Jordan's brief stint in baseball, but I wasn't that smart. Where did my parents even buy this? Did they even buy it? Where did this come from?

These are all questions I ask now. At the time, I was just excited to meet a famous hockey player.

When NHL players weren't visiting my class, I was obsessed with the classroom computer. I always wanted to play the dinky little game on it, probably *Oregon Trail*. Even typing was mind-blowing. Computers in classrooms was a fairly new thing, and I definitely didn't have a computer at home.

My neighbour Brian was helping on that end, though.

Most of the kids at my school talked about the cool video game systems that they had. Kids were playing *Super Mario Bros.* on Super Nintendo or *Sonic the Hedgehog* on Sega Genesis. I didn't have any of that.

Brian did, though. I was over at his house all the time. I used to beg him to play *NHL 96* on Super Nintendo. I specifically remember one time he beat me 33–3. You ever take a video game beating so bad, you remember it over two decades later?

One day, Brian brought this big garbage bag to my house. Because he already had the Super Nintendo and Sega Genesis, Brian gave me his old original Nintendo and over a dozen games.

Santa who? Brian literally just walked across the street with a big bag of everything I've ever wanted. My parents let me keep it and I played it obsessively. *Super Mario* one and three, *WWF Steel Cage Challenge*, *Tecmo World Wrestling*, *Double Dragon* — you name it, I played it. At some point, my parents brought me to the local pawn shop and we got cheap copies of hockey games called *Blades of Steel* and another one that was literally just called *Ice Hockey*. The game's release date was in January 1988, so it was older than I was. The USSR was still a team you could use. But I didn't care about that! I was thrilled.

Video games were life. They also became a great tool for my parents because if I was acting up, all they had to do was threaten to take my Nintendo away. One time, they took it away for an entire week — I swear, it felt like six years.

Luckily enough, my sister loved to watch me play video games. It was like a movie for her. She would get upset when I died because it interrupted her movie. I would provide commentary, too. Unfortunately, some of that commentary involved bad words. The problem was that Rachel would repeat these words. Luckily, she understood that they were basement words she could use only with Steven. But when she did slip up, I would just blame it on Dad, like how you blame a fart on a dog. Hey, I rode in the back of the car while my dad drove — don't think I wasn't listening.

Then came Christmas 1998. I was 10.

My godmother Jo-Anne had just inherited some money from her father. She was generous enough to get me my very own computer.

I was blown away. Who just buys a kid a computer? I couldn't possibly thank her enough. We didn't even have internet at the house. Why would we? We didn't even have a computer! The space on the computer's hard drive: four gigabytes. You're probably carrying a phone in your pocket with at least four times that space right now. You might even be reading this book on it! But to me, it was everything.

The computer came with a free encyclopedia on CD-ROM, and since I didn't have internet, I used to read articles on it all the time. The entry for "hockey" had a video in it from an actual NHL game. I was living in the future!

One winter, Brian and his family were nice enough to get me a present. They delivered it several weeks before Christmas, so it was in my house for a while. We were the type of family who had our Christmas tree up right at the beginning of December, so under the tree it sat. And sat. And sat.

I eventually did what any kid does: try to figure out what the gift was.

When my parents weren't looking, I squeezed the gift like I was testing out a piece of fruit. *Hmm, it feels like there's a box inside. It's about the size of a book, but it's definitely not a book. Wait — is this a PC game?*

Then my parents would enter the room and I would jump up or pretend to be asleep.

Days went by and I was so positive I knew what it was. *If I just move the paper a bit, I'm sure that's fine, right?*

I moved the paper with my finger, millimetre by millimetre. I was like the murderer from "The Tell-Tale Heart."

One day, I went a little too far. I pushed the paper more than I meant to, at least that's what I told myself, and I saw it. It was the tiniest flash of orange. I knew right away that it was a Philadelphia Flyers jersey.

NHL 99! I screamed internally. Eric Lindros was on the cover that year.

It might have been December 23 when I did that, but it could have just as easily been July. I spent every day before Christmas practicing my fake astonishment for Christmas morning. "Wow! *NHL 99*? I had no idea! How could I possibly have known?"

The NHL video game franchise really next-levelled my hockey fandom. Not only did I play it every single day, but it taught me the game as well. Sure, real life hockey doesn't have blocky players and glitch goals — unless you're Alex Ovechkin — but I got to know the stats, positions, and skillset of every player and team in the league. I didn't just know about the Leafs anymore, it was every team.

To say I was obsessed would be an understatement. I scored a Game 7 overtime winner with Sergei Berezin that I still remember. Today they have roster updates you can download. Back then, whenever a trade happened, I had to manually do it myself. When there was a rookie, you had to create them from scratch. I specifically remember doing that for Miikka Kiprusoff — this is the millennial version of "I had to walk ten miles to school, uphill, both ways!"

I played *NHL 99* for two years before getting *NHL 2001* with Owen Nolan on the front, which I played for about half a decade.

How many hockey games can you watch in a night? Two? In video-game hockey, you can watch dozens. This is why I think the NHL video game franchise needs to incorporate analytics, women's leagues, and so on. The games have only gotten better since I was a kid, and they could be such a vital learning tool for kids. Sure, there are lots of other ways to learn about hockey, but this could be a way to teach kids without them realizing it.

Unfortunately, I never got to put this newfound knowledge into practice because I never played hockey.

Like I mentioned before, there was a lot going on with my family around the time my sister was born and the years that followed.

Mom and Dad knew I loved hockey, though, so they put me in skating lessons when I was five. We played on-ice games like What Time Is It, Mr. Wolf? While I got a little red ribbon with a penguin on it for completing the course, I wasn't exactly ready for the NHL after that. My parents found time for those lessons, but hockey and its time commitment just wasn't realistic.

In fairness, I didn't force the issue. I played hockey in the driveway and on the street and had enough fun doing that. I was also enrolled in soccer, which was closer to home, cheaper, and less time-consuming. I never felt left out or cheated when it came to hockey.

When I was about 10, my parents asked if I wanted to try getting into hockey and I didn't bother. All the kids I knew who played were in rep hockey or select, and I barely knew how to skate. I would have been a laughing stock.

Part of me regrets that, but it's hard to blame a 10-year-old for being short-sighted. To really regret that decision, though, I would have to regret the way things have ended up for me, and I definitely don't. Hockey has been good to me, and I never even had to take a puck to the teeth. Hard to complain.

Looking back, there might have been another reason why my parents asked if I wanted to get into hockey: I was getting chunky.

I was spending less time outside and more time playing video games. And I ate cookies pretty much every day. One thing I could definitely say about my childhood is I never went hungry.

It was very difficult to go places with my sister, so my idea of a fancy trip outside of the house was going for lunch at McDonald's. It was an opportunity for Mom to take a break from cooking and for the whole family to relax together outside the house. McDonald's was one of the few places Rachel actually liked going.

I was pretty much raised on McChicken burgers and McDonald's pizza. Remember that?

Right around the fourth grade, I looked in the mirror and went, "Uh oh!" I got picked on for it a bit, too. These kids on the school bus would rip on me, and I couldn't catch them, which made them rip on me even more. I can't lie, at the same time, I picked on some other kids, too. The politics of being a kid can be cruel.

I begrudgingly enrolled in cross-country running with my school. We had a good program with lots of kids, so it was a way to make friends while breaking a sweat.

Hockey was always there, but as I got older, other things shoved their way into the picture. The Attitude Era had struck the WWE, and I was obsessed with wrestlers like Stone Cold Steve Austin. Stone Cold versus Shawn Michaels with Mike Tyson as the special guest referee? Oh, I was amped.

I started to get more and more homework as I got older so there was less time to watch hockey or play video games.

Around 11 years old, girls, y'know, actually didn't seem so bad anymore.

My first crush was on this pretty girl named Jessica. For some stupid reason, one of the kids who used to pick on me was playing hockey with me in my driveway. He was my friend, but he also sort of bullied me. Again, the politics of being a kid, man. In my infinite wisdom, I told him about my crush on Jessica.

By first recess the next day, my whole class knew.

This girl named Rebecca ran up to me that recess with a giant smile on her face and out of nowhere just hit me with "You like Jessica Varello?"

I froze dead in my tracks.

"I, uh . . . shit."

A couple of years ago, Jessica reached out to me because a friend of hers in Australia was watching one of my videos, and she recognized me. She said to keep up the good work. Man, what I would give to show 11-year-old me that message.

By the sixth grade, I had hit a growth spurt. I didn't even realize it, but thanks to cross-country and bike riding, I had trimmed up. Track became my obsession. It was the first athletic thing I was ever actually good at. I went from spare for the track team in sixth grade to the anchor of the relay team in grade seven and eight. I ran my ass off in the 100 metre dash.

My fastest time, unofficially, of course, because we had a teacher with a stopwatch instead of Olympic camera technology, was 11.7 seconds when I was 14. On a good day, I could usually count on hovering around 12 seconds.

I ran every day, I rode my bike every day, and I went to the gym a lot. I developed back problems when I began high school — 14 effing years old — as a result. But I didn't know why. I thought I just had a bad back like my dad and it was genetics, or something. Years later, I found out it was because my legs were wound so tight, my flexibility was awful, putting stress on my back.

I was a total knucklehead. I was pushing 600 pounds on the diagonal leg press to show off, but all the while, I was doing more damage.

You might notice I haven't mentioned hockey for a while. It just wasn't as big of a priority and most of my friends weren't even really fans. I still cared, though. When the Sabres eliminated the Leafs in the 1999 Eastern Conference Final — oh, I cried. I thought I was old enough that that wouldn't happen anymore, but nope. When they lost in the conference final again in 2002, I may have shed a tear or two.

Whether I knew it or not, though, hockey and I were on a collision course.

FIRST
& ONLY

Every hockey game has a story — even the boring ones. The second game I ever went to was a great example of that.

It was December 30, 1996, Leafs versus the New York Islanders at Maple Leaf Gardens. You'll notice the trend with the games I went to: most of them were Christmas gifts. My dad insisted that I go with my mom.

As soon as we arrived, I was kind of disappointed. Felix Potvin wasn't even playing. Some goalie I had never even heard of named Marcel Cousineau was in net for the Leafs. The Islanders responded with Eric Fichaud, a sophomore goalie who was originally a 1994 first-rounder for the Leafs. Toronto had traded him to the Islanders the year before for two picks and Benoit Hogue.

Nobody scored for either team in the first period. Nobody scored for either team in the second period, either. No stinking goals at all, although there was some rough stuff. Tie Domi took a boarding penalty in the second and had to answer the bell about five minutes later, in a fight with Islanders defender Doug Houda. It was actually pretty vicious. Domi basically choke-slammed Houda to the ice after landing a mean right, and both players kept throwing punches while they were down. It's on YouTube, if you want to watch it. It must be the Islanders broadcasters in the clip. One of them said, "Some players play the game to make the game better. Some players are in the game to make it worse."

Some nights it might have been boring to have a scoreless game heading into the third, but this goalie I had never heard of was starting to win eight-year-old me over.

The Leafs finally got on the board about halfway through the third, when Jamie Baker scored a power play goal. Mats Sundin added his 24th of the season with about three minutes left to make it 2–0. And with 28 saves, Cousineau kept the door shut to preserve the 2–0 Leafs win.

It was the first and only shutout of Marcel Cousineau's NHL career.

Insignificant? Maybe. But I think it's super cool. How often do you get to see a player do something for the first time, never mind the only time? This was only the second game I had ever attended in my entire life.

More importantly, I had finally seen the Leafs win in person.

ZOO
STORIES

I can't talk about where my bizarre career path in hockey began without talking about where my work life began.

It was summer 2004. I was 16, had just finished grade 10, and could finally get my licence. For me, thoroughly without a girlfriend, this was great on many levels. *If I could only get my driver's licence,* I thought, *then they'll all flock to my parents' 1995 Ford Taurus station wagon.*

Spoiler: they did not.

Licence and car aside, I also wanted to have my own money. I was tired of asking my parents for an allowance and they were tired of giving me one. I needed a job.

My first stop was the grocery store. *Job application?* I thought. *Don't I just hand in my resume and become a millionaire? Is that not how this works?*

I filled out the application and handed it to the manager. He took one look at it and laughed.

"You don't wanna work weekends?" he asked.

And miss the parties? Yeah, I didn't get that job.

The days went by and still no job. Eventually, my mom came up with an idea. My sister's elementary school teacher, who is an extremely nice person and has treated my sister and family beautifully, was married to somebody high up at the Toronto Zoo, which was close to our home. My mom figured she could help get my resume in there. My mom was absolutely right: I got my first ever interview.

My first ever job interview. Oh God.

What do I wear? I don't know how to tie a tie. What if I say something dumb? Will I get fired? No, they can't fire you from a job you don't even have yet. Unless they can. Can they? What if they ask me to feed the lions? I can't feed the friggin' lions, dude. Screw this, I'll just sell drugs . . .

My parents told me to calm down and be myself. They were trying to be helpful, but that was terrible advice. First of all, they raised me, so they knew I had no idea how to be calm. And be myself? What do you mean? I'm a 16-year-old with no job. I'm trying really hard to not be myself right now, actually.

My mom gave me a ride to the zoo, y'know, because I had no licence and was useless. I thought the interview would be a one-on-one between me and a boss. What's a boss? I don't know, but I'm sure they can fire you. Nope! It turns out that it was actually *two* bosses plus two other applicants.

The first applicant was some dude in his mid-20s who was a manager at a Loblaws, a Canadian grocery store. I couldn't even get a job at a grocery store and buddy here is a manager at one. Great. The other applicant was in her early 20s and earning her master's degree. She was smart enough to be getting a master's, and I was too dumb to even know what that meant.

I remember the interviewers asked about customer service scenarios. The guy talked about times he had to handle customer complaints at his grocery store, which sucked because I had never dealt with a customer before. The girl talked about the customer service experiences she had at previous jobs, which sucked for me because I had no previous jobs.

Wanna guess what I talked about? Go ahead. I'm 16 with no job experience. What could I have possibly cited as some sort of customer service experience?

If you guessed "talking about your experience in the school play," come collect your prize.

That's right. I talked about the school play I was a part of in grade 10. What does that have to do with customer service? Well, the answer that I shoehorned with a crowbar was that the audience was the customer, and I could handle talking to people as a result.

Go ahead and laugh.

The next question was about teamwork and leadership. The guy talked about leading the people he managed at his grocery store, you know, because he was a freaking manager. The girl talked about group projects while completing her master's, because I don't know if I've mentioned this yet, but she was getting her effing master's.

You'll never guess what I talked about.

Bingo! School play.

How does that apply? Easy — it doesn't. I said working on a play is working with a team. You have to treat your crew and fellow cast members with respect and work together to make a great performance.

And what a performance this was. You could smell the bullshit from a mile away, which was especially impressive considering we were in a zoo.

After about three or four other questions, everybody in the room, including myself, had come to the conclusion that the only life experience I had was that I had been in a school play.

So, yeah, I didn't get the job. The interviewers phoned me soon after to tell me they liked me, but I just didn't have enough experience.

How the hell am I supposed to get job experience if you won't let me have any? I thought.

I was so sad. I thought it was a slam dunk. I had help getting my resume in there and everything. I wore a nice shirt. Were they not impressed by my high school acting career?

"So are you just not gonna get a job?" my mom asked.

"I still want a job," I said. "Nobody will hire me."

"Is there somewhere you haven't applied yet?" she asked

again, in that very specific Mom tone — the one they use when they're waiting for you to wise up and figure it out yourself.

"I can't think of any—" Then it dawned on me. "Oh . . . aw, come on."

There was a McDonald's close by that had a giant PlayPlace that I used to play in as a kid. By *as a kid*, I mean like six years before this story takes place.

So I applied to McDonald's and I got the job.

I wasn't over-the-top excited to be working at McDonald's, but I was pretty happy just to work. Besides, a bunch of kids from my high school worked there, too. Maybe this wouldn't be so bad . . .

It was.

I sucked at remembering lists of steps and that's pretty much all working at McDonald's is. "Somebody ordered this. It's made with this, this, and this. Now go make it." Ask me for a list of who played for the 1998–99 Leafs, not if the Mac sauce goes on before or after the lettuce and tomato.

With no experience handling money, I only worked the fryer and the grill in the back. That's right: the pimple-faced 16-year-old who had never cooked a meal in his entire life that wasn't Kraft Dinner got paid to make your food.

I had worked only one three-hour shift at the end of a pay cycle, so my first paycheck was a whopping $21. But, oh boy, was that money burning a hole in my pocket.

I walked to the grocery store that wisely shot me down and bought a box of Trix. When I was a kid, my parents never got me sugary cereal. In retrospect, that was the right move. I was too hyper. Now, though? Ha! I'm a man! I have my own money! I'm buying some damn Trix, Mom and Dad!

I walked through the door, sat down at the kitchen table, and ate the entire box. I felt victorious. And nauseous.

I eventually started to get the hang of the job, though. It took some time but I memorized the steps and was able to churn stuff out at a respectable rate. I remember one time my mom was about to make a grilled cheese sandwich at home, and I was like, "It's OK, Mom. I got this." Oh man, I cooked the hell out of that grilled cheese. I even made Lipton chicken noodle soup to go with it. It's like: Gordon Ramsay, Jamie Oliver, and Steve. I'm on that level, you know?

Unfortunately, I never really liked the job, and I pretty much gave up on it after just two months. With school around the corner, I decided to quit. The only problem was that I didn't know how to quit. My dad told me I had to hand in my two weeks' notice. Realistically, I was 16 and probably the worst employee in the building — they wouldn't have cared if I just never showed up again.

Then it all went bad.

I never stole any food. I don't feel like I deserve a medal for that, but a lot of employees took a few nuggets from time to time. Anyone who has ever worked in a restaurant knows how much perfectly good food goes to waste.

I had way too much of a guilty conscience; I also thought they had cameras on us. I imagined I'd just be casually eating a chicken nugget when all of a sudden a flash grenade would go off and two dozen SWAT cops would burst in. "Put down the chicken, scum bag. Get those hands where I can see them."

On the night of my second-last shift, I saw this guy named Turtle, who was a couple of grades ahead of me at my high school, take a chicken strip. Remember McDonald's chicken strips?

He saw me see him.

"You want some?" he asked.

"No, man." I laughed. "I don't want to risk it."

"What? You've never taken anything before?" he asked.

"No," I replied truthfully.

"What?" He couldn't believe it. "Man, you never make this?" He took another chicken strip, split it in half, poured barbecue sauce on it, and made it into a sandwich. He took a bite and then dramatically closed his eyes and crouched down, clutching stacks of boxes like he was having an uncontrollable chicken strip–induced orgasm.

I was still skeptical about sneaking anything myself, but as the shift passed, I thought, *One chicken strip can't hurt, right? I mean, come on, it's just gonna get thrown out anyway.*

So I ate the chicken strip, OK? I ate it. I was reckless, I tell ya. Just a loose cannon . . .

And to my surprise, no SWAT team. Huh, would you look at that? Time for another chicken strip? I think it's time for another chicken strip.

I did this periodically throughout the night. Around 11:30 p.m., half an hour before the end of my shift, a voice came from behind me.

"What's in your mouth?"

I turned around.

"Are you eating something?" It was my manager.

I looked around. "M'oh," I replied, which was meant to be "no" but my mouth was full.

"Get out of here," she said. "You don't work here anymore."

Just like that, I had been fired from my first job. The weight of it hit me right away. *Dude, how do you get fired from McDonald's?*

My first foray in the working world was a failure to say the least. I had a bit of spending money in my pocket — and it's not like I was missing out on wages since I had already quit — but the zoo specifically said they wanted me to get job experience before I applied there again. I finally got a job and then got fired from it. No reference for next summer.

I told my parents what had happened. They told me to call McDonald's the next day and apologize, which I did. It was humiliating. More than anything, I was genuinely sorry for what I had done. It seems like nothing, but it was technically stealing, wasn't it?

Maybe the biggest benefit that came out of my first job experience was that I appreciated school a lot more after that.

The next summer started terribly but ended strong.

I experienced what I'm now pretty sure were anxiety attacks. I had started dating my first real girlfriend that year. While only four months older than me, she was in grade 12 while I was in grade 11. That meant that when she graduated, she would be leaving not just our high school but the city, for university.

I don't think it was just about her leaving or the anxiety of getting a new job; it was about change, and a lot of it all at once. Beyond crying at the drop of a hat, it felt like a fist was periodically reaching into my chest and squeezing.

At the time, I thought I was just being ridiculous, and I probably was, but it was a problem. I've had a few spats of attacks over the years, but it wasn't until recently that I looked at them as anything other than me being unreasonable or something.

I applied to work at the Toronto Zoo again the next summer and got another interview.

I'm going to get humiliated again, I thought. *What am I going to talk about this time? Should I talk about this year's school play or the McDonald's that fired me?* My anxiety grew as the interview drew nearer.

It was a group interview again, and just like last time it was with a guy and a girl. The guy was this yoked bro and the girl had curly hair, glasses, and was my age. Luckily for me, he wasn't a former Loblaws manager and she wasn't earning her master's.

I said that I had worked at McDonald's and could provide a reference if needed. That was my blind shot in the dark. What if they actually called? Maybe I could get a friend to pretend to be a manager or something? I had to say I worked there, though, or it would have just been me talking about my experience as a high school thespian again.

For whatever reason, I was calm during the interview. I think I just felt so wound up leading up to it that I was happy just to get it over with. Then came the question that likely sealed the deal.

"What would you do if you caught another employee stealing?"

He meant money, not chicken strips.

The bro guy was killing the interview before this, but he whiffed. "Oh, I'd probably just be like, 'Come on, man. What are you doing?' Try to reason with them, you know?"

The girl and I were like, nah, we'd narc, which was obviously the answer they wanted to hear. "Snitches get stitches," some of you might say. But I say snitches get hired at the zoo.

By the end of the interview, I thought I did OK. Definitely better than last time. We all got up, shook hands, and started walking down the stairs. Hopefully they don't ask for references . . .

Oh. My. God.

The girl, who had walked out ahead of everybody, fell down the stairs.

The interviewers freaked. "Are you alright?"

"Yep," the girl quickly answered. "Yep, I'm fine. Thank you. Yep."

All of us offered to help her but she refused. Once outside, she limped over to her mom and quietly started sobbing. Her mom was horrified. Imagine what she must have thought? Like wow, how bad could the interview have gone?

My mom was there as well.

"What happened?" she asked.

"I'll tell you in the car."

For the record, that girl ended up getting a job. The big bro guy ended up getting a job, too, but not handling money. Funny that, eh?

You know who else got hired? Me.

My job was in the rides and retail department. That meant selling tickets for the camel rides, the pony rides, and this big machine called the simulator ride. Basically, it was a little pod with a big screen at the front. It fit up to 16 people. Once everyone was loaded in, a movie played and the pod shook around. Then there was the dreaded stroller rental. Most days, it was boring and peaceful. But some days, it felt like I was Simba in *The Lion King*, dodging wildebeests from trampling me to death.

It was a pretty cool job, and everyone in the department was a character in their own way and I still talk to many of them. Sure, we had to wear full khaki pants in 35 degree heat, but at least we got to work in the sun. Plus it was always cool to say you worked at the Toronto Zoo.

"Steve, you haven't talked about hockey for a while." Well, here it comes.

To pass the time, I talked about hockey with a lot of people at the zoo, but the guy I talked about it with the most was my buddy Karthik, a Colorado Avalanche fan. Karthik and I would be screaming hockey arguments at each other, only pausing to say, "Hi, how can I help you?"

I worked at the zoo for seven out of the eight summers between 2005 and 2012. A lot happened during that time, but here are the highlights.

The camel rides were probably my favourite place to work. The camels didn't belong to the Toronto Zoo, though; they came from the Bowmanville Zoo, a little less than an hour east of Toronto's border.

The camel handlers were a few years older than me for most of the time I worked there. When I started, a guy named Shawn was in charge of the operation. For some reason, he and the other camel handlers had to sleep at the zoo, in a trailer next to the camel enclosure.

Their boss wouldn't let them leave at night, but they were young and bored senseless, so that didn't stop them. One time, I went out with them. We saw a movie and had some drinks.

Shawn asked me if I wanted to come back to the trailer.

"How do we get in?" I asked. "Check with security?"

"No, we gotta climb the fence," Shawn said.

Why I went, I'll never know.

It was pitch black. We were crouched in the grass next to a fence and waited until the coast was clear before starting to climb. I got about halfway up.

"Uh, Shawn," I started. "You're sure you know what's on the other side of this fence, right?"

I was picturing myself on a TV show called *Hey, Check Out How This Idiot Died*. "On today's episode, watch this drunk idiot climb a fence and end up in a cheetah enclosure."

Luckily, we were just on a path, and we stealthily made our way over to the trailer. When we arrived, I still couldn't see anything.

Suddenly, I bumped into a bale of hay. Shoot. OK, just walk around that.

A few paces after that, I bumped into another bale of hay. *Man, these camels go through a lot of hay*, I thought.

Then the bale stood up.

I was face-to-face with a six-foot-something, 800-ish pound camel.

"That's Skoodles," Shawn whispered.

"Oh. Uh, hey, Skoodles. Good Skoodles." Luckily, Skoodles and I were tight, but that was the last time I did that.

I wasn't scared of the animals. I grew up skittish around dogs because I got bit when I was very young, but the zoo helped me get over my fear. Besides, the animals were nothing compared to the customers.

The vast majority of the people I met at the Toronto Zoo were amazing. I like meeting and talking to nice people from all over the world, and the zoo was a great place to do that. But each year, the zoo had over one million guests come through the gate.

Think of all the people you know and deal with on a regular basis. How many of them aren't very nice? How many of them kind of suck? And how many of them are out of their mind? Probably a few, but not many.

Now put that on the scale of over one million people. You're bound to gets some bozos. Oh, and I did.

A few years into my job, I got the opportunity to be a commentator on the zoomobile tour. At the end of the day, we had to put the tour buses away. One day in particular, my friend Rob was driving the bus, and I was at the back — safety first.

We were driving through the zoo's large African section when I saw something that made my heart jump.

Some idiot — some absolute maniac — had hopped into the giraffe enclosure. Hey, at least my camel incident was an accident. This guy knew what he was doing. He couldn't have been more than five or six feet from the giraffe's front legs, and his friend was standing on the non-maniac side of the barrier, taking his picture.

Would you like to know the giraffe part of my commentary from the zoomobile tour? I still remember it.

"The Masai giraffe stands at about six metres tall. Two metres of its height are in its neck, another two metres in its legs, and they give birth standing up.

"A giraffe's heart is roughly the size of a basketball. Believe it or not, they also have the same number of vertebrae in their neck as we do.

"Our guys are nice and friendly, but in the wild, a kick from a giraffe is so powerful that it can crush a lion's skull."

Did you catch that last part?

Rob evidently didn't notice what was happening, and why would he? He had to keep his eyes on the road and it wasn't exactly an everyday occurrence to see somebody chilling in the giraffe exhibit. Plus, humans barely even look real standing next to giraffes. Let's say this guy was six feet tall. Like I said, Masai giraffes are nearly 20 feet tall.

I didn't want to yell at the guy and potentially startle the giraffe. So I grabbed the zoomobile microphone and tried to whisper into it to get Rob's attention.

"Rob," I said, muffled into the mic.

"Rob, stop the bus. Stop the bus, Rob."

He stopped and we got out. Rob quietly called security over the radio and I calmly walked over to these guys to distract them and, more importantly, coax them out of the freaking giraffe enclosure.

Unfortunately, they took off before getting caught by security. On the bright side, however, they weren't turned into pancakes.

Not all the craziness I saw was animal related.

One time I saw a group of students from Connecticut pointing and laughing about something. When they saw me, they flagged me down.

"Hey, how come Canada has so many Asian people?" one asked.

"Um. It's nice here?" What do you even say to that?

"How come everyone here says 'eh'?" the same one asked.

In the most polite, customer service–y way I could muster, I replied, "Oh, I don't think we say it that much." Then I added, "Maybe they say it a bit more out east."

This student looked me dead in my face. "Canada has an east?" she asked.

Has your brain ever melted under the heat of someone else's stupidity? Mine did at that very moment. It was just a puddle in my skull. I had to throw my whole brain out and get a new one.

Some other quick tales:

One time, a gentleman walked up to me at around 5 p.m. and told me he had dinner plans in Montreal that night at 8. For the unaware, if there was no traffic and he broke every law of the road, he still would have been at least two hours late.

Someone told me that they dropped their camera in the Sumatran tiger exhibit, which was extra confusing because at the time, the park wasn't even open yet.

A surprisingly frequent protest to the cost of a camel ride was "I don't know why I'm doing this — I have a camel back home."

One of the older seasonal employees famously refused to give Sylvester Stallone's assistant a free stroller at the stroller rental.

One time, a guy returned a stroller and I gave him his deposit back before realizing that he had left a used diaper in each of the stroller's two drink-holders. I saw them. He saw me see them.

We looked each other in the eyes. Then he turned around and left to continue to be the world's worst human somewhere else.

It wasn't all ridiculous stories of me being a moron and difficult customers. Most visitors were awesome, and I actually liked that job very much.

One time, just as I was about to go home for the day, a couple in their late 20s walked by me in the courtyard with their young son. The child was only about three and looked like he had got into a 10-round fight with the pavement. This kid must have been running full tilt and fell something fierce because blood was trickling out of both of his elbows and knees.

I asked them if they needed any help and offered to call first aid, but they said they just wanted to get home to clean him up. Finally, I offered to patch him up myself — just a few bandages to stop the bleeding while they were in the car. The parents agreed.

I took out the first aid kit, calmed the kid down, and cleaned the wounds. His parents were so happy that they wrote on the zoo's website:

> We want to take this opportunity to thank your staff members for looking after my son Matthew after he fell on Friday, July 23 [2010], while visiting the zoo. Thanks for the care and effort taken to make sure he was OK. In particular, we want to give Steve Glen (we hope we have his name right) a very special thanks. Even though he was on his way home, he stopped to take care and administer first aid to Matthew. He was excellent in the way he treated Matthew, and we appreciate the fact that he went out of his way to help us. Thanks for a wonderful experience at the zoo!

Nearly a decade later, that still makes me proud. My boss used to call those PDMs or positive defining moments; the sort of little one-moment things that could make a guest love the zoo forever. He was obsessed with Disney World and how attentive their customer service was and wanted the zoo to follow their example.

One time when I was operating the simulator ride, famous Canadian golfer Mike Weir walked up with his family. I didn't even like golf, but I knew Mike Weir. He was all over the place when he won the 2003 Masters Tournament. Mike requested a certain ride, and I told him no problem. I got all flustered and accidentally selected the wrong ride. I realized the mistake and went up to greet him after the ride. When the door opened, he gave me a very *that wasn't the ride I asked for* look. Then I told everyone to sit back down because they're getting a free ride. I gave Mike a wink, like, "Hey buddy, I know you're Mike Weir, so here's a free ride on me." No, I was just stupid.

Every summer, the Leafs would send a player to the zoo for an autograph signing. I would either take the day off and show up anyway or wait until my lunch, change into street clothes, and get in line.

It actually became somewhat of a curse. Every time a Leafs player did a signing at the zoo, they weren't on the Leafs by the next summer. It had to be a curse. It couldn't be that the team was consistently trash and had a lot of turnover as a result. No way!

I met Darcy Tucker at one of these signings; he signed a card for my dad for Father's Day. Another time, I met Alexei Ponikarovsky. But the one that sticks out the most was Nik Antropov.

For some reason, I had a lot of Nik Antropov stuff. I had a bunch of cards, an 8-by-10 photo, and I even ripped his page out of a calendar for him to sign.

There's no way he's going to sign all this, I told myself. I needed to get someone to help me.

I convinced Shawn the camel guy to come wait in line with me and get half of my stuff signed. Why I picked Shawn, I'll never know. He wasn't even a hockey fan.

It was a rainy, muggy day, so the attendance at the zoo was sparser than usual, and the line for Antropov was painfully, awkwardly short. I could have just gone up by myself. He would have signed it all. What else was he going to do? There was barely anyone there!

I got my stuff signed and thanked him very much. Now it was Shawn's turn.

"So," he started. "You're a hockey player, huh?"

Antropov laughed. "Yeah."

"And how's that going for ya?" Shawn asked.

"Well, my back's fucked," Antropov replied.

Kyle Wellwood was another Leaf I bumped into at the zoo, only he was just a regular customer. One day, he walked over to the ticket booth I was working in that day, and I recognized him right away.

He accidentally overpaid for something by a dollar. When I noticed that, I said, "Sir, you've actually overpaid. Here's your dollar." I might have even called him Mr. Wellwood.

"Just keep it," he said and then walked away.

I sat there with this loonie in my hand. We weren't allowed to accept tips at the zoo, but this wasn't a tip. This was a souvenir!

I ripped a piece of receipt paper and taped the loonie to it. I taped the paper to the wall of the ticket booth and wrote "Kyle Wellwood's Dollar" on the paper. I made sure to let everyone know if I found out somebody took Kyle Wellwood's dollar, there was going to be hell to pay.

After my final shift, I took home the Wellwood dollar. It hung in my room until long after Wellwood had been a Leaf. One day, I was broke enough that I thought, *Screw it, I could use a dollar right now.*

If you've ever worked at a tourist attraction, especially a weather-dependent one like the zoo, you know it's a lot of hurry up and wait. Sunny Saturdays and Sundays were absolute mayhem, but rainy weekdays were torturously slow and boring.

Being the only one in the ticket booth with no one to talk to was the worst.

I would tear off receipt paper and write out all the Leafs' lines. "Ponikarovsky should get bumped to the Leafs' second line this year. Maybe even first. I wonder if he'll have chemistry with Johnny Pohl?"

Then I would write out all the Leafs' defensive pairings. "What are they gonna do with McCabe this year? Will he ever score 19 goals again? I'd settle for him never scoring on his own net again."

Then I would write out every prospect the Leafs had in the system. Then I would try to write out lines for other teams. A few times, I remember I simply wrote a list of every NHL player I could name.

"Steve, we're out of receipt paper, again."

"Sorry, boss, but I had to figure out the Leafs' bottom six situation."

"Steve, you're fired."

The zoo actually helped me develop skills I still use in my work today. No matter where I was stationed, I was always talking to hundreds if not thousands of people per day. In real life!

The zoomobile in particular helped create many inter-changeable skills. Each tour was 25 to 30 minutes long, and on a busy day, I would do eight to 10 tours. That's four or five hours of talking. How long is your favourite sports radio show or pod-cast? There's a good chance I was talking more than any of them, except I was talking about rhinos instead of Mats Sundin signing with the Canucks, which I refuse to believe ever happened.

And who am I kidding? I probably talked about that, too. I was notorious for going off script. To be honest, I found the script hard to stick to. I never knew when an animal was going to be asleep, away, or hiding, so I had to improvise.

When you bought a ticket for the zoomobile, they gave you a wristband that allowed you to get on and off all day. By the end of the day, a bunch of guests had probably heard the tour, maybe even heard me give it, four or five times.

Around dinner time, I would start asking, "Alright, who has already been on a tour with me today?"

More than half the hands would shoot up, especially on hot days when people didn't feel like dragging their families through one of the largest zoos in North America.

So I would improvise and change up the script. My go-to move was to talk about crazy animal videos I had seen on YouTube. I looked up a bunch of them — half for my own curiosity and half for such an occasion. My favourite video to tell people to look up at the time was called "Battle at Kruger." If you've never seen it, you have to.

There's a giant heard of buffalo in South Africa's Kruger National Park being stalked by a pride of lions. The lions attack and manage to tackle a baby buffalo into the water. As they struggle to haul the baby buffalo out of the water, a giant crocodile comes in and tries to steal the buffalo in a terrible tug of war. The lions win and begin dragging the baby.

Just then, the camera pans out and the entire herd of buffalo comes back, ready to rumble. They chase off the lions, one of them even hurling one of the massive cats high into the air. Unbelievably, the baby buffalo gets back up and runs back into the herd.

It's one of the craziest things I've ever seen and I've seen Mikhail Grabovski score a goal with his head. *National Geographic* paid good money for the rights to the footage, which was crazy back in the earlier days of YouTube. I knew I would never capture a vicious three-way struggle for survival between buffalo, lions, and crocodiles, but it was a tiny sliver of hope for me that yes, I could make money on YouTube.

Working at the Toronto Zoo was an amazing experience. I was so lucky to have consistent work there, have an interesting job in the summer sun, and meet so many great people.

How did I end up working in hockey? It's about time I told you.

GETTING SCHOOLED

The media always interested me. From the time I was young, I always thought it would be great to be on *Hockey Night in Canada*. Lots of kids in Canada have that dream. I just never thought it was realistic.

Come on, Steve. Only former players get those jobs. You don't even know how to stop on skates without using the boards . . .

Nevertheless, being on TV always seemed cool. There were only two things standing in my way:

1. I was terrified.
2. I had no talent.

Other than that, I was well on my way.

It's amazing how random split-second and seemingly insignificant decisions can change the entire course of your life. I mentioned that I was a hyper child, but it's not like I was bouncing off the walls 24/7. I loved drawing. I was pretty good at it, too. I started out drawing my family and cartoon characters. When I got a little older, I drew hockey players and wrestlers, and as a teenager, I drew my favourite musicians. So when high school came around, I decided to take visual art. Why not? It seemed like an easy course and it was one of the few things I actually thought I was good at.

It took only a few weeks for me to decide I didn't like it. For starters, I didn't have many friends in my visual arts class. I had the class after gym, and I didn't particularly enjoy sitting quietly to draw after running around and sweating for over an hour.

One of my oldest friends from elementary school, Adam Rodricks (the one who remembers the pants-down "O Canada" story), convinced me to drop that class and take drama with him, instead. I was skeptical. I liked goofing around with my friends and being a clown in our own little circle, but the idea of getting up in front of the class and reciting something made me want to crawl under my bed. I can now honestly say if I didn't drop visual art in the ninth grade, I wouldn't have my current life and career.

I got comfortable enough in front of my classmates that I did alright in the class, so I took it again the next year, too. Early in the year, our teacher, Ms. Kish, somehow convinced me to audition for the school play. She was a wacky teacher, for sure. She was over-the-top expressive and boisterous, as well as blunt and matter-of-fact in the way she offered criticism. Again, I'd gotten used to my classmates, but the idea of doing a play in front of other people or even just rehearsing in front of people I didn't know sounded terrible.

I had no idea what the hell I was doing. It wasn't any play I had ever heard of, either. Ms. Kish had written it herself. It was called *ConneXtions*.

The character was unlike anybody I had ever met or could even relate to. I played Boone, an asexual guy who came across a businessman who was about to jump off Toronto's Bloor Viaduct. By the end of my scene, I convinced the man not to jump but in the process convinced myself to do it instead. Somehow I got the part.

For a play the whole school could audition for, we were a young cast. There were only seven of us: one 12th grader, one 11th grader, and one ninth grader. Four of us were in the 10th grade, including myself and this guy named Adam Wylde. Apart from a few street hockey games, I didn't know him very well. One of the crew members was a guy named Justin Fisher, a spikey-haired kid caught somewhere between punk and emo. Both Adam and Justin were groomsmen at my wedding. Without this play? Who knows.

I sucked at rehearsals. I had trouble following instructions, and I was easily the slowest at memorizing my lines. The grade 12 student was the only actor I interacted with onstage and he was miles better than me. It wasn't long before the night of the performance in front of the student body that I knew the whole script, and even then I was shaky.

The play was part of the Sears Festival, where they showcased a bunch of Ontario high school plays. There were three tiers: divisionals, regionals, and provincials. Our school, Sir Oliver Mowat, was hosting the divisionals, so we would be performing in front of all of our classmates and parents. No pressure, eh.

I forgot a few of my lines but improvised well enough that nobody noticed. To my shock, I received an Award of Excellence for my performance, and we advanced to regionals. I immediately went from shy guy onstage to aspiring movie star. We made it all the way to provincials and performed in Ottawa in 2004.

I kept up with drama in grade 11 and also gave media a shot, since my newfound confidence made a career in media sound more appealing. It helped that my teacher, Mr. Light, was passionate about the subject, and smart as well as funny. We were one of the first media classes; it had only recently been introduced to the curriculum.

One fateful day in grade 11 sticks out in my mind.

Adam and I have spoken about this. He thinks it was in a class called challenge and change in society, but I'm almost positive it happened in math. I had to pay the most attention in math, after all. I sucked at it and so did Adam. Justin sat with us, too.

One day, Adam, Justin, and I were talking about what we were going to do with our lives. In one year's time, we had to start applying to universities and basically plan out the rest of our lives.

We must have been talking about hockey, too, because I remember Adam saying, "One day you and I will have a sports show together." I didn't think that was at all realistic, but it was something I held on to for years.

Doing a sports show on the radio was something I had definitely thought of. I used to call into *Leafs Lunch* hosted by Jeff Marek, on a station called MoJo Radio. I really liked Marek's style. I remember calling in after the Leafs got eliminated from the 2004 playoffs — that damn Jeremy Roenick goal — and complaining about Nik Antropov for some reason. I said, "I'm only sixteen, but I don't think I'll ever see a Stanley Cup in my lifetime." When I hung up, either he or his co-host said, "Wow, I don't think I've ever heard a sixteen-year-old sound so jaded." They even played the clip again after the commercial break. I mean, if I can ace a radio call like that, I can probably handle my own sports show, right? How hard could it be?

Another thing that was born late in high school: *the* name — "Dangle."

Because I knew I wanted to get into media, and journalism specifically, I started writing for the school newspaper, *The Mowat Missprints*. Our editor-in-chief, a classmate named Diana Bailey, wanted to carry on a tradition. For some reason, all writers had to take on some kind of ridiculous fake nickname that would be printed in the middle of your first and last name in the newspaper.

One day, Diana brought in a book by an author who, for whatever reason, had a chapter dedicated to homeless people who had given themselves strange names.

My eyes fell upon the name "Floyd Dangle," which I thought was hilarious for some reason. When I was published a little while later, I was Steve "Floyd Dangle" Glynn. Fisher wrote for the paper, too, and he was Justin "The Sexwise Elf" Fisher. Looking back, my writing was dreadful and I made arguments about things I'd punch myself for if I could time travel, but, at very least, I found Floyd Dangle.

Unfortunately for my school, I ran to become publicity rep in grade 12. I cracked a few jokes in my speech and made fun of my big head, and I even used MS Paint to superimpose my face on top of Keanu Reeves's face on *The Matrix* poster and plastered it all over the school.

I actually won, which meant I got to do the morning announcements every day. Each morning, at the five-minute warning for the bell before first period, I got to play music, and I chose everything from Sean Paul to Flogging Molly. One morning, I even played the *Halo* theme song. How could you not be ready to crush the day after that? During announcements, I'd stumble over my words and use a stupid high-pitched Elmo voice from time to time. Why they never kicked me out, I'll never know.

Another impulse move in high school, this time in grade 12, changed everything for me.

Today, there are many good journalism and media programs in Canada. In 2005, however, choices were slimmer. The journalism school with the best reputation in the country was Ryerson University in Toronto, which was great because I couldn't afford to move away anyway.

When I was in grade 12, the Ontario University Application fee was $100, and you got to apply to three schools. Each additional school you applied to was another $33. I applied to the journalism program at Ryerson, journalism at University of Toronto's Scarborough campus, and, for some dumb reason, the English program at York University. I picked that one randomly, because I liked writing. I had no idea what I could do with an English degree (my wife who is a teacher has an English degree).

I had tunnel vision for some reason. It must have just been the word "journalism" because Ryerson also had a well-known and well-respected media program called radio and television arts, or RTA for short.

I remember the night that applications were due. The deadline was midnight, and I was sitting at my computer with less than half an hour to go. Both my parents were fast asleep.

I found myself looking into Ryerson's radio and television arts program more and more. Should I have applied? Their journalism program is so hard to get into. But then again, so is this one. Do I really want to go to U of T Scarborough, just down the street? Why the hell did I apply to York? Forget the program — commuting there is going to be a freaking nightmare. I've made a huge mistake.

Panic set in. I woke my parents up — to ask them for money. My parents love me and everything, but I wouldn't have blamed my mom or dad if they karate chopped me in the throat.

Through groggy eyes, however, my mom understood that I was actually thinking about my future, so she got out of bed and helped me apply to a fourth school, just 10 minutes before the deadline.

York didn't even notify me when I got in. U of T Scarborough did, though, with a big letter in the mail. I was so proud and so were my parents. Neither of them went to postsecondary school.

Finally word came from the Ryerson journalism program: waitlisted.

Basically, "Hey, you're not quite good enough for our school, but you might be if some more qualified students decide this program is beneath them." That was a bit of a gut punch, especially because I had wanted to get into that program for so long.

The radio and TV application process was intense. I had an 82 percent average, just a hair above the minimum 80 percent needed to get in. After my initial application passed the smell test, I was invited to take part in the next portion of the process: an online test. Adam Wylde had applied for the program, too, so we took it in the library together, under the supervision of our grade 12 media teacher, Ms. Andrews. The questions were incredibly bizarre. I don't remember much, but I distinctly remember something random about a squirrel. Adam and I were both convinced we bombed terribly.

To our surprise, we both got to the next phase: an essay.

The essay I wrote was called "Sour Grapes," and it was about how Don Cherry could get away with saying literally anything on-air. They must have liked it, because I was selected for an interview, the last part of the application process. Adam got one, too. The night before the interview, I realized I was missing one of the forms I was supposed to have. I was an absolute wreck; I had a nervous breakdown. After everything I had done to get this far, I had screwed it all up because of a stupid form. I'm screwed! I'm completely screwed!

Turns out, it didn't matter. What a ball of stress I was, though.

I was told the interview topic would be current events. A rumour had spread that a girl who had applied to the program couldn't name any local, provincial, national, or even international events. Allegedly the interviewer asked, "Are you serious?" and laughed her out of the room. I made sure to find a story for each of those.

The day of the interview, students were told to wait in a room together. Unfortunately, Adam wasn't scheduled for that day. Every nervous applicant in there had to make idle chit-chat.

One of the other applicants was this long-haired guy from Brampton named Clay. We immediately clicked, maybe because he was the only person who was louder than me. Everyone was actually having a great time and even cracking jokes, until one of the girls in the room told a story.

"What did you guys put on your applications under experience?" she asked.

We all listed off a few things.

"Did you hear about the girl with the violin?" she asked.

A few people shook their head.

"There was this girl who heard that if you say you play

59

a musical instrument, they were more likely to accept you, regardless of whatever program you applied for, because it shows dedication. She put down that she had played the violin for 12 years. Because who could possibly check that, right?

"So she gets to the interview, and when she walks in, sitting right there on the chair is a violin. They asked her to play it. She admitted that she had lied about it. They told her that because she lied, they were going to alert the other schools in the province and have her blacklisted."

That sucked all the fun out of the room. Everyone seemed more nervous than when they had arrived.

On the other hand, I couldn't help but feel like I had heard this story before. I was pretty sure it was just an urban legend. Did she tell all the other applicants that story just to throw them off? She ended up getting into RTA, but I never quite trusted her after that.

Finally, it was my turn for an interview.

The professor interviewing me was an unassuming-looking academic. Imagine if Bill Nye had a subdued, WASPY uncle. I didn't mind, though; supposedly one of the more eccentric professors was notorious for dying his hair blue during interview week just to mess with the applicants.

To this day, I don't think I've ever aced anything like I aced that interview. I was confident in my answers, well prepared, and well spoken.

The defining moment of the interview was when he asked me for some local news in my neighbourhood. I had thorough answers for international, national, and provincial, but I was genuinely stumped for my own neighbourhood. There just wasn't much going on at the time.

What do I do? I definitely can't make something up. How do I BS my way out of this one?

Rather than try to impress him, I just told him the truth.

"Honestly, I live in east Scarborough. I know Scarborough is often on the news, and not always in the best way, but not much has happened recently."

I mentioned a few older stories and something that was happening at the community centre in the summer. That was all I could muster.

He just stared at me in silence. It was probably for only two seconds but it seemed like an entire weekend.

"You know, I'm from west Scarborough, and I totally know what you mean," he said. I felt like I had just won 10 grand at the poker table with a handful of nothing. We started bonding over Scarborough and critiqued how it was conveyed in the media.

"If it were up to me, I'd accept you into the program today," he told me.

I lit up like a Christmas tree.

"But it's not up to me," he explained. "So I'll let you know."

When I walked out of there, practically floating, I saw Clay. I guess his interview went well, too, because he was smiling ear to ear. We compared notes for a bit, said goodbye, and as I was leaving, I said, "See you in September!"

I didn't even mean to say it. It just came out. In that moment, I knew I would be getting in. Unfortunately, Adam didn't have the same kind of experience. His professor had asked him what courses he planned on taking in semesters seven and eight.

"What the hell?" I said. "What did you even say?"

"I said I don't know," Adam told me.

Apparently the professor was not impressed. I guess Adam's answers made it seem he hadn't done his research on the program. But who the hell even looks at that sort of thing? I didn't even know what courses I wanted to take in first year, let alone fourth.

This is one of the many things I'll always respect about Adam. Kids at our high school knew his mom is Marilyn Denis, a famous Canadian radio and TV host. All he had to do was say that during his interview, and I bet he would have gotten in. I mean, that's pretty relevant information, don't you think? He had been around radio and television his entire life. She was the perfect mentor to have and he lived in her freaking house.

But he wanted to do it on his own. I got in; Adam didn't. He attended Ryerson for a bit but not for the program that he wanted. But now look at him: Adam has been working in radio and television since he was 18, working a combination of overnights, evenings, afternoons, and even mornings in Barrie, Halifax, Calgary, and Toronto. His resume is longer than this book. Oh, and later, we'll get to that little sports show we talked about in math class.

Sometimes I think back on it all and it's a bit overwhelming.

What if I hadn't decided I was too sweaty to draw? What if Adam Rodricks hadn't suggested I switch classes? What if I didn't audition for that play? What if I never wrote for the school newspaper or chose that stupid nickname? What if my mom didn't get up and help me apply for another school? What if I didn't ace my interview? What if I got the same interviewer as Adam Wylde?

What's the lesson here? Try lots of things? Say "yes" more often? Certain things are just destiny? Or maybe life is just a lot of dumb luck?

It's scary how much these little, seemingly nothing decisions you make as a teenager can follow you for the rest of your life. Thinking about it freaks me out.

FIRST YEAR

In one of my classes during the first week of university, we went around a circle and everyone said who they were, what they had done, and what they wanted to do.

Half of the class had a story along the lines of "Hi, my name is . . . and I volunteer with Rogers."

For the non-Canadians, there are basically two giant telecom companies in eastern Canada: Rogers and Bell. There are a few more options, but those are the main companies. Rogers owns a whole bunch of local TV stations, where people could volunteer and learn all kinds of things: camerawork, lighting, sound, floor directing — you name it.

After like a dozen of those stories, it was my turn.

"Hi, uh, I'm Steve and, uh, I used to do the morning announcements."

It was like talking about my school play at a job interview all over again. *How the hell did I even get into this program? How was this happening, again?*

That first year, I struggled with a few things — most prominently the technology.

Our first semester was dedicated to audio. We barely even touched video. "You can't learn to edit video before you learn to edit audio," we were told.

One of my classes recommended we all get noise-cancelling

headphones, which I didn't even know was a thing. One friend bought a pair of $300 headphones. Meanwhile, in my first week, I was doing some math and wondering, *Can I even afford to take the train this much?* I used ear buds, and when those proved to be borderline useless, I borrowed a pair of cheap headphones from my dad that looked like I had two soup cans strapped to my head.

I still remember wearing those headphones on the train one day, changing CDs in my portable CD player, and these kids who looked a few years younger than me were sneaking glances and laughing. Man, five years ago I begged for this thing — now it's corny? Damn.

In another class, we had to learn Flash, an older graphics program. I sucked at that, too. I made this little cartoon guy dribble a basketball and shoot it, but I couldn't get the ball to go through the hoop.

For that class, we had to get a one gigabyte flash drive. Go ahead and guess how much one of those cost? Remember this was 2006.

They wanted $40. Forty. Damn. Dollars. They give those things away at events like pamphlets now. Most of you reading this probably have a bunch of bigger flash drives lost somewhere in a drawer in your house. Hell, some of you are probably wondering, *What the hell is a flash drive?*

Easily the most inhibiting thing was not having the actual software at home. For audio and video editing, we used Sony Vegas. For Flash, we obviously used Flash. I didn't have either of those programs. They were too expensive.

"Why didn't you just bootleg it?" some of you might ask. Some of my classmates did, for sure. Honestly, though, I think my computer would have exploded. I was still using the computer my aunt had given me — it was so old, it was ready to die. The fan literally sounded like a motorcycle.

"Why not just stay behind and use the school's computers?" I did. A lot. But I was a commuter. *I've already been downtown all day for my classes, I have all this homework to do, I have to get up early again the next morning.* After class, I could spend maybe an hour or two playing with the software but not all damn night.

One girl brought me back to reality, however.

I was in the student lounge with Clay, lamenting my commute. He had to commute from Brampton himself.

"Do you know where Blaise commutes from?" he asked.

"Where?"

"Waterloo," he told me.

"What?"

"Yeah, man. She takes the bus. Every day," Clay explained.

Two hours there. Two hours back. Four hours round trip. Every day. I found her in the student lounge shortly after.

"You're Blaise, right?" I asked.

"I am," she said, surprised.

"I heard you commute from Waterloo," I told her.

She just laughed. Apparently I wasn't the first to ask.

"Yep," she said.

"I'm never going to complain about my commute ever again," I said, which was a dirty lie.

I kept complaining and I still do. Who the hell likes commuting? People send me a lot of nice messages about my podcast these days, but the ones that mean the most to me are "Thanks for making my commute suck less." The whole greater Toronto area is commuter hell in business hours and most of the rest of Canada is sprawling and spread out. If I can make the whole affair suck less, then I feel like I've done a good job.

While I was discouraged — and wondered what I was even doing in the program, and felt underqualified, and contemplated dropping out — I didn't know what else I would do. Plus the idea of my parents murdering me was . . . unappealing. So I made it work. Everyone has goals in life, and sometimes, to achieve them, you have to make a choice. Want to eat a cookie? Alright, pay for the cookie. Don't want to pay for it? No cookie for you then.

Sometimes, the currency is your time, effort, and sacrifice. Want to learn how use this software? Alright, well, the cost is two hours of your time and effort each night for the next two weeks, plus the sacrifice of missing a few Leafs games and not seeing your friends. You can take it or leave it, but that's what it costs.

One nice benefit of the program, however, was I really liked my classmates. I started to make new friends, including the Thursday Hangout Crew: me, Clay, Katrina, Carly, and this journalism student named Derek Rider.

Derek had all the charisma in the world and, like Clay, this uncontainable Energizer Bunny filled any room he was in with his energy. Despite getting into Canada's premiere journalism program, and despite that fact that he seemed to be succeeding in it, he never had much interest. He spent more time hanging out with us in the RTA lounge than with his peers in the journalism lounge.

Derek had an October birthday and we wanted to celebrate. We were all under 19, so going for a drink was out. We decided to go to the grocery store across the street and get him a cake.

We pooled our money and got him one of those rectangular cakes and asked them to write "Happy Birthday Derek" on it. They told us there wasn't enough room, so we settled on "Happy Derek."

We ate the cake until we felt like barfing. There was still a lot left, so we looked out the window onto a downtown Toronto street and saw a homeless man.

"Let's go down and give the rest to him. I bet he'll really appreciate it."

"Hello, sir. Would you accept this cake from us? We left you a fork, too."

"I will if you give me two bucks," he replied.

We weren't expecting that. We gave him the two bucks, for some reason.

When we went back upstairs, we looked out the window, and to our surprise, we saw two guys just having a donnybrook right on the sidewalk, throwing wild lefts and rights at each other.

"Oh my God! Somebody's robbing him for his cake!"

We were about to run down when we realized, he wasn't one of the guys fighting. He was just standing a few feet away from them, watching the fight and eating his cake.

Out of nowhere, a fire truck pulled up and at least four fire-fighters jumped off the truck to break up the fight.

Then our friend hiked up his pants and walked off into the sunset, box of cake still in hand.

I kept in touch with my high school friends, too. My good pal Justin Fisher was studying English at U of T Scarborough, right near where we lived. That winter, knowing I was utterly single and alone, he told me about this girl he had met.

"She asked me if I knew any boys," he explained. "Her name is Sarah-Louise. I think you would like her. She's pretty funny and she'll probably knock you down a peg or two."

Funny enough, we didn't really want to meet each other. Fisher had a recent track record of disastrous relationships, so we were both like, "Um, yeah, not sure I trust your judgment there, bud."

In spite of our better judgment, we decided to meet each other at another mutual friend's house. When I got there, they were already baking cookies. That's a good start; just a pro move.

She was as funny as advertised, had these big pretty eyes, and was sharp as a tack. That last one might have something to do with her being born in Scotland. We went in expecting to come out of it going, "Justin, what the hell was that?" but after meeting once, we both liked each other.

Want to know another great thing about Sarah-Louise? She worked at Future Shop, an old electronics franchise in Canada. You know what's great about that?

Discounts!

She told me she could use her employee discount to get me some of the stuff I needed for school. One thing in particular I wanted, for both school and personal interest, was a webcam.

One day she posted on my Facebook wall.

"Wonderful news, I can get you a $77 webcam for 23 bucks. See yah."

I was planning on asking her out the next time I saw her, so that's all I was thinking about.

The night after my final exam in first year, we met up at Justin's and I asked her to be my girlfriend.

On April 25, 2007, I left Fisher's house with a girlfriend who would eventually become my wife and the webcam that would kickstart my career.

I didn't know that at the time, though . . . I was just happy that a girl liked me.

SEAT FILLER

A frequent thing I tell media students is "The most valuable thing you'll graduate with is your phone." Sure, you might have paid an astonishing, wallet-crippling amount of money for that fancy degree, but the saying, "It's all about who you know" is actually very true.

That "someone" doesn't have to be a rich, powerful person sipping expensive brandy in their office at noon. Sometimes it's an 18-year-old classmate who hears about a neat opportunity and is awesome enough to share that information with you. For me, that awesome classmate was Chloe Perelgut.

Chloe was in my program, and we'd hang out in the student lounge. I'd goof around, and she'd work, and we'd talk about nerdy stuff together.

Her boyfriend made a stop-motion YouTube video called "Thriller Metru." It was all of the Toa Metru characters from the Lego Bionicles dancing to Michael Jackson's "Thriller." It was perfectly choreographed, comprised of 1,300 pictures, and took him two months to complete.

I thought I was a geek, but their nerdiness was NHL-level and mine was barely Junior B. In fairness, over a decade later I'm a grown man who makes YouTube videos in a room full of toys for a living, so who's the real dork?

On May 23, 2007, Chloe sent me a message on Facebook.

"Just passing this along. I don't know who else likes this sort of thing."

Chloe had received an email from CBC, Canada's national public broadcaster, that said:

"We are on the lookout for seat fillers for the 2007 NHL Awards on June 14. This is your chance to see all your hockey heroes in person.

Tickets are free, but there are some strict rules involved:

Maximum of two tickets per person.

No autograph seeking.

You must be 18 years of age or older.

No wandering off into restricted areas.

There is a formal dress code involved.

Seat-filling is like a game of musical chairs. This is not a ticket to the event, but a volunteer opportunity to fill a seat for a limited amount of time while the ticket holder does not occupy it.

If you are interested in being a seat filler, or have further questions, please email me."

Holy. Eff. Yes. I am interested.

I sent an email to the organizer, never expecting to actually hear back. I sent them my resume and everything, as if you need some kind of qualifications to be a seat filler. "I may hate the Ottawa Senators, but with the incredible acting skills I picked up from a play I did in grade 10, no one will ever know!"

To my utter shock, they emailed me back and said I could come. And with that, I was officially a seat filler for the 2007 NHL Awards.

They mentioned that they wanted a few seat fillers to show up early in the afternoon to help out and stand in for things if they were needed. I made sure that I had the day off at the zoo, determined to get as much out of this as possible.

When the morning of June 14 came, I could not wait to get ready. I got showered, put on the suit I had worn to prom almost exactly a year earlier: black shirt with a white tie, pretied by my dad from the last time I had worn it. Ready for prom night 2.0, I took the train downtown to go to the Elgin Theatre.

The Elgin Theatre is an older venue in the heart of Toronto's downtown core, near Yonge and Queen. I passed it on my walk from Union Station to school every day. It opened in 1913, making it older than the National Hockey League.

When I arrived, I was one of first people there. My job at that point was pretty simple: stay out of the way.

The theatre is full of red seats with gold trim. The seats definitely had a "grandparents' curtains" feel to them. I wouldn't have been surprised if they had been the same seats from when the theatre was restored the year before I was born. I specifically remember walking over to the right of the theatre — stage left, for my fellow drama dorks — and sitting down in a random chair. About 10 rows down from me was a group of three or four people, one of whom looked familiar. Wait a second — is that George Stroumboulopoulos?

It was. I grew up watching Strombo as a VJ on MuchMusic and had even watched his talk show *The Hour* a few times. *The Hour* was the first podcast I ever downloaded in video form. I remember the first time I got to watch it on my iPod Touch while on the train, looking at all the morning commuters around me and thinking I was in an episode of *The Jetsons*. It turns out George was there because he and famous Canadian WWE wrestler Trish Stratus were presenting the Vezina Trophy to the NHL's best goalie that night. They ended up doing this bit about how they were Greek and that there were no Greek-born players in the NHL because none of their names would fit on the back of a jersey.

George was having an animated conversation about some party he went to where the host had his Xbox hooked up in an IMAX-style theatre. I heard him say, "So I'm just sitting there like Jesus Christ!" as he leaned back to reenact what it was like to play video games on the ceiling.

Yes, I was eavesdropping, but this was probably the most famous person I'd ever seen at that point, talking about the coolest thing I'd ever heard of. He might as well have been talking about hitting up Studio 54 in the 1970s.

After a minute or two, George finished up his conversation, got up, and started making his way up the aisle. Just before he walked past me, he saw me gawking at him and shot me a quick wink. I gave him a quick nod back and smiled. Like, "Hello, peer."

Listen, I know it's stupid, but I was a 19-year-old trying to "make it" in media, and I had just had a non-verbal exchange with George Stroumboulopoulos. This was the most famous I had felt since kindergarten, when my school play got picked up by the local news.

After George passed, I noticed the chair I was sitting in was labelled "Phil Kessel." At the time, I didn't know what kind of (allegedly) hot dog–eating pariah he would become in Toronto or the Stanley Cup champion he'd become in Pittsburgh. I only knew Kessel as the Boston Bruins player who had beaten testicular cancer, missing only 12 games in the process, all as a rookie.

Phil was a lock to win the Bill Masterton Trophy for perseverance, sportsmanship, and dedication to ice hockey. Wait — was I sitting in Phil Kessel's seat?

As I realized where I was sitting, one of the seat's arms wobbled and flipped around 90 degrees.

Ah! Did I do that? No, no. I didn't do that. I found it that way. What if Phil Kessel — *the* Phil Kessel — had to sit in this seat with a wobbly arm? The guy was here for the Masterton Trophy. Hadn't he been through enough?

I got up and told the nearest person who was not some hyper teenager with a rapidly growing crush on a former MuchMusic VJ and who was actually working there. He said thanks for letting him know. I sat down and patiently waited for my inevitable "Employee of the Month" plaque.

While the production crew continued to set up, I took a new seat at the opposite end of the theatre. I saw longtime *Hockey Night in Canada* rinkside reporter Scott Oake on the big screen onstage, reciting lines from outside the theatre while they tested the camera and adjusted his microphone levels.

"What up? This is Scott Oake," he said into the mic, as I probably laughed a bit too loud.

Just then, Ron MacLean appeared right there, onstage and in the flesh. I'm not sure I even knew he was hosting that night.

The aura surrounding Ron MacLean is hard to describe. As he paced around the stage, asking questions and giving out instructions, he was equal parts calm and confident. He wasn't rude or bossy at all, just friendly but all-business at the same time.

After what had to be less than five minutes, Ron had finished whatever it was he needed to do and left. He was just in and out like a pro who had been there before and could get on national television in his sleep. Here I was, cheating on George.

After Ron left the stage, one of the people in charge of coordinating the event called out to me. Oh man, this was my big chance to impress!

She pointed to a seat a few rows above me. "Can you sit over there for me?"

I sprung up and sat exactly where she told me to go. They moved a couple other seat fillers as well. Once we were all seated, the screen changed. It was split into three. They were making sure all the cameras were set up in the right spots to capture all the nominees for each award when their time came. Except instead of the world's best hockey players staring up at the screen, there were three way-too-impressed seat fillers, myself included. They tested out the graphics, too. I had "Roberto Luongo" written below my face at one point.

It was only about two hours until show time when the camera crew was done fiddling around and everyone took a break to eat. We got to know each other, talked hockey, and ate some of the free sandwiches they set out.

Once I was done free-fooding, I took a random seat in the middle of the theatre.

"Hey! I didn't know you were gonna be here!" someone who had sat down near me said.

Who is this guy talking to and why does he look so familiar? Do I know him? Have we ever met? Wait a second. That's —

"Kelly Hrudey," he said as he held out his hand.

Long before he was an analyst for *Hockey Night in Canada*, Kelly Hrudey had been an NHL goalie, most famously for the Wayne Gretzky–era L.A. Kings. Being an NHL goalie was all I ever pretended to be when I was playing in my driveway, and this was the first time I ever had the chance to shake hands with one. And for some reason — he approached me!

"I thought you were just doing a video thing," he said.

I was so confused. This was months before I started making YouTube videos about hockey, so he definitely wasn't talking about that.

"Uh, well, I was on the screen a little while ago," I explained. "You know, just helping them get set up and stuff."

He looked at me for a minute.

"Wait. Sorry. You're not him, are you?" he asked.

"Who?"

"John Tavares."

Back in 2007, John Tavares was a junior hockey phenom tearing it up as a 16-year-old sophomore with the OHL's Oshawa Generals. Even though his draft year was still a couple of years away, everyone said he would go first overall. And now he's a damn Maple Leaf!

You know what John Tavares wasn't in 2007, though? Me. Although, I will admit that back then, we actually did look a lot alike. So alike, in fact, that Kelly Hrudey thought I was him.

"Oh!" I laughed. "No. I'm just a seat filler." I don't think I even told him my name.

Kelly apologized and went on his merry way.

Not long before the show, the seat fillers started to scatter throughout the still mostly empty theatre.

Then it happened. In walked Sidney Crosby. The Sidney Crosby. Sid the Kid. The guy who was pretty much a slam dunk to win MVP. My first thought was *God, I wish I had his rookie card*. It was going for like $400 on eBay and I was pretty broke. Then Joe Sakic walked in, too. He was one of the few Colorado Avalanche players I just couldn't bring myself to hate despite being half a Detroit Red Wings fan when I was younger. I think I remember seeing at least one of the Staal brothers, as well; Jordan was nominated for the Calder Trophy for rookie of the year.

While I was gawking, one of the other seat fillers I had been talking to pointed at the screen and yelled, "Look!"

I looked up and saw the same setup as before with the screen split into three, only this time it showed me, one other seat-filler, and the actual Sidney Crosby.

Man, I wish I had something better than a flip phone so I could've taken a picture of that. After my extremely brief screen time with hockey royalty, more players began to stroll in and seat fillers were called to the back.

Once we all got there, it became hilariously apparent that they had let way too many people volunteer for this thing. There were several dozen of us. What did they think was going to happen? Every time a player won an award his entire team would walk up?

We were all standing there in our suits and dresses, and one of the floor coordinators in charge of us explained all the rules again. No asking for autographs, no this, no that. Whenever someone leaves their seat, go fill it. If they come back, get out.

While they were going through the spiel, I realized there probably weren't enough seats for all of us. Screw that! I was going to get a seat at the damn NHL Awards! Before the show started, I weaseled my way to the front of our little seat-filler pack and spotted a single seat. As soon as the show began, I made a beeline for it.

My heart was pounding when I sat down. I felt like I had stolen a ticket to an award show. Any moment now, I would be found out and the cops would come and arrest me for party-crashing. I don't know why I thought that way — it was literally my job.

As politely as I could, I told the people on either side of me that I was a seat filler and asked if somebody was supposed to be sitting there. *Steve, shut up! There's a show going on!*

Once I shut my yap, I surveyed the scene. I was sitting in the very bottom row of the top chunk of seating, meaning all that separated me from the NHL's elite was about a dozen feet of carpet. *Where's Crosby sitting? Did they ever fix Kessel's armrest? I hope he's comfortable.* Here I was sitting in the thick of all those players whose hockey cards I had been collecting since I was a kid and the legends who I had seen on TV thousands of times.

Sitting nearby was a player I recognized very well: Nicklas Lidstrom, sitting with his wife and kids.

Lidstrom was the reigning Norris winner as the league's best defender, and he had just put up another stellar season of 62 points in 80 games.

Not only was he likely to win the Norris Trophy, but that would mean he'd be on TV. If he got on TV, that means *I'd* get on TV!

Sure enough, he won!

I was such a dork. I made sure my posture was all prim and proper and put way too much thought into how I was clapping my hands. *Stay strong and rigid! Wait, no, stop, you look like a robot. Relax a little. Not that much, spaghetti arms!*

Luckily, that was my only on-screen time at the awards — clearly I could not handle the pressure.

Throughout the show I kept waiting for somebody to come and claim my seat, but nope, I got to sit and watch it all, live and in person, for free. With a resume like this at just 19 years old, I figured I was on pace to become Canadian prime minister by the time I was 25.

After the show, when everyone started to clear out, two girls walked up to me. They were about my age, had brown hair, and definitely weren't wearing their prom dresses.

"Hey," one of them said.

"Uh, hey," I said back. I had no idea what these girls wanted, but my teenaged instincts went into full-on panic mode.

"Um," one of them said, "are you Rod Brind'Amour's son?"

This definitely rubbed me the wrong way. I didn't care if he had just won the Frank J. Selke Trophy as the NHL's best defensive forward. No — I was not the son of smelly Rod Brind'Amour whose smelly Carolina Hurricanes beat my Toronto Maple Leafs in the 2002 Eastern Conference Final. How dare you?

I didn't say that, though. What I actually said was a confused and stuttered "No."

I took my sweet time getting out of the Elgin Theatre that night. I didn't want the night to end. Maybe there was some crazy after-party I could get into. After all, I had been able to drink legally for a whole three months at that point. Any minute now, Sid Crosby and Alex Ovechkin would walk over to me and say, "Whoa, you're that seat filler with the great clapping posture! Love what you did out there tonight, man. Here's ten thousand dollars. Wanna come party and friend us on Facebook?"

Just as I exited the building, however, I noticed Kelly Hrudey and Scott Oake signing autographs. I thought, *Screw it. I'm not on duty anymore. What are they gonna do? Fire me?*

I summoned some courage and asked them to sign my program. No, they weren't current NHL stars, but one of them was a former player and they were both on *Hockey Night in Canada*, which was more than cool enough for me. I even jokingly reintroduced myself to Kelly Hrudey as John Tavares. I don't think he remembered, but he politely laughed anyway.

I stared at the autographs the entire train ride home that night. I was riding such a high. Sure, I was mostly just a fly on the wall, but I had rubbed shoulders with hockey royalty that night.

When I had started school, I never thought working in sports was a possibility. After all, I had never played the game. After that night, however, I had thoroughly gotten the itch.

GAME OF BOUNCES

On February 4, 1998, at nine years old, I attended my third-ever Leafs game. This time I finally got to go with my dad, and with tickets in the lower bowl, it was the closest I had ever sat. Dad drove us downtown to see the Leafs play the old blue, gold, and red St. Louis Blues.

Felix Potvin played in 67 of the Leafs' 82 games that season, but yet again, I didn't get to watch my idol. The Leafs were starting Glenn Healy, and the Blues were starting the legendary Grant Fuhr.

Childhood hockey memories are funny because stats ruin them. When I was a kid, I thought Fuhr was unbeatable. Turns out, he had a weak .898 save percentage that season. I get told the same thing about Felix Potvin's stats. Whatever, dude, I'm nine, I'm not in school right now, and you can't make me do math. Just let me watch the game.

The fans booed Brett Hull when his name was announced. I didn't understand why — Hull was one of the best players in the league. I used to play that old handheld Game Boy–style video game with Brett Hull and Wayne Gretzky on it, until the battery died or my thumbs blistered — whichever happened first.

My dad explained it to me in the same cartoony way he would explain who a bad guy was in a movie.

"He was born in Canada," he said, "but he plays for the States."

"What?!" I asked. I couldn't believe it. Why would anybody do such a thing?

I remembered watching Hull and the Americans beat Canada at the 1996 World Cup of Hockey. Hull had actually led the tournament in scoring with seven goals and 11 points in seven games. I remember hating him for beating Team Canada, but I had no idea he was a traitor, too!

Hull, who was born in Belleville, Ontario, had dual citizenship. The Calgary Flames had drafted him in the sixth round in 1984, and he played his college hockey at Minnesota Duluth. Canada had the opportunity to select Hull to the 1986 World Junior team but snubbed him. As a result, Hull made Team USA and basically made it his mission to make Team Canada pay. So really, Canada kind of created its own monster.

My dad could have explained all that boring nuance stuff to me or he could just have fun with his son at their first hockey game together. He chose the latter, so, "Boo Brett Hull, you suck!"

The Leafs took a penalty early in the first because, as I'm sure you all know, all refs are against the Leafs and are smelly butt-heads and what the heck this isn't even fair! Because the Leafs are the best team, however, Igor Korolev scored a shorthanded goal, making it 1–0, Toronto. It's OK, guys — hockey is fair again!

Midway through the period, Al MacInnis tied the game up for the Blues with Craig Conroy and smelly stupid traitor man Brett Hull getting the assists. God I just hate him!

Before the end of the period, Conroy beat Healy for a goal this time, and the Blues carried a 2–1 lead into intermission. Sorry, everyone. My mistake. Hockey is rigged again.

At the beginning of the game, I hated poophead-hates-Canada-for-no-reason Brett Hull, but as the game wore on through the second period, I couldn't stand Grant Fuhr. The Leafs just couldn't score on him. I could've sworn it was the best non–Felix Potvin performance in hockey history, and he was single-handedly ruining my first hockey game with my dad. In reality, Fuhr faced just 21 shots that night. You think that's bad?

Healy faced only 17! The late '90s, man. There's a reason they call it the Dead Puck Era.

Third period: it's do or die time. Just eight seconds in, Chris Pronger took a hooking call to put the Blues down a man. Do you know how badly you had to hook somebody to get called for hooking in 1998? He must have practically shanked the guy.

With Toronto on the man-advantage, at long last, the Leafs solved Grant Fuhr. Derek King scored a power play goal to tie the game at two. It was a back-and-fourth nail-biter in the third, complete with certified stars and villains. Just awesome!

With six and a half to go, the Leafs were buzzing. They were attacking in the Blues zone, which was right in front of us on our end of the ice. A Swedish sophomore for the Leafs named Freddy Modin put a shot on goal.

I can still picture it.

Either the puck was deflected or Fuhr got a piece of it. It fluttered in the air just above Fuhr's head and started to drop. Fuhr didn't know where it was. When he turned around to see where it was, he batted the puck into the net with his own head.

The place exploded. I went nuts! I was cheering and laughing my head off. It was a beautiful combination of all the things I thought were great as a nine-year-old: the Leafs winning and somebody hitting themself in the head.

That proved to be the game-winning goal, too. Glenn Healy shut the door from then on and the Leafs won 3–2. Take that Brett Hull, you bum (who was also a league MVP and one of the best goal-scorers ever and the winner of two Cups)!

But that's hockey. Just like in life, bounces can happen at any moment.

WELCOME TO YOUTUBE

I didn't exactly know what to do with my webcam. For me, it was a video camera backup for school in case I got desperate. Other than that, I couldn't think of a practical use for it.

Enter YouTube.

I created my YouTube account in February 2007, but I didn't want to use my real name. I remembered my silly "Floyd Dangle" nickname from my high school newspaper and made my username SteveDangle. It had nothing to do with the hockey version of the word dangle at all, which means deke.

I mostly just wanted to upload videos from class projects. The oldest video on my channel was uploaded on March 1, 2007, and is an old first-year sketch called "Gus Bundy and the Manchu Runs." It was a dumb little skit we made about a salesman trying to pitch the idea of a completely no-touch bathroom. I invented the name Gus Bundy because, I don't know, I'm an idiot and thought it was funny? And manchu runs is based on Manchu WOK. Get it? Wok like walk, but now it's run? Shut up. I thought it was funny.

Then came my second year of university, and with it, the next hockey season. I was still a frustrated Leafs fan. After a few promising-looking seasons of going two or even three rounds deep in the playoffs, the year-long lockout hit. After that, the Leafs missed the playoffs by one stinking point two years in a row. But this year, the 2007–08 season? Oh, this one was going to be different, baby!

The Leafs lost their first game to the Ottawa Senators 4–3 in overtime. Dany Heatley scored the game-tying goal for Ottawa in the third period, then the overtime-winner as well.

I don't know when I saw it, but the *Toronto Sun* had a front page that grinded my gears. It read: "Leafs, better luck next year!"

In the spring, when I got my webcam, the Leafs weren't in the playoffs, so I guess I didn't have much to talk about. During the summer, I had tried to make a couple of YouTube videos, but without editing software on my computer, they all sucked. Now it was October and newspapers were already ripping on my hockey team — you bet I had something to say!

For some reason, I took my navy blue baseball cap my dad bought me at our final game together at Maple Leaf Gardens and turned it sideways. I got one of my Leafs flags and started waving it like a cartoon hummingbird. Then, in a voice that sounded a lot like my dad's impression of a drunk person, I made a one-take, 16-second video.

"Hey, did you see the Leafs game last night? Oh my God, they lost their first game by one goal in overtime! They should probably trade the coach and trade all the goalies and I don't know why."

I swiped the hat off my head and went back to my regular voice.

"Shut the fuck up! It's the first game!"

I stopped the recording. I played it back a few times. I was pretty pleased with myself for the "They should trade all the coaches" line. It's hilarious, because, well, you can't trade a coach. Master of comedy, right here.

I uploaded it to my YouTube channel. Once it was up, did I put on Facebook? No. Did I tweet it? No. I didn't even have Twitter in 2007. I used the best promotional tool I could think of: I put the link to my video in my MSN status. Yes, Microsoft Messenger. If you're too young to know what that is, it was an ancient form of communication used by the Byzantine Empire. Don't even ask about ICQ. Thirty-four people saw that video the first day it was online, followed by 26 the next day, and only five the next. That was more people than I thought would watch, honestly. I wasn't expecting anything more than a few laughs from some friends.

In game two of the season, the night after losing their season opener, the Leafs lost to Ottawa again, despite erasing a two-goal deficit and outshooting the Sens 43-29. Daniel Alfredsson scored the game-winner for Ottawa in the third. Yuck.

But I'm a Leafs fan, dammit! I'm there for my team no matter what! Back to the webcam.

This time, it was a 58-second epic. Compared to my first video, this was the entire Lord of the Rings trilogy. "Hey guys," I started in my same drunk impression voice. "It's me again, the Toronto Maple Leafs' biggest fan. Ha! And so did you see the other day the Toronto Maple Leafs lost their second game to Ottawa? Oh my God. That game-winning goal. Alfredsson, just, whoa!" and I imitated a wrist shot.

"And Toskala's like, 'Where'd it go? I don't know! I still don't know where it went!'" as I spun around in my computer chair.

"Oh my God, I read this article on the cover of the *Toronto Sun* that said, 'Hey Leafs — wait 'til next year!' Ha, it's funny because they'll probably have to wait 'til next year for the Cup again because, you know, we can always judge what the season's gonna be like after the first two games, right, guys? Ha! You know, I believe everything the *Toronto Sun* says. It's the best newspaper. The Leafs are on the cover of it every day. I was reading this article where they said they should trade Tucker and Sundin and Newbury and basically the whole forward line and —"

I took off my hat and switched voices again.

"You know what? The *Toronto Sun* is not a real newspaper. It never will be. The only good thing about it, sort of, is, y'know, they've got the Sunshine Girl. Well, it's good if you like bearded chicks."

I can't explain how painful it was to watch that video again and actually write down everything I said. I don't even know where to begin. Bearded chicks? Steven? Really? The whole forward line? What's the whole forward line? Stop it with that stupid laugh! The front cover of the *Toronto Sun* doesn't even have an article on it, you idiot!

It was 58 seconds and almost everything I said was a bad idea. Once again, I would love nothing more than to go back in time and fist fight my former self. Please don't go watch it. If you do, then I would have just watched it for nothing.

That Saturday, October 6, I inadvertently made the best career decision of my life.

I was out with my girlfriend and her friends. They were heading downtown for a birthday party. I couldn't go with them for some reason, but I joined them for the pre-party. Correction: pre-drink. Maybe it had been earlier that day, maybe it had been earlier that week, or maybe it was right there at that party with a few beers in me that I made the decision: "I'm going to make a video after every Leafs game."

Why not? It'll be fun to try it. I know a lot about hockey, and I'm pretty sure all my Leafs opinions are bulletproof. Did you know that Matt Stajan is the most underrated player in the league? Well, he is. I say so! Everyone's going to love these videos, right? Why wouldn't they?

I also looked at it as a sort of internship. It would make me more comfortable on camera. If I'm going to do a video after every single game, I'll have to learn discipline. Plus it will build my profile. Wait a sec . . .

If I was planning to become a famous millionaire by next month, I should change my YouTube name. I don't want people to know my real name. Then people would, I don't know, siege my parents' house or something. What would I do when they all showed up? Feed them? My mom can't possibly make that much macaroni and cheese by herself.

To my surprise, my username was SteveDangle. I had forgot

I had even made it that. Ha, Dangle. That actually kind of works. It's a hockey channel. Alright, screw it, I'll leave it.

When I got home, half in the bag, I made my third reaction video, this time about the Leafs' first win of the season. Tomas Kaberle scored the overtime winner against Montreal.

I missed only three or four videos over the course of the first season, but for the most part, I stuck to it. The videos usually topped out around 50 views, probably because that was basically all my MSN friends. The numbers helped keep me going, though

It also helped that the Leafs' start to the season was wacky. They'd lose to Carolina 7–1 one night, then beat the Islanders 8–1 in their very next game.

Then people who weren't my MSN friends started tuning in.

I have no idea how they had found it, but *blogTO*, a blog dedicated to Toronto, embedded one of my videos on their website. This was huge. Nobody was really on Twitter, and Facebook was still relatively new, so getting your video boosted to someone else's audience wasn't as simple as a retweet. Somebody had to discover your stuff, find it at least somewhat noteworthy, and feel the need to talk about it on their website.

A few dozen views turned into about 150. I was over the moon.

The Leafs' seventh game of the season was against the Buffalo Sabres. With Buffalo on the power play and with just five seconds left in overtime, Leafs defender Bryan McCabe accidentally swatted the puck into his own net. Everyone was talking about it. It was on all the highlights non-stop. If fans weren't already running McCabe out of town by that point, everybody else had picked up a torch and pitchfork after that.

At the time, there was a viral video going around of this kid named Chris Crocker. It was 2007, which was the height of the "Let's harass Britney Spears until she completely loses her mind" obsession. Crocker, who was obviously an enormous Britney Spears fan, made this extremely dramatic video in his bed, as he cried hysterically and defended her.

"Leave Britney alone!" he famously screamed, mascara running down his face.

I had the idea to do my own parody version of that called, "Leave Bryan McCabe alone." I used my blue bed sheets as a backdrop and I dramatically fake-cried in Bryan McCabe's defence.

The video got picked up by a website called BryanMcCabe Sucks.com. The site was run by this 15-year-old kid named Jeff Veillette. Online he went by Jeffler.

That video picked up steam, more subscribers came on board, and all of a sudden I was getting 250 views per video. I still remember logging onto my channel one day in the RTA student lounge and glowing.

Another cool thing about starting a YouTube channel and having very few viewers is you actually get to know them individually. They were a fascinating mixed bag: some men, some women, some older, some younger. Subscriber 15 was Morgan, and she still watches today.

Pierre was a man in his 50s from Quebec. He told me I reminded him of his estranged son. He messaged me pretty much every day for a long time. I don't remember ever giving out my address, but he sent a package to my parents' house. Luckily, it was just an NHL-themed Monopoly game; still, it was a jarring experience for a 19-year-old just figuring out the internet. He was a very nice man, just lonely, I think.

One day, he sent me a message that he had finally gotten back in touch with his son. He thanked me but said he didn't feel like he needed me anymore. True to his word, he only contacted me about half a dozen times after that, maybe less. I hope everything worked out for him.

I showed the numbers to everybody I could. I was a bit more reluctant to show them the videos, though, because, well, they would think I was a lunatic. This little experimental self-appointed internship was cool and all, but my classmates were getting real internships and practical experience in media, while all I could do was rattle off animal facts.

My classmate Nate Hershenfeld, a friend I often talked to about the Leafs, had an internship at the Fan 590, Toronto's big sports radio station. "Why not try getting one there?" he asked.

He gave me the office line of the station's program director at the time — a man named Doug Farraway.

That number sat there on a piece of lined paper in my binder for a long time before I finally called it. No answer.

I waited a few days to call again. No answer.

I started calling around 1 p.m. every day for weeks because that's when I had time between classes, and Doug never answered.

Here's why you do your research, folks. Do you know why Doug never answered his phone around 1 p.m.? It's because he was on the air.

One day in February, I called him at a different time. Wouldn't you know it — he answered! When I finally heard his voice, I was shook. I forgot what I was even calling him for. I finally managed to ask about an internship, and he told me to come in for an interview.

The interview was after my morning classes. I walked a few blocks north from Ryerson, up to the sprawling Rogers campus at Bloor Street and Jarvis Street.

I got up to Doug's office. He was bald with glasses and when he spoke, you had to wonder what he would be doing if he weren't in radio. For some people, the "radio voice" is put on, but others seem to just have it naturally. Doug was a natural. He asked me some questions about myself, my interests, what I was doing at school, and what I wanted to do after. I'm honestly not sure what I told him. Prior to starting my YouTube channel, writing was the only thing in my program I felt confident enough in to say I was good at it. Sports broadcasting hadn't even occurred to me. I wanted to be a staff writer on a sitcom or something.

Doug seemed less concerned with my answers and more caught up in other happier things. After I talked about what

I was hoping to do with my life, he started talking about his retirement plans and how he was going to travel.

"How far away is that?" I asked.

"Two years, I think," he smiled at the ceiling.

I genuinely had no idea if I was acing this interview or not. I remember he asked a question about the Canadian Football League, and I was totally lost. I didn't even mention the YouTube videos; I was too embarrassed and didn't want to come across like an immature kid.

But you can't put a price on a great mood, and Doug must have been in one that day. To my surprise, he gave me an internship right then and there. I started the next week. I couldn't believe it. I shook his hand, walked out of his office, and practically tap-danced all the way out of the building and down Yonge Street.

I called up the Thursday Hangout Crew and a couple others and we went out to celebrate. I spent all the money I didn't have, but it didn't matter — I was officially an intern.

It was an unpaid internship, and because Bloor Street is so far north of the train, I had to take the subway to get there on time. That meant an extra $12 per week, maybe more if I had intern shifts on nights where I wasn't already downtown for classes. That zoo money was going to run out at some point. But my parents understood what this meant to me, how important it was, and what an opportunity it would be. They were proud and seemed happy, as long as I promised to be quiet when I got home from my shifts, around 1 a.m. My girlfriend even baked me an amazing cake. On top of it she wrote, "I'm your biggest Fan . . . 590." That's wife material right there, folks.

My first shift at the Fan was pretty much just training. All the interns worked alongside the producers as they prepped their shows in this room called the bullpen. It was probably only about the size of your kitchen, maybe slightly bigger, and had six desktop computers. The walls were plastered with awesome clippings from magazines over the years. Big photos of Michael Jordan, Yao Ming, Vince Carter, Tiger Woods, Mats Sundin, and so on. There were literally hundreds of them. In fact, after I had interned there for a while, I helped fill in a few blank spaces with hockey cards from my collection.

The person showing me the ropes was named Jaspreet Mangat, a soft-spoken guy who went by Jas (pronounced Jazz). He showed me around the place, introduced me to people, and taught me how to use the station's audio editing software, Burli.

Right away, it struck me that I was going to learn a lot more here than at school. Lectures with professors were fine and practicing on the school computers was OK, but this was the real deal. Everyone who worked at the Fan 590, many of them from different parts of the country, were there because they worked hard, knew their stuff, and deserved to be there.

It was also a glimpse into the real media world.

I still remember on the first day of RTA, a professor said to never swear in front of a live microphone. After about five minutes of being at the Fan, I realized that wasn't a rule here.

My shifts were typically 5 p.m. to midnight, but they would let me slip out around 11:30, so I could rush to make the last train home. I was expected to clip little sound bites from guests of *Prime Time Sports* with Bob McCown, the station's longtime big-name host. Another one of my duties was to get Bob's coffee order along with that of his co-host, the late Jim Kelley, which actually wasn't coffee at all. Both drank tea. Bob was a large tea — milk, double sugar — while Jim was a large tea with cream. Hard to forget that one. Who puts cream in their tea?

After *Prime Time*, I was expected to cut highlights from whatever sports were on that night: NHL, NBA, NFL, CFL — you name it. Most were exciting and easy to clip. Golf and curling were hard. It was usually just a ball whizzing through the air or a curling rock grinding on the ice while someone periodically shouted, "Whoa!"

For the most part, I kept my little YouTube experiment

a secret. I was there to gain professional experience, and my YouTube videos were anything but professional.

But one day very shortly after my internship began that became tough to avoid.

Today, YouTube has its trending pages. You can upload a video, and if it gains some traction, it might get on YouTube's trending page for your country. In 2007, the equivalent of that was getting featured. For whatever reason, they featured my Leafs Fan Reaction video for game 63 of that season.

It was a disjointed, crappy monologue about what Mats Sundin meant to the Leafs. I think the reason it got featured was because that was the season fans and management started pressuring Mats Sundin to waive his no-trade clause, so the Leafs could trade him to a contender for a bunch of picks and prospects.

Why did they have to feature this damn video, though? I only uploaded it to stay disciplined and not miss a video. I had just gotten my wisdom teeth out when I shot it. My face was still swollen, I wasn't even talking properly, and I was literally on drugs.

A lot of people hated the video, which sucked. I wasn't used to that many people telling me that all at once. It was my number one fear coming to life. However, a lot of people seemed to dig the video, too.

By that time, I was averaging maybe 300 views per video, but after getting featured on YouTube Canada's homepage, the views rolled in by the thousands, ending up somewhere around 25,000 to 30,000 within a few weeks. I still remember discovering this in the RTA student lounge. I thought it was a mistake. I thought I had been hacked.

I was happy to get the attention, but I hated that they chose that video. I tried sending them messages to use my next video instead.

After game 64, I penned an even more glowing, on-camera love letter to Mats Sundin, only this time I added something new: jump cuts.

I watched this YouTuber named sXe Phil, who you might know today as Phillip DeFranco. He was one of the first YouTubers I ever saw use the jump-cut style that is now famous, or maybe infamous, on YouTube today.

I downloaded a free video-editing software on my computer called Windows Movie Maker. I had never used it before, but I taught myself how to use it that night.

I was bouncing off the walls, using props and everything. I wasn't on drugs anymore, but my mouth was still swollen and I was talking funny.

"This video is not about a man but a legend — Mats Sundin!" I proclaimed.

It was unlike anything I had ever shot before. Oh, it was still pretty bad and I made a bunch of awful mistakes, but at least it was different: high energy and with quick edits. That said, I still yell at the screen whenever I watch it: "Stop looking at your face on the screen and look into the camera, you idiot!"

YouTube Canada featured this next video yet again, and it did even better, eclipsing 30,000 views and edging closer to 40,000 over the coming weeks. Before getting featured on YouTube Canada's homepage, the most views I had ever received on my channel in one day was 1,349 and it was the only time I had ever eclipsed 1,000 views in a day. Most of the time, I hovered around 500 or so. Now I was getting 10 or 11 times that per day. Between the time I started making Leafs videos and February 25, 2008, about five months, I had 52,829 views total. Over the next 33 days alone, after the featured videos, I had over 93,000. The views obviously died down after that, but compared to before, they were still up. In total, my first full season of hockey videos amassed 167,000 views in about six and a half months.

It was more than I could handle — a mental hurricane. The high of so many people watching and saying they liked it combined with the shattering low of hundreds of strangers telling me I suck and I'm a loser was a tough thing to process.

I only mentioned it to a select few people at the Fan 590. Who knows if they told other people, "Check out the dumb intern!"

Should I tell everyone at the Fan about the videos? I honestly wasn't sure. What if they had already seen it? What if they thought it sucked, too?

TAKE ME OUT TO THE BALL GAME

With the school year finally over and the Leafs unfortunately out of the playoffs, it was time to go back to the zoo while interning at the same time. I arranged my schedule so that I was working at the zoo five days per week, while the other two days were at the Fan at night.

Oh, so you stopped partying with your friends, Steve?

Ha! No! I was 20. Hangovers are a myth. Sleep is for the dead. Let's go!

When baseball season rolled around, interns were given a privilege that I didn't even know about: we would get to be the visiting room reporters for the Toronto Blue Jays. This meant that whenever the Jays were playing at home, actual Fan employees would go interview them after the game while the interns got to handle whichever team was visiting that day.

That was always a funny thing to me. When the Jays are great, they create a huge buzz around the city. But in 2008? Dude, I would much rather be covering the visiting team. The New York Yankees, the Boston Red Sox — are you kidding me?

April 16, 2008, was my first Blue Jays game as a reporter. I put on my prom shirt again, trying to look my smartest. I was nervous as all hell, which by now you might have noticed is a theme.

I wonder if I'll be able to catch the last train? I thought. It was a 7 p.m. game. The last train wasn't until midnight. In my mind, that was plenty of time to go to the game, get some interviews, go back to the station, dump the audio and equipment, and run to the train.

As luck would have it, the game went 14 innings. Blue Jays starter A.J. Burnett had to join the game as a relief pitcher and ended up picking up the loss, with the Texas Rangers winning 7–5. During the game, I was sitting next to an older reporter for the Canadian Press. When he found out I was going into the visiting locker room, he asked me if he could borrow my audio to use for his game recap.

"No problem," I told him, having no idea whether or not that was allowed.

I went in the Rangers room and held my mic out for their manager, never dreaming of working up the courage to ask him anything. Baby steps.

One of the player scrums had already began. I couldn't find a way to squeeze in through the mass of bodies, microphones, and cameras. I tried reaching my microphone in, when a TSN cameraman suddenly turned and I accidentally punched him right in the face. I was mortified, but he brushed it off like a pro.

Fun side note about scrums and why it pays to be a good person: a story circulated among the interns that one time, an intern was in the visiting room and couldn't find a way into the scrum. A reporter named James Cybulski, who worked for TSN at the time, took the intern's microphone right out of their hand.

The intern froze, thinking that a reporter from a competing network had just stolen their microphone. To their surprise however, Cybulski reached the intern's mic into the scrum along with his own to capture everything the player was saying. After the scrum, Cybulski just handed the intern back their mic.

The Fan 590 had about 20 interns and almost all of us were still in school or had just recently graduated. All of our networks of friends and peers were trying to get into media in some way, shape, or form. If you were cool like Cybulski was in this story, we knew about it. If somebody was a dick? Oh, believe me, we knew about that, too, and we talked endless smack.

Interns turn into employees, who turn into your coworkers, maybe even someone with influence, and maybe even your boss. Be nice to interns for your own benefit, if just being a decent person isn't a good enough reason for you. Respect is earned, intern or vet.

When I got back to the press box, the Canadian Press reporter asked who I had spoken to; I told him my list of names and he was pretty happy, until we couldn't figure out how to get the audio onto his computer. After about 10 minutes of struggling, we came to the conclusion that I had accidentally deleted the audio somehow, if I had even recorded it at all.

"It's OK," he said unconvincingly. "It's fine. Don't worry about it."

When I walked away, I heard a pretty distinct and exasperated, "Fuck!"

Always good to make friends on your first day . . .

I returned the recording device and microphone to the Fan. I couldn't figure out how to get the audio out of it there, either. For whatever reason, most of it wasn't even there.

My first game was a failure, pretty much a total waste of time, and I missed the last train.

I called a friend of mine who lived in an apartment downtown. She was out of town, so she told one of her roommates to leave the door unlocked for me. Apparently the other roommates were asleep, so they didn't know I was coming. I was worried I would open the door and one of them would deck me with a frying pan.

I tried to sleep through a headache but was unsuccessful. I got up early enough for the first train in the morning and went home. "Well," I told myself, "you can only go up from here."

There were a few highlights for me that season. I got to be in the same locker room as Ken Griffey Jr. before he retired. He came to town with the Cincinnati Reds. He wasn't the most

96

memorable part of their visit, though. Pitcher Edinson Vólquez was talking in a scrum I was a part of, and early on, he accidentally rubbed a giant booger onto his nose. It just sat there as he spoke. Several minutes passed before the scrum ended and someone finally told him.

Volquez wasn't happy.

There were no cameras, and I guess we didn't want to interrupt him. At the same time, we let him just have a booger on his face. Our painful politeness was actually rude. The lesson I learned: if the person you're interviewing has a giant booger on their nose, tell them.

When the Minnesota Twins visited, Twins manager Ron Gardenhire was getting ready to talk. Just as everyone had pressed record on their devices, I accidentally held my microphone near a speaker, causing a horrible squeal of feedback that filled the room for a few seconds. Gardenhire looked at me and said, "That didn't sound like it was supposed to happen," but it sounded an awful lot like, "Don't let that happen again." That's exactly why the Fan gave interns this job, though: to learn difficult lessons. I never made that mistake again.

Another thing I learned was a lesson in mercy. The Oakland Athletics were in town, riding a horrible losing streak. They were fully in control of the game, up three or four runs on the Blue Jays late in the game, when A's relief pitcher Huston Street came out to the mound. The Jays lit him up, took the lead, and Oakland's losing streak continued.

Athletes often talk about forgetting bad games and brushing it off. So soon after the game, however, Huston Street wasn't ready to brush things aside. He said something along the lines of taking all the blame for this one and not being able to sleep tonight. He sounded like he was about to cry.

That might have even been the first answer. The scrum had only been going on for a minute, maybe less. When he said that, every reporter looked around and simultaneously lowered their mics to let Street go about his night.

You might say that we should have kept asking questions. Maybe he says something even more heartbreaking. Maybe you'd even see a tear or two. But this is sports, man. He's a relief pitcher, not the secretary of state. It was also a random regular season game. He didn't just blow it in Game 7 of the World Series. You're there to get a sound bite that captures the game. The pitcher who blew the game for his team just said he's not going to be able to sleep. What more do you want? Take your pound of flesh and go.

I also got to witness the spectacle that is the New York Yankees.

The size of the media contingent varied from team to team. Some teams only had a writer or two follow them, and many of the Toronto-based outlets wouldn't even bother sending a reporter into the visiting room. Other teams had more writers, as well as a radio reporter or two, and maybe even a camera, while several Toronto-based outlets would send people to cover them as well.

The Yankees had the most North American media I had ever seen, with loads of print reporters, radio reporters, and TV cameras, and I think the manager's press conference was even broadcast live. Every Toronto outlet and their dog were there, as well. Even more amazing still is that the Japanese media in attendance might have been the same size, if not bigger. Somehow I ended up squished at the front of the scrum right next to Joe Girardi, with my microphone arm bent into a chicken wing.

My baseball knowledge wasn't the best, but the Yankees were so star-studded, I knew a lot of them. Jason Giambi, Hideki Matsui, Derek Jeter, and Alex Rodriguez were there, just to name a few. I remember thinking, *Holy crap, Johnny Damon's got a big head!*

But the team I remember covering the most? The Boston Red Sox.

One time, I was in the corner of the Blue Jays press box. A short, stout man who I had never seen before sat down next to me. I looked down at his hand and he was wearing a ring the size of a golf ball. Wait a minute. Is that a . . .

I had to introduce myself to him. Being a smartass, I gestured to his hand and said, "You must be pretty important." He appreciated the joke and turned out to be quite the smartass himself.

His name was Carl Beane, the Red Sox announcer at Fenway Park. He travelled with the team and was an internal reporter for them on the road.

His ring was indeed a Boston Red Sox World Series ring, emblazoned with the markings of two championships. He said he was with the team for both championships — 2003 and the previous summer in 2007 — and joked that Dustin Pedroia had only one. He knew I was just an intern but gave me all the time in the world and talked to me all game.

He joked that he walked by some Yankees fans who mocked his Red Sox gear.

"How many World Series rings you got?" he asked them.

"Twenty-six!" they told him.

"No — how many do *you* have?" he asked them again.

They didn't get it.

"Well, I got two," he said, proudly holding up his fist to show off the ring.

He loved that ring. It clearly meant a lot to him. He said one time he fell down the stairs, and when he told his family, they asked if the ring was OK. Before I left that night, he let me take a picture with it, and despite being a lifelong Blue Jays fan, I left with a soft spot for the Red Sox.

Unfortunately, Mr. Beane died four years later in a car accident caused by a heart attack. I'll never forget how kind he was to me that night at the Rogers Centre.

Another legend my internship led me to was Don Cherry. I was walking into the office kitchen to heat up some leftover meatloaf. I was sleep-deprived from school and barely focused on where I was walking.

All of a sudden, this booming voice yells, "Are those cookies?" The voice scared me half to death.

"What?" I said.

Then I realized, *Holy crap, that's Don Cherry.* He was wearing the same black track pants and sleeveless shirt that he wore whenever he lifted an octopus out of the water for a Stanley Cup Final intro. Full gun show.

"Are those cookies?" he asked again, pointing at my container.

The words just tumbled out of my head.

"Oh. No. It's, uh, meatloaf. My mom made it."

"Oh, OK," he said. "I thought they were cookies." Then he left the room, presumably to find cookies.

Did you just tell one of your childhood idols that your mommy packed your lunch for you? Yeah, that took a few years to get over.

Jack Armstrong, long-time commentator for the Toronto Raptors, had a radio show on the station when I was there. Jack commuted to work in downtown Toronto from Lewiston, New York, every day. Can you believe it? After his show, he would always call up his kids on the phone. "Hey, buddy, how are ya? How was school?"

One time, he offered to pay for my dinner while I was making my daily coffee run. I turned down the money and told him he was extremely kind, but I couldn't possibly accept it. Jack looked at me like I had slapped him in the face. Like all he wanted in the world was to help out this poor intern, and he couldn't believe I said no.

I never spoke to him much, but he's one of the nicest human beings I've ever met. Not a mean bone in his body. He's one of a handful of people I've met who makes me want to fight anyone who doesn't like them. Same with Leafs TV's Paul Hendrick, by the way. Someone tweeted something at him over half a decade ago and I still can't help but judge them for it.

Lastly, the internship taught me an important lesson about money. Yes, I was still broke. I knew I was making money at the zoo, but I had to make that money last. School plus the Fan plus the zoo was a grind, but I didn't want to give up my internship and I didn't want to stop making money. The solution seemed obvious to me: get a media job that paid.

Just because the answer is obvious doesn't mean it's easy to achieve. The 2008 recession was in full swing. It absolutely hammered the broadcasting business. How do radio and television make money? Advertising. You know what companies cut when there's a recession? Advertising. Media companies are letting people go, not hiring them.

Still, it didn't hurt to ask.

One day in the bullpen, I was talking to a producer named Dave Cadeau. He was working on the Fan's mid-morning show with Mike Hogan and Mike Toth.

"Dave, I'm just an intern," I started. "Do you know any ways I could get a paying job while balancing school as well?"

He paused for a moment to think.

"Get a job that pays commission," he said.

"Oh," I said, surprised. "I didn't know there were media jobs that paid commission."

"There aren't," he said. "I mean like an electronics store or something. I worked at Future Shop for a while."

This wasn't the answer I was expecting or hoping for, but it did confirm something: there were no shortcuts. There was no easy way to success. I had gotten the opportunity to do a few cool things, but I still had a long way to go.

By the end of the summer, I had learned quite a bit. With the Blue Jays failing to qualify for the postseason, my summer covering baseball was done.

But I still had a few curveballs coming my way.

FLAMINGO

As an intern or as someone just starting out in their respective field, "more" does not always translate to "better."

About four months into my internship at the Fan 590, an unbelievable opportunity came my way. Well, that's what I thought it was, anyway. Some people at the station kind of thought it was a bit of a joke.

Whenever there was a big international tournament, the interns got assigned to go to bars and restaurants that represented one of the countries that were playing. Maybe it was to spice things up with a little on-air variety. Maybe it was just the station throwing the interns a bone. Either way, I looked at it as an opportunity.

In this case, it was the 2008 UEFA Euro.

The gig was simple: you got assigned a game, and at the end of the match, you did a 15-second on-air phoner from the bar.

I can't imagine the phoners were good for listeners. In fact, while on the air one day, Bob McCown even clowned on the interns doing this. I got bent out of shape about it at the time. *This guy has some nerve. Where would Bob McCown be without the interns? Nowhere, that's where! He'd have to get his own damn tea!*

Looking back, he was right. We stunk. At the very least, I stunk. There were probably a lot of listeners who found McCown's jeers hilarious because they also didn't want to listen to a bunch of over-eager go-getters give a stuttering recap of a game they had just watched in a noisy restaurant. Bob was just saying what a lot of his listeners were thinking. That's good radio. Enough about Bob, though. Back to the real star of the show: 20-year-old me.

Like pretty much everything when I was an intern, I thought this was my potential big break. I imagined my boss working away in his office. He picks up his coffee, brings it to his lips, but then my sultry voice blesses the airwaves. It freezes him in his tracks — his eyes wide and mouth agape. He drops his mug and shards of ceramic fly, leaving caffeinated carnage all over his desk.

He wind-sprints down the hall.

"Who was that?" he asks breathlessly.

"I believe that was our intern Steve, sir," someone responds, equally awestruck. "He's been with us for four months."

My boss turns around to Bob McCown and slaps him in the face so hard that his sunglasses go flying.

"Bob, you're fired. This kid's gonna make us rich!"

The first game I was assigned was Spain versus Russia. The game was at noon on a Tuesday, a day when I had my usual 5 p.m. to midnight intern shift. It was going to be a long day.

Then a brilliant idea dawned on me. I had wanted to shadow the morning show producer Jeff Sammutt for a long time. On top of being the show's producer, he also made funny skits that would air on the show. He had a stereotypical Italian character named Vito from Woodbridge, who was basically just an over-the-top version of a typical sports radio caller. It was a blend of sports and comedy, so I wanted to see how it was done.

The plan was to shadow Jeff in the morning, go somewhere to watch the game and do my radio hit, then come back in for my regular seven-hour intern shift at night.

I thought it was bulletproof. I'm going to learn a lot, get an on-air opportunity, and be visible to everybody in the station. They're going to think that I'm the hardest worker in the building. People are going to walk up to me in the halls and hand me $50, just because. This will be great.

I got up at the same time as my dad: 4:30 a.m. The older I get, the more I respect my dad for getting up for work at a time of day that shouldn't even exist. He always took the first train in from Rouge Hill to Union Station around 5:30 a.m. This got me downtown for a little after six, I took the subway up and was at the Fan before 6:30 a.m.

The morning show was already in progress when I got there. I got a couple "Whoa, what are you doing here?" questions and told them my whole little plan.

Oh yeah, buddy. I already look like a rock star. Great start.

What impressed me while hanging around Jeff that morning wasn't the skits or jokes he made; it was his work ethic. Jeff would get up at like 3 a.m. to get himself ready, get to the studio on time, and prep. Then he would work on the show, and after that day's show was done, he would do some work on the next day's show. He would then go home, have a nap, and be back in the studio for another show he was working on in the evening. Then he would go home, sleep, and do it all again.

That just made me feel even more confident about my plan. I'm going to show everyone I can work that hard, too.

When the morning show wrapped up, I went to the bullpen. More people were there now and they also asked what I was doing there. I told them my plan and I could've swore that they were going to invent an "intern of the month" plaque just to give it to me.

With some time to kill, I did way too much research on the Spain-Russia match. I can talk about hockey in my sleep, but I had no idea what was going on in most other sports, especially soccer. All I knew about the world's best soccer players came from my *FIFA 2001* game.

"Filippo Inzaghi is going to help Juventus win it all this year! What's that? He hasn't played there in seven years? Silly me!"

I was always insecure about my lack of knowledge of other sports and didn't want to look like an idiot. After I had been at the Fan for a few months, Bob McCown's producer Ryan Walsh was put in charge of the interns. Getting an internship with him at the helm was much harder, or would have been for me, anyway. Why? Because he gave interns a sports test.

One day we were talking about it in the bullpen, and he turned to me with a smirk. "Can you name five guys on the Raptors right now?"

"Chris Bosh," I started with confidence. "Andrea Bargnani. Um, what's his name? Oh! T.J. Ford! And the Spanish guy. Um. Oh! José Calderón! One more . . ."

My mind raced through the empty Raptors Rolodex in my head. I had been cutting Raps highlights for so long. How don't I know this? Oh God, people are watching.

Then a light bulb went off.

"And Graham Humphrey!" I shouted with confidence.

"Ha! He actually got it," one of the other producers laughed.

"Wait," Walsh stopped. "Who was that last guy?"

"Graham Humphrey?" I responded.

"Do you think that's one person?" he asked.

My face got hot. "Um. I hope so?"

"Joey Graham and Kris Humphries," he said, breaking the bad news. "Those are two different people."

He was absolutely right. And I was absolutely wrong. Graham Humphrey was a friend of mine from high school.

"Oh my God," Walsh said. "You wouldn't have even passed the intern test."

If that's not a cue to shut up forever, I don't know what is.

The current me was trying to avoid that mortifying moment by printing out sheet after sheet about Team Spain and Team Russia. As a matter of fact, let's print out something about the UEFA tournament's history. And maybe a bunch of the other teams in their group. Wait — who's in their group? Ah! It says here Sweden and Greece. Is that good? I should check. And actually why don't I print out the directions to this place, too. Wouldn't want to get lost.

I killed a tree with anxiety that day.

Then I arrived at Plaza Flamingo. It was a sky-blue building with what looked like a handpainted scene of a Spanish village out front. There was a flamingo, too. There had to be one. Not having one would have just been silly.

I went in expecting it to be packed with rambunctious Spanish spectators with giant flags and painted head to toe in red and yellow.

When I got in there, it was me and five people.

The Euro tournament was a big deal and all, but not too many people were willing to blow off work at noon on a Tuesday to watch Spain spank their first opponent in the group stage.

That day, though, there were a few staff, a handful of customers, and a 20-year-old me sitting alone at a table quietly mumble-rehearsing to himself like a lunatic.

I let one of the staff know I was there and what it was for. You know, in case they wanted to know what all the commotion was. Why did I think they would even care? All I had to do was make a phone call. For all they knew, I was on the phone with my mom.

With every minute that passed, full time drew closer, and I got more and more nervous.

Hold it together, man. It's no big deal. You're just going on the radio. Oh my God, I'm going on the radio. How many people are going to be listening to me? What if I suck and they hate me? What if someone hears how much I suck and it turns out they work with my dad and then the whole lunch room at my dad's work is laughing at me and he can't even claim me as his son so he just has to live in humiliation?

At least nobody could ever accuse me of not caring, right?

David Villa put Spain up 1–0 in the 20th minute. Ah, OK, good. I'll write that down.

Villa scored again in the 44th to put Spain up 2–0 at half-time. Oh man, this Villa guy is the real story here. I'll have to talk about this Villa guy. Wait — is it VEE-ah or VILL-ah? Has to be VEE-ah, right? He's Spanish. It's like tortilla, or something. Oh my God, I don't know soccer, I don't know names, I don't know anything.

Is my phone charged? Looks charged. I better keep it charged. That's enough charge, right? If my phone cuts out while I'm live on-air, I'll probably be fired and arrested.

During half-time, one of the staff asked if I wanted something to eat.

"No, thank you," I told them. "I'm so nervous, I think I might barf."

They finally got me to accept a glass of water after they convinced me it would actually help with my nausea.

Once play resumed in the second half, Villa scored again in the 75th minute. The hat-trick! Absolutely perfect! It's not like I could talk about the finer points of the game, so something simple yet significant like a hat-trick was perfect.

Russia answered with a goal in the 86th minute from Roman Pav— oh man, please don't make me say this on the air. Roman Pavlyuchenko? Sure.

As the game winded down, I called the station to ask when they wanted me on. Honestly, it might have even been taped, I don't even remember. That's not as cool, but it would have made a lot more sense than allowing some idiot who doesn't even know soccer to call in and talk about players he's never heard of with names he can't pronounce live on-air.

Fabregas scored in the dying minutes of the game to complete Spain's 4–1 win. What's his first name? C-E-S-C? How do you even say that? That's a typo, right?

No time for that now, Steve. It's go time.

I couldn't even tell you what I said or talked about. I blacked out. I just went into super-broadcaster mode, man. I probably turned into a soccer expert, too, and started calling it "footy" and chatting about the condition of the "pitch." All I remember is that once it was done, I felt a little pride and a lot of relief. I could do it. I just did it! Now that I've done it once, I'll have no problem covering my next match: Germany versus Croatia, two days later.

Once I arrived back at the station, I realized how tired I was, and I seriously regretted not eating. When I walked in, I expected to get a rapturous applause from everybody in the room like mission control at NASA when they successfully launch a rocket into space.

Nope. Just business as usual.

My regular shift was just as it always was. Cut clips from guests on *Prime Time Sports*, get Bob a tea, and cut some sports highlights. Tonight, the Blue Jays were taking on the Seattle Mariners and it was Game 3 of the NBA Final between the Boston Celtics and L.A. Lakers.

You think the night folks were impressed with my crazy, all-day plan? Nope.

They knew the work rate I was capable of and because my brain was basically tapioca pudding at this point, my performance got worse and worse as the night went on. I took too long to get things done, and when I did, there were too many mistakes.

Finally, around 10 p.m. or so, I was asked to do something incredibly basic. I don't remember exactly what it was, maybe send a file to someone or something, and I had learned how to do it in my first week there.

"Do you know how to do it?" the producer asked, kind of frustrated.

I just stared blankly at the desk, trying to think. Nobody was home. If you could have gone inside my head, all you would have heard was elevator music.

"Just go home," he finally told me.

And I did. I feel bad for whoever had to sit near me on the train because I had to be snoring. I even set my alarm so I wouldn't miss my stop.

At the time, I thought I had done a great job. By the time I got home, I had been up for about 20 hours. Nobody made me do that. It was all my choice.

I figured I had gotten the attention of some people I needed to impress. Sure, I'm young, but look at me: I'm here all day and putting in work.

I thought I had made real progress. In reality, I looked like a total idiot.

My heart was sort of in the right place, but it was misguided. I got some knowledge out of my morning with Jeff, so that was good. Going to Plaza Flamingo to talk about the Euro was a valuable experience that would hopefully help me act like a regular human on the radio.

But in terms of visibility, do you know what I accomplished?

Everybody saw me that day; unfortunately, they saw me making a dumb decision.

What I thought would come across as a go-getter attitude probably made me seem cocky and overambitious. They want you to put in work, sure, but not at the cost of you not being able to do your job.

Anyone who was there in the morning probably thought, *This kid's gonna burn himself out*, and anyone who was there at night got to see that, yep, I burned myself out and was sent home early for being useless. Does that sound like a career-advancing move to you?

I did what I thought would be best for visibility, not what would be best for my ability to work and learn, which was my whole job as an intern. Well, I wasn't able to work and couldn't demonstrate that I learned anything.

In an industry this small, it takes no time to develop a reputation, but it can take a long time to change it.

TEA & TRUCULENCE

How badly have you ever messed up at work?

My worst screw-up as an intern was *bad*. The crazy thing is it could have been worse.

Interns usually fetched guests from the lobby to bring them up to the main studios on the fifth floor. I loved that because it meant I got to take a break from doing work and meet famous people. And not just any celebrity — these people were famous in sports. What if I got to meet somebody I grew up watching as a kid? It would give me something to brag about to my friends that they actually cared about, instead of reminding them my last video got 300 views on YouTube.

Interns didn't always get to greet the guests, though. Often it was whoever was producing the show who got the honours. Back when I was an intern, the producer of *Prime Time Sports* with Bob McCown was the guy with the intern test, Ryan Walsh. When it wasn't him who greeted the guests, one of the older interns would do it. It made sense — they had seniority, and, let's face it, the guests probably would have sensed that I was just a sports-loving eight-year-old trapped in a university student's body.

On one particular day in 2008, for whatever reason, I got to fetch all of McCown's guests. It was a star-studded lineup. First, I got to meet Michael "Pinball" Clemons, the legendary

Toronto Argonauts player and coach. Americans reading this right now might roll their eyes and think the Canadian Football League is cute, but Pinball is legitimately one of the most universally beloved athletes in Toronto.

Standing at just five-foot-six and weighing about 170 pounds, Pinball would fearlessly bounce into and off defenders twice his size. His tenacity along with his infectious energy and charisma have made him one of the most recognizable sports figures in town.

The first thing I noticed about him, besides his height, was his uncontainable energy. You know the episode of *The Simpsons* where Bart pranks Homer by shaking up a can of beer in a paint-shaker to the point where the can is literally vibrating? Pinball Clemons is that in human form. He seemed like the kind of guy who at any time could say, "You wanna race?" and take off before you had the chance to respond.

He's one of the celebrities I've met that I wish I could go back in time and calm myself down before meeting. I was so in awe of being in the presence of a Toronto sports legend that I was barely paying attention to anything he was saying. All I remember is that he would respond to simple questions with "*Yehhhs*, yes, yes," with his patented perma-smile.

After the interview, I got to lead Pinball back down to the main lobby. *I'm in the elevator with Pinball Clemons!* I thought. I'd call it youthful overexcitement on my part, but I would probably have the same reaction today. If you ever get to meet him, you'll understand.

The next guest was very different: famous UFC referee Big John McCarthy.

Big John stands at about six-foot-four, 260 pounds, and his job is to prevent trained killers from killing other trained killers. Big John McCarthy is one of those guys whose height and weight don't properly describe his size. You can't fully appreciate how massive he is until you're standing next to him and feel like an insect.

Once he was done upstairs, I led Big John back to the lobby. He certainly wasn't mean or anything, but he was definitely one of those guys whose silence can feel threatening.

The third and final guest I picked up was the most intimidating because of how important he was to the show: Doug MacLean. This was before MacLean himself worked for Sportsnet. In fact, this day was probably only about a year or so after he was fired as GM of the Columbus Blue Jackets.

The significance of MacLean's appearance was that he had frequently phoned in as a guest on *Prime Time Sports*, but he had never been in studio. Ryan, the producer, was hoping that MacLean would surprise Bob on-air.

I didn't want to let Ryan down. This wasn't just any guest; this was precious cargo. If I help Ryan, that's gotta look good on me, right? After introducing myself to Doug in the lobby, we got into the elevator. When we got to the fifth floor . . . nothing.

It should open any second now.

Still nothing.

I clumsily beeped my security pass to get the door to open, but nothing happened. *Dude, am I actually trapped in the elevator with our most important guest?*

Doug awkwardly stared at the ceiling while I fumbled with pretty much every button on the elevator. I don't know what the hold-up was with the stupid thing but it eventually opened. After a few minutes of waiting, Bob threw to a break and Ryan introduced the two longtime phone pals. It was a great moment, and as far as Ryan knew, everything went smoothly!

I proudly walked back to the bullpen down the hall to cut some clips.

Once Bob had thrown to break, it was time to get his tea. I got up from my desk and started to walk out the door.

Just then, the older intern who was working with me that day drew my attention to the TV screen above him.

"Whoa, are you seeing this?" he asked.

"No, what?" I asked.

"Brian Burke is resigning," he said.

There was no sound, but there on the TV was Brian Burke standing at a podium, talking to the media.

This was enormous news, especially as a Leafs fan. At the time, Burke was the general manager of the Anaheim Ducks, the team he had recently won the Stanley Cup with. At the same time, the Leafs finally appeared to be gearing up for a rebuild. Despite the fact that he was still with the Ducks, rumours were rampant that the Leafs were going to snag Burke somehow.

Now with all those rumours swirling, Burke just up and quit?

"Whoa, that's crazy!" I said.

I ran down the hall toward the studio and told Walsh right away.

"Did you see the Burke news?" I asked.

"What Burke news?" he asked.

"He just resigned from the Ducks."

"What?"

"Yeah! Look at that," I told him, pointing up at the television.

We both looked up and there was Burke, still at the podium.

Ryan told Bob, and Bob and his newfound friend, Doug MacLean, looked up at the screen and saw Brian Burke standing at a podium.

While they all debated what to do next, I went back down the hall to get Bob his usual. As I walked by the bullpen, I stuck my head in.

"Hey, I told him," I announced to the other intern.

"Told him what?" he asked.

"Bob. I told him about the Burke news. How he resigned."

The other intern's smile dissolved completely and his eyes became as wide as dinner plates.

"*WHAT?*"

"Yeah, I figured they would want to talk about it on-air. It's kind of a huge deal . . ."

That's when he dropped the bomb.

"Dude, I was kidding . . ."

Knowing I was a die-hard Leafs fan, the other intern thought he would play an innocent little prank by telling me that Brian Burke had resigned from the Ducks. He knew the wheels would start turning in my little Leafs brain and I would think that Burke was coming to Toronto.

Here's the real problem: Burke's press conference was to deny ever asking to leave the Ducks in favour of the Leafs.

In other words, I had just told Bob McCown the exact opposite of the truth and he was about to announce it to a national audience.

Right away, everyone in the room started buzzing the main studio to try to tell them what had happened before they went to air with the news. When I say I sprinted down the hall, I mean I went full-on Donovan Bailey. If somebody were to walk around the corner at that exact moment, I would have destroyed them Madden style.

"It was a mistake!" I yelled.

Bob, Doug, and Walsh all looked confused.

"The Burke thing," I said, sucking wind. "It was a mistake. He's not quitting."

"We're like thirty seconds from going to air," Walsh said. "We almost hung up on our guest. Are you serious?"

"Yes," I told them. "I'm sorry."

Bob seemed a bit annoyed, but he mostly shrugged it off. Doug didn't really care; he was just a guest, after all.

Walsh? Oh, he cared.

I walked back down the hall to the bullpen.

"Did you get a hold of them?" the other intern asked with dread.

"Yeah," I said meekly. "Yeah, I told them."

After that, we just sat quietly, cutting clips.

This is it. Not only am I so all-the-way fired, but I'm never going to get hired anywhere in media ever again — not even as an unpaid intern. I'm screwed.

We didn't exchange a word as we waited for Walsh to come back to the bullpen to give us the most well-deserved cursing out ever. I had to stop myself from just getting up and leaving right there.

After a little while, Walsh walked in. He paused for a moment while looking at the floor in front of him. *Here it comes*, I thought.

"Did we learn something today?" he asked.

The other intern and I nodded our heads and said, "Yes."

"Good."

With that, Walsh walked out, and I was left completely shitting myself, in utter disbelief that I wasn't fired and thrown out of the fifth-floor window for almost ruining the credibility of the biggest personality in Canadian sports-radio history.

Me and the other intern didn't say much else that night. There wasn't really any bickering. He knew he was at fault for picking on the youngest and easily the dumbest intern. I knew I was at fault for *being* the dumbest intern.

I think a big problem I had as an intern, and a big problem a lot of interns and young professionals have, is believing that it takes one big thing to get you noticed. If you can knock it out of the park one day with one grand gesture, then you're set — all the bosses will respect you and they'll give you a job the second one pops up. In my experience, that's almost never the case. Sure, they'll take note when you do good work, but what they seem to appreciate the most is dependability and consistency. They want to know they can rely on you to do your work and do it properly. They just want you to put your head down and do your job.

I was definitely not that kind of intern. Talking about sports in the office of a sports radio station is perfectly fine, but don't let it get in the way of your work. If you start falling behind because you're talking about the latest trade with your buddies, then what are you there for? People who hire interns want people who help out, not hang out.

Not to mention that if you're actually paying attention to your work, you'll have a better grasp of the details. You'll make fewer spelling mistakes, avoid editing errors, and, most importantly, you won't accidentally tell everybody that Brian Burke had just quit when he hadn't.

JUNIOR

There's making your own luck and then there's dumb luck. Getting my opportunity with *Junior Hockey Magazine* was a bit of both.

After interning at the Fan 590 twice a week for about eight months, I'd become one of the more senior interns, despite being just 20. Most of the other older interns either got hired or had moved on. I was taking a full course load at the time, but I was a straight B-/C+ student, so grades weren't a huge priority. I was also working at the zoo during the summer but made time for the Fan at least a couple of times each week. That helped open the door to the opportunity that would affect my entire career.

One day, I was asked if I wanted to apply to become a writer on a show called *RBC Junior Hockey Magazine*. Since I had never heard of the show, and since I'm an idiot, I thought it was an actual paper magazine. But of course, I was wrong. Turns out *Junior Hockey Magazine* had been around since I was three and was Canada's only nationally syndicated junior hockey radio show. They needed somebody to write scripts for the weekly show and to book guests. To top it all off, the host was Gino Reda, the TV personality who had covered hockey for TSN since 1988, the year I was born. He's best known for his show *That's Hockey*.

Junior Hockey Magazine was viewed around the office as a bit of a grinding gig but also as a tremendous opportunity. Writers for *Junior Hockey Mag* almost always went on to work in sports media. Some of the people who had done the job in the past include current Sportsnet 590 the Fan program director Dave Cadeau, Sportsnet's Toronto Raptors insider Eric Smith, and longtime TSN Flames reporter Jermaine Franklin. To sweeten the pot, the job paid $75 per week. You might laugh, but that was $75 per week more than the zero dollars I was making during the school year. And think of all the nasty dive-bar beer you can get with $300 per month.

I figured there was no way I would get the job ahead of interns with more experience — heck, at the time I was just proud when I didn't screw up the coffee orders. But here's where the dumb luck came in.

I went for an interview with the show's executive producer Colin Campbell. No, not the Colin Campbell who was executive vice president and director of hockey operations for the NHL — different guy, same name (but pronounced the much more common way). When I got to Colin's office, nobody was there. I even called out a few times. I walked around this creepy, abandoned-looking office expecting *Resident Evil* zombies to jump out and eat my face. Just as I was about to leave, I heard someone call out, "Hello?"

"Hi, uh, it's Steve. I have an interview?"

"Oh, hi Steve!"

It turned out they were moving offices and pretty much everything had been cleared away except for Colin's desk.

The interview started the way most do. I basically explained a little bit about myself, what I was doing in school, and how I heard about the job.

"How much do you know about junior hockey, Steve?" he asked.

I had nothing. "Um . . . John Tavares?"

Back in 2008, even if you knew nothing about junior hockey, you knew about John Tavares.

"OK . . ." he said, hoping for more.

"Honestly," I continued, "I don't know a lot about junior hockey, specifically, but I'm an enormous hockey fan. Whatever I need to learn, I'm confident I can learn it quickly."

Just like with my interview to get into university, I was honest about my limitations. It seemed like that was a good enough answer. The one thing I did continue to keep secret was my YouTube channel, which still wasn't even a year old. I didn't want him seeing my screaming rants and thinking I was a weirdo, and I for sure didn't want to be known as the "YouTube kid."

"One more question," he said. "If you were offered another job in media that paid more, would you leave our show mid-season?"

I had to laugh. "I'm twenty years old," I explained. "That's not gonna happen. Besides, I'm a full-time student during the hockey season." We shook hands, and I left.

Even though the interview had been fine, I didn't think I would really get the job. Had my junior hockey knowledge even been average, which it wasn't, my age and lack of experience would keep me from getting hired.

It turns out the opposite was true.

The two other people who were interviewed for the job were more experienced and a few years older. Of course they would leave the show mid season if they got a better offer.

I should mention that those guys are doing well. Travis MacKenzie is the producer of the *Jeff Blair Show* and *Baseball Central* at Sportsnet 590 the Fan, while Josh Gold-Smith is a senior editor for hockey at the Score and also produced the *Marek vs. Wyshynski* podcast for a while.

Despite how green I was, and because I had the ability to string a few sentences together without vomiting during the interview, I became the new writer for *RBC Junior Hockey Magazine*. I immediately realized I had a lot more than just junior hockey to learn about.

My first day with *Junior Hockey Mag* was overwhelming. I

had never done anything like this before: it was actual paid work in the industry, so the stakes were higher, and if I failed, I would be letting down Gino Reda, someone who I had watched on TV since childhood. Luckily, I wasn't alone. The previous season's producer, a guy named Brandon, joined me for the first episode of the 2008–09 season to train me.

The show was very structured, with a few key sections. First, there was the "news and notes" section, where I would find quick snippet stories from around the Canadian Hockey League. Ideally there would be a story from each of the three leagues within the CHL: the Ontario Hockey League (OHL), the Quebec Major Junior Hockey League (QMJHL), and the Western Hockey League (WHL). I needed to find an audio clip for each story, and more often than not I had to call teams around the league to get a few quotes.

After that came our insiders. Our OHL insider was Jim "the Hitman" Cressman of the *London Free Press*. Our QMJHL insider was Stephane Leroux of RDS. Finally, our WHL insider was Rick "the Bear" Wyle, the longtime sports director for Radio NL in Kamloops, B.C. Every week, I was supposed to call each of the insiders, discuss the topics they wanted to talk about, and write them into the script.

Oh, yeah, there was a *script*. Not bullet points — an actual full script for each show that I had to write. If Gino just came in and winged it every week after a long day at TSN, recording the show would have taken way longer. With the text ready, Gino would just come in, read, record, and . . . voila, we had a national show.

Then the most important segment: the featured guest. Each week, I had to find a new guest from around the CHL. General managers, coaches, players — the bigger the name, the better. Usually, I would just book the guest and write out question suggestions, but sometimes, due to scheduling conflicts, I would have to conduct the interviews myself, then we would fake it like Gino had been the one asking the questions.

Before you gasp in horror, that's not an uncommon practice. Believe it or not, a lot of teenagers don't want to be conducting phone interviews at 8 p.m. They've got homework, friends to hang out with, and noobs to pwn in *Call of Duty*. Plus, sometimes the show was put together on a game night and they literally couldn't do the interview at that time.

After that, we had one more interview segment: the Junior A featured guest. If you don't know, Junior A is one tier below major junior. It's also the path that players in Canada who want to go the college route take, since playing in major junior makes you ineligible for college hockey. Junior A has churned out plenty of NHL talent in recent years — guys like Zach Hyman and Tyler Bozak. Brandon Pirri was our Junior A guest at some point that season.

Finally, I had to choose the Globesports.com player of the week.

I should probably mention that even though the show was recorded, it was vital to finish the script on time. The guys didn't want to have their night delayed because the dopey kid they hired couldn't get the job done. Also it was a nationally syndicated show that aired in various markets around the country from Friday through Sunday, but it aired in Toronto on the Fan 590 on the same day as it was recorded on Thursday. We couldn't afford to get held up if the show was going to make it to air in every market.

To say I was intimidated by all of the steps would be an understatement.

Whenever we were looking for guests, they wanted us to try to find potential first- or second-round picks for the upcoming 2009 NHL Draft. We definitely nailed it, booking Windsor Spitfires defender Ryan Ellis, who now plays for the Nashville Predators, for our first show that season. Even our Junior A guest that day was a good choice: a 2008 draft pick of the Leafs named Andrew MacWilliam. Wow — we're having a Leafs prospect on the show? I didn't care that he was a seventh-rounder. He's a Leafs prospect, man!

Producing that first show definitely didn't go smoothly, though. After making sure I understood how to use the phones, which I quickly learned I did not, Brandon wanted to take off the training wheels. He couldn't just make the show for me. He wanted to see me run an interview myself.

We got a hold of the WHL's Vancouver Giants for a potential news and notes story. The player we spoke to was Evander Kane, who just happened to be a potential top 5 pick for that upcoming draft. To call the interview a train wreck would be generous. I had the poise of a newborn fawn. My voice was trembling and I had no confidence when I asked Kane my questions. Why? I still barely knew anything about junior hockey.

I can still remember the worst moment. I was staring down at my paper of questions while Kane was talking. I was honestly probably six inches away from the page as I was reading it, like I was trying to absorb the information like some kind of X-Men character with super crappy powers. When I asked the next question, Kane paused, laughed, and went into his next answer. While he was talking, Brandon muted our mics.

"Dude, weren't you listening?" he asked.

That's the thing — I was concentrating so hard on the next question that I wasn't listening at all.

"He's laughing at you, man," Brandon said. "He already talked about that in his last answer."

I don't hold it against him. Imagine if your friend asked you a question, you answered, and then they asked it again. You'd ask them what the hell was wrong with them. Now imagine doing that with a stranger. At least Kane was polite enough to give an answer.

How was I going to impress a seasoned broadcaster like Gino Reda when I was literally getting laughed at by a 17-year-old?

In the end, we didn't run the Kane interview at all. For one, it sucked. Second, we already had enough clips for the show.

With the script ready on time, all of our clips gathered and all of our guests lined up, it was time to record the show.

Colin Campbell was there. The producer, a guy by the name of Chris Clarke, was there to work the boards. "Clarkey" as we called him, had been working with *Junior Hockey Mag* for years, was part of the Fan 590 when it originally launched in the early 1990s, and had worked with Leafs TV since its inception.

They were obviously extremely respectable broadcasters in their own right, but I hadn't watched them talk about hockey on TV for all of my childhood. Then Gino walked in.

Look, I know I'm hyping him up like Charlie Murphy talking about Rick James's orange aura on *Chappelle's Show*. When you're as hockey mad as I am, that's how he seemed to me, OK?

He shook my hand and introduced himself. Some TV and radio people have a completely different voice on-air than they do it real life. Not Gino. I honestly felt like I was shaking hands with the TV.

We recorded the show and it went off without a hitch. I survived week one.

It was a tradition for everyone to go out to a pub downtown after every show to eat chicken wings. I was dying to make a great first impression and tell the guys more about myself, but honestly, I was dead tired and had a splitting headache. I still remember popping an Advil at the table and hoping they wouldn't judge me like, *We're one week in and this kid barely even made it?*

At some point in the week between my first and second episode, the guys on the show told me to basically forget most of what Brandon had taught me. Apparently, they didn't think that Brandon had done the greatest job the year before, and he didn't like them much either. OK, cool, all I have to do is re-learn everything.

The next week I knew I had to do the show on my own. On top of that, Gino wasn't available, so TSN's Cory Woron filled in. But it doesn't matter. This was my job now and I had to figure it out.

What's the worst that could happen? I asked myself with confidence.

You could get fired, another voice in my head shot back.

I started by booking our feature guest. That way, the most important part of the show would be out of the way early. Unfortunately, I couldn't seem to lock anybody down.

OK, no problem. How about news and notes?

This is when I was confronted with something I didn't think about enough when I was younger and it's something a lot of people who want to get into sports don't think about: sometimes it's serious. I got into hockey because talking about hockey is fun. Serious stuff, though? That can be uncomfortable.

Sure enough, one of the biggest stories that week was that a player for the Mississauga St. Michael's Majors, William Wallén, had suffered a brain aneurysm during a game. There's something ghoulish about calling up a team and asking about a player who was in the hospital, but that's journalism. If you want to tell a story, sometimes you're going to have to make uncomfortable phone calls and ask uncomfortable questions.

I spoke to Mississauga's head coach at the time, Dave Cameron, who would eventually go on to coach Canada's World Junior team and later the Ottawa Senators. "There's no time frame on it, but the prognosis is a full recovery," Cameron explained. "Full recovery means that at this point there's no reason to think that he can't resume his career."

Just one week earlier, there was a story about two Kitchener Rangers suffering minor injuries in a car accident. Unfortunately, in January there was a story you never want to have to happen: a death. An Everett Silvertips and Winnipeg Saints player named Jordan Mistelbacher was found dead. Just two days later, I called the team and spoke to their head coach Doug Stokes.

It was an awful call to make.

"I think this really puts hockey into perspective," Stokes said. "It's just a game, in the end. Unfortunately, there are things that are more important than this. It's something that's overwhelming for all of us."

If you're looking to get into sports broadcasting for the fun of it, which I think is why most of us get into sports, you need to ask yourself if you're willing to make that phone call. If you can't, you're not doing your job.

Luckily, William Wallén recovered from his aneurysm and went on to play another full season with Mississauga before heading to play pro in Europe.

As a small aside, the next news and notes clip from that week's show came from a QMJHL coach named Guy Boucher, who currently coaches the Ottawa Senators. I had both of the Senator's two most recent coaches on the show that week, just to show you the names you can speak to when you cover junior hockey.

To my surprise, I was pulling it off. *Junior Hockey Mag* was coming together. I gathered some clips, spoke to the insiders, and even booked a Junior A guest. Still, I was missing a feature, and without one, I didn't have a show.

I called the WHL's Lethbridge Hurricanes and asked if I could speak to one of their draft eligible players. They had lots of highly touted prospects for the 2009 NHL Draft.

Unfortunately, they could only give me an interview at 6 p.m. eastern.

My only option was to do the feature interview myself in just my second week on the job.

Lethbridge agreed to give me a player named Zach Boychuk, who ended up going 14th overall to the Carolina Hurricanes earlier that year.

I prepared some questions, one being particularly cringeworthy: "What's with you and teams called the Hurricanes?"

Even more awkward, I explained to Zach that he needed to refer to me as "Cory" for the whole interview. Luckily, Zach was so awesome and willing to help. More importantly, he answered my crappy questions like they were good. It couldn't have gone better, given the circumstances.

With the show completed in the nick of time, we were ready to record.

"Who's tonight's guest?" Clarkey asked.

"Zach Boychuk. I just recorded the interview," I told him.

Clarkey and Colin just looked at each other. On one hand, I almost didn't finish the show. On the other, it took some balls to do the feature interview myself on my first solo show.

It was stressful, nerve-racking, and the script almost didn't get done in time, but I did it. Yes, I still had a lot to learn. But it didn't matter — I had done it. This was my job. I can do it. I can work in this business.

We had loads of guests that year who ended up playing in the NHL, but there's one in particular I remember: Calvin de Haan. Today, de Haan is a defender for the Carolina Hurricanes. Back in fall 2008, he was a draft-eligible rookie defender for the OHL's Oshawa Generals. He had a great start to his OHL career after spending the previous season in Junior A.

I met Calvin when I covered a Generals game for the Fan 590. They got me a press pass and I was eager to see the John Tavares show, but de Haan caught my eye, too.

After the game, I asked to talk to both Tavares and de Haan.

Tavares is much better these days now that he's an NHL superstar, but when it came to interviews, teenaged Tavares was torture. I simply asked him, "How are you?" and he answered with game talk.

"Oh, I guess the interview started!" I said internally, as I rushed to turn on the mic.

Then I got to speak to de Haan: he was great, and I grabbed his cell number to have him on as a guest.

When I called him not too long after, he seemed taken aback. I asked him some pre-interview questions, and he seemed kind of nervous.

"Alright, when do you want me?" he asked.

"Oh, it'll be sometime around 8:25 p.m.," I told him.

"OK. Where is it?" he asked.

"What?"

Calvin thought I was telling him to show up to the studio, and because he's a beauty, he was totally going do it. I said thank you but a phone interview was more than enough.

We were late getting to his interview that night due to a technical difficulty.

Oh my goodness. We were going to lose de Haan. He'd be offended, curse me out, and the Gens would never let me speak to their players ever again.

I called him up. I might have even called him sir.

"I'm sorry," I started. "We'll only be a few more minutes."

"That's OK, man," he said. "I'm just sitting here, playing *Call of Duty.*"

In that moment, I realized something: this guy is just a guy.

For some reason, maybe because I grew up idolizing athletes, I looked at them as these untouchable, all-powerful deities. They are all to be pampered and tended to, strictly on their terms, lest you be bound, gagged, and executed for wasting their precious time.

No, no. It's a 17-year-old who plays video games. He was only three years younger than me. Interviews became instantly easier to do when I started talking to athletes like they were human beings.

Calvin did something that night that no other guest did all season.

When I was on the train heading home, my phone rang. It was de Haan.

"How do you think I did?" he asked.

I didn't really know how to answer that. "Uh, you did great, man," I said.

We were just shooting the breeze about random stuff when

I asked him if he knew what his draft ranking was. NHL Central Scouting had just released their preliminary draft rankings for the 2009 NHL Entry Draft.

"Oh, I don't know. Like fifty-second?" he said, trying to sound like he was guessing.

Sure enough, I checked and he was ranked 52nd. He knew. Of course he knew. If the NHL had me in the draft rankings, you bet I would know exactly where I was.

THE
MINORS

Meanwhile, my second season of YouTube videos, which I had dubbed Leafs Fan Reaction videos, or LFR for short, was well underway. After a strong end to the season with those two YouTube Canada homepage features, I was worried I had lost momentum. I needed to switch it up. It was going to be a lot more work, but I decided to switch to jump-cut edited videos full time. The videos were just straight up better that way. I also made an intro for my videos with quick-cut edits of me flying around my room with a wicked guitar riff from a song called "Fighting for Love" by my high school friend Al Rowe's band, Aberdeen.

Viewership was up but only a little. Again, it would have been nice to have a Twitter account with over 100,000 followers that I could tweet all my stuff from, but that was just a fantasy world in 2008, unless you were Ashton Kutcher.

Someone sent me a message on YouTube one day. "Did you see you've been Puck Daddy'd?"

I didn't even know what that meant. Apparently, Greg Wyshynski of the *Puck Daddy* blog on Yahoo Sports had linked to one of my videos in a post of his. This wasn't some random fan blog. This was Yahoo Sports. Wysh did that for me a few times that season, and you could tell by the spike in viewership every time.

Early that season, I got another sign that my videos were starting to gain some traction. This one was a lot less expected.

I received an email from a guy named Trevor van Knotsenburg. He said he worked in media relations for the Toronto Marlies, the Leafs' American Hockey League affiliate.

Today, the Marlies usually draw a pretty strong crowd. Back then, however, they had only recently relocated to Toronto and attendance was one of the worst in the AHL.

In an effort to get more fan attention, they offered me press credentials for their games.

I was caught so off-guard, I called him to make sure it wasn't a prank. He was serious. When you think about it, it was an innovative move back in 2008, and it was a brilliant way to get authentic grassroots exposure for the hockey team without spending a dime. On the other hand, he was taking a huge risk because I might have been a shmuck.

If you're wondering what a smart guy like that is doing these days, he now works with the Tampa Bay Lightning. You could say he got called up.

I took the Marlies up on their offer and covered some of their games. It was a different experience. I was always taught "there's no cheering in the press box," but that didn't apply to some of the reporters I met. I tried not to get sucked into that. If I started cheering in this press box, I might've accidentally cheered in another.

This was a totally different feeling than covering the Blue Jays. For one, it was hockey, so I was much more confident in what I was doing. While I didn't have the safety net or guidance of the Fan for these games (they already sent reporters to cover games for them), I was totally free. I was my own boss. I wrote and asked the questions; I owned and published my own content to my own YouTube channel.

I used this freedom to my advantage.

After a game against the Iowa Chops, the AHL affiliate of the Anaheim Ducks at the time, reporters were asking then

Marlies head coach Greg Gilbert some questions. Gilbert was a straight shooter and real prickly when he wanted to be. The questions he was being asked seemed boring to me, and they produced equally boring answers.

The Iowa Chops' logo was just a really angry looking pig. I don't know why the question came out, but I just asked, "Do the Iowa Chops have the dumbest logo in the league?"

His face totally changed and every reporter was like, *What the hell did that kid just say?*

Gilbert gave a very diplomatic answer about how he actually thought the logo wasn't so bad and that they had slick-looking jerseys. When he finished his answer, he raised his eyebrows, smirked at me, and walked into the locker room.

The other reporters looked baffled.

"It was worth a shot," I said, smiling.

I went to some great games that year. I got to see Tim Stapleton set the Marlies' team record for scoring in a season: 79 points in 70 games. When he got called up to the Leafs for four games that season, I was like, "Hey, I know that guy!"

Another fun guy to cover was a player named Max Taylor, who been called up from the ECHL. Taylor already had two goals, and the Marlies were killing their opponents 5–1. Late in the game, Taylor buried his hat-trick goal with 2.4 seconds to go. He went bananas, like he had just scored the OT winner. His teammates poked fun at him after the game.

One cool thing about covering sports is you get to be there for those moments. Taylor scored eight career AHL goals and three of them went in that night. That was his final year of pro hockey. On the other hand, I got to see and cover James Reimer's first pro hockey game in Toronto, after he was called up from the ECHL's Reading Royals, that led to a long NHL journey in which he ended the Leafs' playoff drought, got the city to chant his name, and became a millionaire.

Then there was Jeremy Williams.

Williams is a bit of a legend in Leafs Land. He got called up for one game with the big club in 2005–06 and scored a goal. The next season, he got called up for one game and scored again. The following season, he did it a third time. Now, in the 2008–09 season, which thoroughly sucked for the Leafs, Williams was a little ray of sunshine, scoring five goals and seven points in just 11 NHL games.

Once he was back with the Marlies, I covered one of his post-game scrums. After the scrum, he looked at me and said, "My mom showed me your videos. She loves them."

Getting on the radar of the Marlies media guy was one thing. Being acknowledged by an actual professional hockey player and a Leaf, no less? I couldn't believe it. I never dreamed this would happen when I decided to make Leafs videos on YouTube — a decision made while half in the bag.

Then, as I looked over his shoulder and saw the Marlies enforcer Andre Deveaux, a colder thought occurred to me. *Oh God — have I ever said anything about him? Were they nice things? I really hope they were nice . . .*

Meanwhile, I still had *Junior Hockey Mag* going on. Even after almost a full year, I tried to keep what I considered to be my professional life, which was the Fan 590 and *Junior Hockey Mag*, separate from my amateur hobby, my YouTube videos.

Finally, the inevitable collision happened.

"WE'RE GONNA MAKE YOU A STAR"

Clarkey offered to drive me from the Fan to Union Station one day. It's technically a short drive, but since it's Toronto, it can take anywhere from five minutes to two hours.

Remember I said Clarkey worked at Leafs TV? Well, he started telling me about this cool new idea they had.

"It's called Leafspace," he said.

The idea was basically to create a site like MySpace but specifically design it for Leafs fans. You could connect with other fans, post pictures, blogs, and even videos.

Clarkey told me that the plan was to make a weekly half-hour Leafspace TV show, featuring the videos that fans posted to the site. It was gutsy at the time.

He mentioned that if the site got a few people who regularly posted videos, they'd be golden.

I sat quietly in the passenger seat. Should I tell him? No way, dude. You're finally getting the hang of this job. Don't screw it up. But what if it works?

I just went for it.

"You're gonna think this is stupid," I started, "but I already kind of do that."

"Really?" he asked.

"Yeah, I have a YouTube channel. I've been making videos about the Leafs since last year."

"Oh! You didn't tell me that," he said. "Send me a link and I'll take a look."

After I sent him the link, I briefly wondered if I had just made a huge mistake but mostly forgot about it.

Three days later, I was walking through Dundas Square after class when my phone rang.

"Dude!" Clarkey yelled into the phone. "You are *exactly* what we've been looking for!"

I didn't know what to say. I had never heard him this excited before.

"Really?"

"Oh my God — absolutely." Then he said something I'll never forget: "We're gonna make you a star."

What did he say after that? Great question: wish I knew. I blanked after that. That was all that mattered, wasn't it?

When I hung up, I wanted to climb one of the signs at Dundas Square and hang off it, roaring like King Kong until the cops came. I've been a Leafs fan all my life. I knew I wanted to be in broadcasting, but I didn't know in what capacity. I was wandering around with no confidence and no real sense of worth or professional meaning. Then out of nowhere: "We're gonna make you a star." It was the stuff of movies.

I knew exactly what I wanted to do with my life: talk Leafs. Not so fast though, junior. You've still got other commitments. Remember school? Also *Junior Hockey Mag*. Oh, and don't forget to do a video after every Leafs game, too.

My shifts at the Fan basically stopped. I just couldn't do it. There literally weren't enough hours in the week. Luckily, because of *Junior Hockey Mag*, I still got lots of face time at the station.

I was lucky to work on *Junior Hockey Mag* that season. I got to speak to Jordan Eberle that year, which was the same year he scored against the Russians with 5.4 seconds left at the World Juniors. I was getting all these cool opportunities, and as much as I wanted to come across as professional, I had watched him score that goal while I sat in my parents' basement and literally ran around the house in my boxers afterwards — so it was difficult, to say the least. (Also, apologies for the visual.)

I also spoke to P.K. Subban that year, as well as Brayden Schenn, Zack Kassian, and Ryan O'Reilly — if you were a big-name draft prospect in the CHL, we had you on the show.

After the World Juniors, on the eve of the OHL trade deadline, I had our entire show written and prepped by 3 p.m. Then the Oshawa Generals traded John Tavares to the London Knights and effectively blew up my world. I basically crumpled up the whole script and threw it away.

The Generals traded Tavares, defender Michael Del Zotto, and a goalie to London in exchange for three players and six draft picks.

I tried calling Knights GM Mark Hunter — no answer — and Generals coach and GM Chris DePiero — again, no answer. Neither team was even answering their office line. What about Tavares's agent Pat Brisson? Nope. I called Calvin de Haan and he answered, but all he said was that it sucked, which is true, but that's hardly a feature interview.

Someone at the Fan saw I was flustered and asked what was up. I told him my situation and he pointed at the marker board in the bullpen that had a list of the past week's guests. They kept track to make sure shows didn't have the same guests.

"Did you try the mayor?" they asked.

"I'm sorry," I said. "What?"

"Yeah, somebody had the mayor of Oshawa on for something recently. John Grey, I think his name was. Get his number and give it a try."

So I called the mayor of Oshawa. First ring: "Hello, John Grey speaking."

Are you kidding me?

So I interviewed the mayor of Oshawa about the John Tavares trade.

Luckily, Gino had anticipated that the show had been torpedoed, so he called to tell me not to worry and that he had handled everything. We had London Knights assistant coach Pat Curcio on, which, given how the day went, was a huge get.

Most CHL teams were happy to give you any guest you asked for because they needed the publicity. There was even a QMJHL team whose owners barely spoke English, but they were so accommodating that they told me to send them my questions in English, then they translated them to French, answered them in French, wrote down the translation in English, read that translation, recorded it, and sent me an email with the files.

It was nearing the end of the season and we hadn't had John Tavares, the likely first overall pick, on our national junior hockey show. Gino challenged me to find a way to book him.

I was excusing myself from class to make calls, sending emails, everything. Finally, I scheduled a call with John. I was working on a stressful school assignment at home when I was supposed to do a pre-interview with John, which I had to do. I call, no answer. I call again, no answer. I wait, then I call again, no answer. I can't concentrate on this damn assignment; I haven't slept in a week. *Can someone answer the damn phone?*

Finally, the Knight's PR guy called.

"Hi. Did you get my voicemail?" I asked.

"Yeah," he said. "And I saw the other six times you called, too," he shot back.

The red mist set in. I might be 20 and even younger than some players in the OHL, but don't talk down to me when you're the one in the wrong.

"Listen," I snapped. "I called at the time you told me to call. I have things to do. I didn't want to call you six times. I was hoping to be done with this all by now, actually."

I can't believe he didn't hang up and tell me to screw myself.

To this guy's credit, he actually called back later to apologize to me, some 20-year-old. It was nice to actually feel like an adult and be treated like one for once. After we did our thing with John, the PR guy said I could have any player I want for the rest of the season.

"We have this kid," he said. "Nazem Kadri. He's supposed to go pretty high. He's great, you'll love him."

The second I hung up the phone, I thought, *If that guy wants Nazem Kadri on this show, then Nazem Kadri will never be on this show.*

When the draft rolled around a few months later, I was so excited because the Leafs had the seventh overall pick, and odds were, I had their pick's phone number. *I hope they pick Jared Cowen,* I thought. It was a very different time.

When the Leafs picked Kadri, I could have cried. That's why you don't hold a grudge, kids. Looking back, thank goodness they picked him.

There was a constant internal struggle that I faced. On one hand, my YouTube channel was doing better and better, and there was this great new Leafspace thing that I was getting a lot of praise for. Some classmates would come up to me and say, "Dude, you were on the TV at the bar last night!"

On the other hand, there was *Junior Hockey Mag.* Expectations rose as the season went on. Little mistakes that were forgivable in the first couple months soon became cardinal sins.

One time, I made a minor mistake in the script that Gino pointed out. I asked if it was really that big of a deal.

"No," Gino said nonchalantly. "It's fine if you want to work at a radio station in Orangeville."

Sometimes your boss might be a jerk, which is totally how I viewed stuff like this at the time. But looking back, he was right. Make a mistake once? Fine. A second time? Shame on you. A third time? Dude, figure it out!

The fact that it wasn't a big mistake wasn't the point. Gino wouldn't have told me that, he wouldn't have pushed me to be better, if he didn't think I could be better. I remember after one show, I stewed for the whole train ride home because I had done such a bad job. When I got to my parents' street and made sure the coast was clear, I started crying.

Again, looking back, that was good. I wasn't a child. I cried because I was disappointed in myself, not because my boss was mad at me.

I used to drive Gino nuts with maybes. "Maybe" does nothing for him. Odds are, "maybe" doesn't do anything for your boss, either. When they want to know something, they're not interested in what you might know; they're interested in what you do know.

Either you know or you don't. That's it. "I'm not sure" is useless unless it's followed by "but I'll go find out." After enough slip-ups, that one's thoroughly burned into my brain.

Once the season was over, Gino and the guys told me I actually did a really good job. As a whole, I think I did, too. Certainly not perfect, but I helped make our show a good one.

One day, I had mentioned to Clarkey that making videos for every Leafs game was getting difficult with my work and school load. Plus Leafs TV wanted the videos to be around four minutes or so, they couldn't have any swear words, and they had to be done by a certain time in order to get them into the show. It was getting to be more than I could handle. Soon after that, Clarkey invited me to the Leafs TV studios to talk to his boss, John McCauley.

"Steve," John began, "we really like you and we really like your videos. What can we do to help you to continue making them for us?"

I don't know what he expected me to say. Probably money? But I had a different idea.

"I need an internship," I told them. "Next year will be my fourth year, and I need a fourth-year internship in order to graduate."

Judging by the looks on their faces, they weren't expecting that answer.

They said yes.

The 2008–09 hockey season was a disaster for the Leafs, but it was easily the most successful year of my professional life up to then. I took some lumps, but I learned a lot and got a ton of really cool opportunities. In fact, Leafs TV wasn't even the only TV channel I was on.

Somebody named Josh Wilder emailed me. He was a producer for CBC, the Canadian Broadcasting Corporation. He told me that he had seen my videos and thought it would be interesting if I made one for their playoff preview show. If it was any good, they would use it.

You probably could've seen my smile from space. I told my parents; I told my girlfriend; I told anybody who would listen.

Want proof that the world is a teeny tiny little coffee shop? The guy who showed Josh my videos was none other than Jeff Marek, the guy whose radio show I used to call during high school.

Jeff hosted a segment on CBC called the "iDesk." Broadcasters are better at integrating online content today, but in 2009, it was basically an isolated "OK, here's our internet segment" thing. Hey, I'm amazed they talked about the internet or hockey blogging at all, let alone allowing a hockey blogger to make a video on his crappy Logitech webcam and then broadcast it on national television.

I stayed up all night making my video — literally all night; I went to bed at 6 a.m., after my dad had some breakfast and went to work. It had to be perfect.

The first video was like four minutes long. Josh said, "That's great, but can you make it closer to thirty seconds?"

I started over and made a 30 second video. I had quick one-liners about each upcoming series for the 2009 Stanley Cup playoffs. Yes, I worked in a Leafs joke, even though they weren't in the playoffs.

Jeff invited me in to the CBC office that day. There was a live studio audience for the playoff preview show, with a full panel and Ron MacLean hosting.

I didn't get to watch from the studio itself, but I was watching on a TV in the building when they threw to my video. Just like that, I was ranting and raving about hockey on national TV. Once they cut back to the studio after the video, you could hear a split second of the audience laughing at what I ended with. I also heard Ron MacLean chuckle through my name. "Alright — Steve Dangle!" he said as he threw to break.

BRING
YOUR
LAWYER

In the spring of 2009, I got a message on YouTube from someone who had questions about my channel. They asked to see some of my analytics to find out who watched my videos for a "case study."

Case study? I thought. *It's probably someone in high school doing a boring project for social studies.*

Thinking that I was just helping out a fellow student, I gave them all the information they asked for. YouTube has statistics for the age and gender of your viewers, as well as the country views come from.

A few days later, the "student" messaged me back. They told me that they had reviewed the information and that they would like to meet with me to talk about a potential business deal.

Meet me? In person? Hell no! Who the hell is this guy? I just want to make videos about the stupid Leafs, man. I'm not trying to get abducted and turned into this guy's new rain jacket.

I responded by declining the offer. I gave them some wishy-washy answer and basically implied I wasn't that comfortable meeting some random stranger from the internet.

I figured that would be the end of it, but sure enough, the YouTube Serial Killer messaged me again.

They insisted that we could meet wherever I wanted in downtown Toronto and they could make it close to my school if need be. They also mentioned that they would be paying — which changed things. I'm always down for a meal, but a free one? Forget all my plans, let's go order 40 pounds of wings right now.

One part in particular made me realize this was for real: they told me to bring my agent or my lawyer if it made me feel more comfortable.

Agent? Lawyer? Who do they think I am? I'm a student who lives with his parents. They've seen my videos — haven't they seen my bedroom? I don't even have a credit card.

Since it seemed legit and because this is exactly the kind of message I had been hoping to receive for a while, I knew I had to meet whoever this was. I also knew I couldn't go alone. What if it was a scam? What if I signed something and severely screwed myself over? What if I got sued for all the money I didn't have?

Then it dawned on me: Derek.

My friend Derek from the Thursday Hangout Crew had told me about a law course he was taking. What kind of law, you ask? It was probably a glorified, next-level version of high school law class. It didn't really matter because regardless of how advanced or elementary his class was, Derek had to know more about law than I did.

I also knew that Derek had bandied about the idea of starting his own business one day. He even got an internship for the Business News Network. I was just picturing all the boring business-type jargon he probably heard all day long and figured he could talk the talk.

Derek worked at a bank as a teller, which meant he had to wear fancy clothes to his job, and to top it off, Derek has the kind of smile and charisma that makes you want to keep him away from your house just in case he leaves with your mom. Think of the kind of guy who would clean up at a PTA meeting or a taping of *The Marilyn Denis Show*.

"Hey, Derek, can you wear a suit to school?" All lawyers wear suits, right? Sure. Yeah. Everyone knows that.

Like the true friend that he is, Derek said yes.

This will be perfect. He'll show up, throw on the Derek charm, and we'll be millionaires before we even graduate.

I messaged back the YouTube Serial Killer and told them my lawyer and I would meet them at the Elephant & Castle, just north of the Ryerson campus. When the big day came, I felt terrible. I had some kind of spring cold, but it was probably because I was a nervous wreck.

Being the nervous Nellies that we were, Derek and I showed up to the restaurant about 20 minutes early. I was in my student clothes and Derek — always clutch — had on his lawyer suit.

We sat down at a table and talked about what we thought was going to happen. We barely had any information to work with. All we knew is that they wanted to discuss some kind of business idea involving my YouTube channel.

For all I knew, they could have been from some tiny website, offering me exposure instead of money, or they could have said, "Don Cherry is retiring and he specifically hand-picked you to be his replacement. Here's ten million dollars." The serial killer option was also still there, plus now I had gotten my friend killed, too.

"No matter what they offer you, act like you were offered it yesterday," Derek told me.

That got me hyped up. No more of this foot-in-the-door crap. I need to get paid. They need to make this worth my while. I'm Steve Dangle, damn it! Wait — should I introduce myself as Steve Dangle or Steve Glynn? Maybe just Steve. Who bothers with their last name in an introduction? How should I shake their hand? Firm? Firm, yeah. Establish dominance. What was I thinking about? Oh, yeah, no matter what they offer you, act like you were offered it yesterday. Great advice, Derek. This is why you're my lawyer.

After Derek and I had built up enough fake confidence and a sufficient amount of faux male bravado, two men named Elliot and Craig came through the door and walked over to the table.

They were extremely friendly with big, genuine smiles. Elliot had particularly big eyes and nice teeth. *Wait, Steve, are you here to check this guy out or become a millionaire? Focus.*

Handshakes were firm yet friendly. Pretty much perfectly down the middle. Derek stood with a pumped-up chest and greeted them with something to the effect of "Gentlemen," trying his absolute hardest not to sound like a 20-year-old.

The two guys made some chit-chat and ordered food.

Since I was so gross and stuffed up, all I ordered was some soup. The two guys told me I could order more than that if I wanted, but I wasn't hungry. It figures, the one time I get a free meal from someone who isn't my parent and I'm not even hungry. That never happens. *Oh God, is this a sign? Do they think I'm weird now? No. The handshakes were good and Derek still has his suit going for him. We're gold.*

After a few minutes of friendly banter, the guys told me that I had to sign some papers before we could officially talk business, for legal reasons.

Legal reasons, huh? Well, good thing I brought my lawy— uh oh.

Derek and I spent a few minutes shuffling through the papers and trying to read the fine print. Every time I didn't understand something, I would look over at Derek, who would be reading with his "I'm definitely a real lawyer and not just a 20-year-old wearing a suit because my idiot friend told me to" face.

Derek — say something, man! I screamed internally.

After a few moments of reading in silence, the two men asked if we had any questions.

Yeah I have a question: What the hell does any of this mean? I thought.

"No, not yet," I told them, trying to sound calm and casual.

Finally, I read something that I actually understood: a "non-compete clause."

For those of you who don't know, a non-compete clause basically means you can't work for a competitor of theirs for a certain amount of time after signing the agreement. I remember learning about them just the semester before, in the one media law class I had taken and achieved a mediocre grade in. I should also mention that the only reason I took that class is because I had to drop one of my evening classes because it was right after Rammertime. That's when the student bar, the Ram and the Rye, had $2.75 beers.

So, hey, thanks, Rammertime.

"What's this non-compete clause?" I asked.

The two guys looked at Derek assuming he would answer, but he just continued reading silently.

They explained what I pretty much already knew: after signing these papers, I couldn't work for a competitor of their client's for six months, whether we actually came to an agreement or not.

"I'm not sure I can sign this," I said.

They explained that things couldn't continue if I didn't sign the agreement.

"The issue is that I don't know who you represent," I said. "Let's say you're representing The Score. We might have a nice conversation but if nothing comes of it and if I want to try to get a job with Sportsnet, then I wouldn't be allowed to?"

It looked like Craig was about to say something. Before he could, Elliot interrupted him and looked me dead in the eyes with his head tilted down.

"The client is Nike."

I wish someone from the Guinness Book of World Records was there to clock how fast I signed that contract. I'm surprised I didn't rip through the paper with my pen.

I can still hear Elliot's words, "The client is Nike," in my head. I was so shocked that it's permanently burned into my memory, right next to the Leafs winning the 2016 Draft Lottery.

Is this really happening? I thought. *What the hell does Nike want with me? Do these guys think I'm actually in shape? Wait — do these guys think I can skate?*

It was hard to keep my mind from racing, but I tried as hard as I could to listen to what these guys had to say. It was one of those things where you actually realize how life-changing this moment could be while you're experiencing it.

Unfortunately, my legal counsel had to leave the meeting shortly after this enormous revelation. I think he told them that he had another engagement to be at, but I knew damn well he just needed to catch a bus back to Brampton to have dinner with his parents.

When Derek got up to leave, he shook hands with both men and then gave me a casual smile and nod. The way he walked away was hilarious. He was trying so hard not to laugh or even make eye contact with me. I could tell he was concentrating super hard because it looked like he forgot how to use his arms.

Elliot and Craig started going through the idea they had for me: an Olympic campaign. The plan was to bring me to the Winter Olympics in Vancouver, so I could interview some Nike athletes from a variety of sports, including hockey. Their big hockey guy was Jarome Iginla, one of my favourite players growing up, even though he was never a Leaf.

This was insane. Just six months ago, I was too intimidated to talk to junior hockey players on the phone and now these guys think I can talk to Olympic athletes in-person? I wasn't about to tell them they were nuts. *Bring it on*, I thought.

The rest of the meeting went well, I finished my free soup, and we shook hands. The second I walked out of the restaurant, I pulled out my Blackberry Bold, called Derek, and we both freaked out like we got Nintendo 64s for Christmas.

Unfortunately, I didn't hear much from those two in the months that followed. School ended, the Leafs' season ended, and soon after the junior hockey playoffs came to an end, so did my season with *Junior Hockey Magazine*.

Back to the zoo I went. Luckily, I went back armed with a powerful weapon: my phone.

"EBS" & FLOWS

Transitioning back to the zoo in late April was difficult. Elementary and high school students weren't even out of school yet. Weekdays were painfully quiet. After the year I'd had, I'd become used to constant hustle and bustle. You'd think that I would be happy for the change of pace, but I actually preferred busy days at the zoo to quiet ones. I was bored out of my skull.

It was technically against zoo policy to have your phone on you during work hours. I took that as more of a suggestion. One day, I was looking through my contacts: Jordan Eberle, Taylor Hall, Ryan Ellis, John Tavares.

All of a sudden, I missed *Junior Hockey Magazine* a lot. I wasn't even worried about getting harsh criticism anymore; I just wanted more hockey.

What's strange is I don't think I ever once mentioned in my videos that I was doing that show. Looking back, that was the dumbest thing ever. Why wouldn't I promote the fact that I was doing this wicked-cool job? I still had this weird inkling to keep my professional life and YouTube life separate, even though that was getting more difficult to do.

Then a light bulb went off. My classmate and friend Joseph DeBenedictis is a good video editor and a gifted cameraman. Plus he is a huge Leafs fan, so we used to talk hockey all the time. As an added bonus, he lived close by, in Pickering.

What if I could call these guys up — these junior hockey stars — do an interview with them, get Joseph to shoot and edit videos, and then post them to my YouTube channel?

Joseph was down. Alright! Who should I try first?

I decided to go with the player who I had spoken to the most times throughout the past hockey season and one who answered his phone whenever I called or texted: Jordan Eberle. Go big or go home, right?

So we arranged the interview.

It was a pretty bootleg yet brilliant setup. Joseph had his professional camera shooting me, but what about Jordan? We didn't know how to record a video call at the time. What were we going to do? Point the camera at the computer screen?

I had an idea, but it required Jordan's cooperation. I would call Jordan on the phone, he would put me on speakerphone and have his phone sitting off-camera. Then he would record himself on his personal webcam and send me the video file.

Jordan, being the absolute beauty that he is, agreed to do it. After he sent me his footage, we edited it with my own webcam footage and Joseph's camera footage.

Joseph's computer and software was agonizingly slow, but eventually we made the interview into a proper video where Jordan and I were both on the screen at the same time.

My questions stunk, but Jordan was a good sport. I think he realized he was doing me an enormous favour. This comment from user Vagrant_88 left back in 2009 was actually pretty on the nose: "You have so much potential in terms of the access you have to players and the fact that, being an independent journalist, you don't have to stick to the standard script. I think that is an asset you should utilize in your approach. Being a young guy, you also have the potential to ask some questions that could really generate some funny answers. Don't serve so many meatballs next time! Still, though, a very good, albeit fairly generic, interview. Keep 'em coming, man!"

I probably read that at the time and thought, *Shut up, idiot! My questions were great. I am a legitimate journalist!*

The criticisms were fair, though. This was a unique opportunity and Vagrant_88 didn't want to see me squander it. There's a lot of pressure that comes with that. I asked Eberle about the adversity of missing the WHL playoffs with the Regina Pats and the famous goal against Russia, but that news was over five months old by then. *Dude, ask him if he's got 5.4 painted on the roof of his car yet or something — jazz it up!*

The simulator booth at the Toronto Zoo became my office. I was texting and emailing players and PR folks from all around junior hockey. I remember I once spoke to the Windsor Spitfires PR guy and Taylor Hall on one of my lunch breaks.

I arranged even more interviews to do with Joseph. Calvin de Haan was second; he didn't need any convincing. With Eberle and de Haan on board, it was easier to go to other players and say, "Well, hey, these guys did it."

We went to Guelph to interview Peter Holland, a Guelph Storm player and likely first-rounder. We spoke to Ethan Werek, a Kingston Frontenacs player predicted to go somewhere in the first or second. Can't get John Tavares? Go to Oshawa and talk to his coach, Chris DePiero.

We couldn't get all our guests in person or over the computer, so we tried something else.

My buddy Fisher was a station manager at Fusion Radio, U of T Scarborough's campus radio station. At some point, after a brief period of screwing around and talking about silly random crap on another show, we started a hockey radio show, simply called *The Steve Dangle Show*.

One day, I arranged a show with the following lineup:

Tyson Barrie, a Kelowna Rockets defender now with the Colorado Avalanche.

Carter Ashton, a Lethbridge Hurricanes forward who went in the first round and played 54 NHL games with the Leafs.

Robert Slaney, a Cape Breton Screaming Eagles forward who had just signed with the Leafs.

Michael Latta, a Guelph Storm forward with over 100 NHL games played.

Taylor Hall, star forward for the Memorial Cup Champion Windsor Spitfires, eventual first overall pick, eventual Hart Trophy winner, and former Edmonton Oiler. Sorry, that last part was unnecessary.

We had them all on the phone one after the other. One guy backed out, though: my buddy Brian Barton. We became friends when he worked security at the zoo, but he also played Junior A. He had an offer to go play roller hockey in Italy, which I thought was cool, so I invited him on.

"I can schedule you in right after Taylor Hall," I told him.

"What?" he yelled. "Dude, forget that! I don't belong on there with Taylor Hall."

Yeah, that was kind of a lot of pressure I guess, huh?

After the draft, I managed to get one last in-person interview with two newly drafted Leafs prospects: second-rounder Jesse Blacker and none other than Nazem Kadri. See? We got to talk after all.

Were any of these interviews good? Well, I can't even stand to watch them today, so I'll say no. But they certainly gave my channel some legitimacy.

Another thing that gave me clout: a YouTube partnership.

Around this time, YouTube invited me to become a YouTube partner, meaning they could put ads on my videos and I could collect money from it. That's right, baby! YouTube money! I only had like 900 subscribers, but who cares? I'm gonna buy a gold-plated house with a chrome pool and fill it with chocolate milk!

You used to need to have earned at least $100 in a month to get a YouTube cheque. After about three months, I finally got my first cheque.

I know that's not much, but it was a lot to me at the time. I needed all the money I could get heading into fourth year. Also, the idea of it meant a lot.

When I stood in line at the bank with my first *Junior Hockey Mag* cheque I was like, *This is it — my first hockey cheque. I can make a living off hockey.* Now it was *This is it — my first YouTube cheque. I can make a living off YouTube.*

There was one nasty hiccup that summer, though.

The Fan 590 saw that I got all these interviews with recently drafted hockey players. They asked me if they could feature them on their website.

"Are you kidding?" I said. "Of course you can!"

They were up there for a few hours before I got a call from Clarkey. Apparently, somebody above him was pissed off that my stuff was getting used on another outlet's platform. They had been showing my videos on Leafs TV throughout the summer and didn't want it looking like I was a personality for another outlet.

Writing this book has allowed me to look back on a lot of things I once resented and consider them from a more mature, understanding angle. But this is one thing where I'm still like, *Nah, that was bullshit.* Why couldn't I get exposure on the Fan's site? I had interned there for long enough. Also, I wasn't even a Leafs TV intern yet. What was their problem? This could have been huge for me, and if my profile grew and earned respect, wouldn't that just make Leafs TV look good?

It made no sense (still doesn't) and I was fuming, but my future looked like it was heading toward Leafs TV more than the Fan, and I didn't want to jeopardize my school credit internship.

I called Doug Farraway to deliver the bad news.

"Well," he began, "it sounds like they've got you by the balls, Steve."

They took my videos off the Fan 590 website. It was a long time before I got another opportunity with any Sportsnet-related platform after that.

As the summer ended, the 2009–10 hockey season was set to begin, and with it, my fourth and final year of university. That meant completing a practicum project, which was a giant group project that you had to pitch to professors in order to get approval. This final year also included the mandatory fourth-year internship.

I looped back with Leafs TV. They were still down to give me an internship for school but only under the condition that I begin right away in September. The cherry on top: it was a paid internship. It was only $300 per month, but that was $300 per month more than most internships pay.

It was completely different working in a television studio than a radio one. They had sets with cameras and a green-screen backdrop. One guy who worked there was Jon Sinden, their social media expert. I couldn't believe that was even a thing. It was like pulling teeth to get companies to embrace social media and that was this guy's entire job? Awesome!

And there was Brocky, a producer who put together a lot of the station's shows. He taught me some great lessons, and whenever I was feeling down after getting scolded for making a dumb rookie mistake, he was always there to be the good cop. I needed that. At just 21, I was probably the youngest person in the building on most days.

Leafs TV proved to be a great place to learn. They taught me how to edit video highlights as I produced the *Game in Six* highlight packages that they still put on the Leafs' official website today. I worked alongside a girl named Heather on most nights. She was lightning fast and taught me almost everything I knew in that department. She saved my ass on more than one occasion.

They also put me in charge of updating parts of the Leafs TV news ticker. I got behind-the-scenes access to the server, so I could make updates from home. Of course, this was also the 2009–10 season, and the Leafs totally sucked, so it was difficult to post any stats that were flattering. I still remember being like,

"Carl Gunnarsson is second among NHL rookie defencemen in plus minus." If that's the best stat your team has, your team sucks.

Another time, Brocky walked up to me with a big camera and asked, "You know how to use one of these?"

"No," I told him truthfully. I took mostly writing courses in school. I was useless when it came to tech.

"Well," he said, "you're gonna learn today. I need you to shoot something."

I figured out record, zoom, and focus, but that was about it. How do you white balance again? How much footage is too much? Oh God, the battery's dead! If the best way to learn is making mistakes, then I was a great learner.

Slowly but surely, however, my camerawork improved. My video editing was getting pretty decent. Then again, I was making six-minute hockey highlight packs, not *Avatar 2*. With more and more on-camera opportunities, and with my YouTube channel continuing to grow, I had to get more comfortable on camera.

The 2009–10 season was definitely a test for my creativity, both with making highlight packs and my YouTube channel. That was the infamous season where the Leafs traded for Phil Kessel, only to go 0-7-1 in their first eight games. I remember after one loss, I pulled out a gong that my dad had in the basement — you know, like all dads have — and blasted it. The Leafs were literally a gong show.

Back at school, I was a ball of stress.

Nate and I, along with our friend Tom, pitched an idea for our practicum project that was half in Toronto and half in Montreal. We would be making a documentary about the rivalry between the Toronto Maple Leafs and Montreal Canadiens. I was confident I could arrange interviews, Nate had a job editing highlights at Sportsnet, and Tom was doing lots of things with CBC. We thought our pitch was really good.

Our idea was shot down, however. At the time, I told myself it was because our professors were biased against sports. After all, there was only one sports-related course in the entire program at the time and, on more than one occasion, different students complained that professors turned their nose up at sports ideas.

One student in particular, during his interview to get into the program, kept referencing sports because, well, that's what he wanted to do with his life. After a number of questions, the interviewer cut him off before he could answer another.

"Let me guess," the professor said. "Sports, right?"

That student was waitlisted before he ended up getting in. Today, that former student works at TSN and was the artistic mind behind the famous documentary *The Butterfly Child* about Ottawa Senators fan, the late Jonathan Pitre. So yes — *sports*.

Realistically, though, we were probably shot down because we didn't understand how much money it would cost. This was the difficult thing about practicum: you had to have a good idea and have a plan for how to make it happen financially. One practicum pitch involved an idea with a budget of about $20,000, but it was accepted because they actually had a plan for how to achieve it. We thought our idea would be only a couple grand. Really? Between renting equipment, travel, food, and maybe hotel for our entire group, and incidental expenses? I don't think so.

Luckily, my pal Joseph DeBenedictis's idea, a pilot for a reality show about a used car dealership, did get accepted, so Nate, Tom, and I joined in. It was called *Deal with It*.

We had seven fourth-year students working on the project with a budget of about $7,000. We didn't have the money, so we had to get creative. We made t-shirts and sold a few dozen, which didn't cover much. I set up shop in the atrium of one of the university buildings and literally tried to sell my hockey card collection.

Joseph's dad owned a small sporting goods store — Metrosport the Soccer Store — and hired me to work there part time for a bit of extra cash. I steamed stop signs and name plates onto hockey jerseys for local teams. I remember working on some jerseys for the Ajax Knights.

It was a fluke we even ended up at this car dealership. Joseph had a place lined up, but after the project was approved, they bailed. One day, Joseph saw a different dealership on the back of a licence plate and just called the number, a total shot in the dark. For some reason, they agreed to let us film them for three days.

I was in charge of making sure we had a story that made sense, which was surprisingly difficult. All in all, we had about 60 hours of footage between three cameras that we needed to smush into one 22-minute television episode.

We poured our entire lives into this project. We didn't sleep, but we got it done. I was officially broke as a joke. Worth mentioning: today, Joseph is an editor for Pegula Sports & Entertainment, makes videos for both the Buffalo Sabres and Buffalo Bills, and has won several Emmys. He turned out OK.

Along the way, I learned a valuable lesson: get your invoices in on time.

Overwhelmed in the middle of the project, I submitted my monthly invoice to Leafs TV about a week late.

Clarkey just goes, "Sorry, you're too late."

"What?" I asked.

"They're not going to accept that. You should have submitted it when I told you," Clarkey said.

I didn't understand.

"So, like, they're just going to tack it onto my next invoice?" I asked.

"No, Steve. It's just too late. They're not going to accept the invoice," he told me.

I was shocked. I started telling him about one time when I was late getting my bank information to the zoo but that they ended up paying me all the money I was owed. After all, I had done the work!

He leaned over his desk. "Do you think I'm fucking you?" he asked exasperatedly.

"No," I said, startled, "But if I don't get this money, I *am* fucked. I literally can't afford to take the train to get here without this money."

Reminder that this whole argument was over $300.

I ended up getting paid. It's possible that whole incident was a story he invented to teach me to get my invoices in on time. Regardless — point taken.

To add pressure to my life, I finally got the call: Nike.

Elliot and Craig were back in the picture. After some time to think about it, maybe sending a 21-year-old to the Olympics for a major campaign was a bit risky. They had a new idea, though.

"We saw your Jordan Eberle interview," they told me. "How'd you pull that off?"

I reminded them of my time at *Junior Hockey Mag*. They asked who else I had spoken to. I was keeping a close eye on Canada's potential World Junior roster and rattled off all the players I had spoken to who had a chance of making it. I didn't realize it until I said it, but I had spoken to well over half the potential team.

The new idea was to go to the 2010 World Junior Hockey Championship in Saskatchewan that upcoming December to make videos and interview players, and if that campaign was a success, we could go to the Olympics.

No pressure, eh?

We agreed on a dollar amount for the whole campaign, and I couldn't believe it. My parents couldn't believe it. It was a lot less than they would have paid somebody with any kind of actual clout, but it was also exponentially greater than what my internship was paying me and way more money than I ever thought I would make in hockey. More importantly, I had train money for the rest of the school year.

SWOOSH

Just before Christmas break, I took a trip to the unveiling of Canada's World Junior roster. It was my first time on a plane: a night flight to Regina, Saskatchewan.

I was nervous, but the guy sitting next to me, a total stranger, had been on a lot of flights, so he calmed me down.

After landing in Regina, I picked up my bags and went outside. It was stupid cold. I expected to see a lot of taxis, but there weren't any. After a minute or two, the guy who I sat next to on the plane pulled up in his car, with his wife in the driver's seat.

"Need a ride?" they asked.

Against my better judgment — and oh my God please never ever do this — I got in the car.

I called my mom just to have someone on the phone in case I got abducted. But what was going to happen to me? These two literally looked like characters from *Corner Gas*.

They drove me around and told me all these facts about Regina.

"That park on the right is actually the biggest inner-city park in North America," she said. "People think it's Central Park in New York, but no — it's this one."

Then they dropped me off at my hotel, wished me luck on my trip, and drove home. Saskatchewan, man.

The roster unveil at the arena was a huge thrill. For starters,

Nike hooked me up with loads of free clothes — nicer clothes than anything I was wearing at the time. Second, the entire Canadian sports media contingent was there. Forget the athletes, this was everybody I had been watching on TV since I was a kid.

Whoa, that's John Lu! I thought. *"John Lu, TSN, Regina."*

I got to interview four players that day: Nazem Kadri, Ryan Ellis, Alex Pietrangelo, and team captain Patrice Cormier. It was a very different interview experience. For one, they were in-person, and I hadn't done many of those. Second, I was surrounded by other people, which was awkward as hell. There were agency people and Nike Canada folks, who were keeping an eye out for things, like forbidden logos, phrasing of questions and answers, and so on. Last, it was a corporate interview, which I had never done. The questions needed to be pointed in a certain direction: training, hard work, determination, patriotism — things like that.

At the end of the day, we all went to the airport to fly home. In and out, just like that.

"What the hell is that?" one of the Nike guys asked.

I had packed all my stuff into this powder-blue faux-leather suitcase that my parents let me borrow for the trip. My mom must have bought it in 1983.

He just laughed. "I'll, uh, make a note to get you a bag."

We left for Saskatoon shortly after Christmas. Saskatoon is a fair bit farther north than Regina and even colder. I've heard of instantly freezing nose hairs before, but I thought people were joking. Nope — booger icicles in five seconds or less.

It was about -35 degrees Celsius. A local man rode by on his bike in sweat pants and running shoes. I asked him how the hell he was doing that. He told me about how he couldn't go out the other day because it was -50 and his gears froze. In saying that, I realized that had his gears not been frozen, he probably would have gone out that day like it was nothing.

We covered games and practices and made videos. We tried

different skits and attempted to follow the content plan set out by the agency. The issue was that we didn't have Mark, our editor, with us in Saskatoon. We had to send all the footage back to Toronto over the hotel internet. It was so slow that we literally considered mailing him the hard drive. Finally, Nike just said screw it and flew him out.

I was so green. I kept asking this woman named Laura, who worked for Nike, when we were going to lunch or dinner.

Finally, she just said, "Dude, just get room service!"

"That's allowed?" I asked.

We had already been there for like four days. "Oh my God," she slapped her forehead. "Get food!"

"But I can't afford a thirty dollar room-service burger," I told her.

"Oh my God," she smiled again. "We pay for that, man."

OK, this has already been the best thing in the history of ever and now I get free room service? I tried to push the limits and call her bluff and ordered like $50 worth of stuff for dinner that night. I felt like Macaulay Culkin in *Home Alone*.

Laura was great, but she was under a lot of pressure to make the campaign a success. Darryl the cameraman, Mark, and I had all these ideas for the videos, but she was constantly nitpicking to make sure everything was on message. Halfway through the trip, however, she got sick as a dog and had completely lost her voice.

Finally, we just said, "Look — stay here at the hotel. Get better. We'll go out, shoot a funny video, and it'll be great. If you hate it, then never let us do it again."

We went out and shot a ridiculous video in the middle of a Saskatchewan field. Maybe it was exhaustion setting in, but we all thought it was the funniest thing ever, including Laura. We earned her trust, and therefore Nike's trust, and the videos got better and easier to make after that.

Most games, even the games that didn't feature Canada, got great attendance. People just wanted to watch hockey. At about a quarter of a million people, Saskatoon isn't the smallest town, but there's a small town vibe. One night we went to watch *Avatar*, which had just come out. They were showing it on three different screens and we got the last tickets to the third one. Even *Tooth Fairy* with The Rock was sold out. I always say, "There's nothing to do and everyone's at the nothing." Trust me, I say it with love.

The town was buzzing and everyone seemed to have their own World Junior gossip. The lady in the hotel gift shop said that she saw a kid from Team Latvia, who had been staying at our hotel, walking around with a black eye. She heard he tried to dance with somebody's girlfriend on New Year's Eve, but her boyfriend showed up and socked him in the face.

Sometimes I think about that poor kid.

"How was Canada, Aivis?"

"Well, Mom, we lost every game, Canada beat us 16–0, and I celebrated New Year's by getting punched in the head."

Canada went to the gold medal game that year. With only minutes remaining and Canada down by two, Jordan Eberle, Canada's 5.4-second hero from last season, scored a pair of goals to force overtime. That game-tying goal is still one of the loudest pops I've ever heard in any arena.

It's only matched by the deafening silence caused by John Carlson's overtime winner for the States. Literally the only people you could hear were the players on Team USA.

We spoke to a few players after the game and obviously they were all crushed. I still remember Brandon Kozun's face. He was born in the States but played for Team Canada. I couldn't help but be reminded of Huston Street. That scrum lasted maybe 20 seconds.

Another thing I couldn't help but notice throughout: cut-eye from certain journalists.

I told myself it had to be in my head, but there were definitely a few people there who rolled their eyes with every question I asked. Sometimes just seeing my face was enough. Was it because I was wearing Nike gear instead of a dress shirt? Was it because I was there for a corporate campaign and not as a journalist? Was it because I was a young weird blogger guy? All I knew is that it made me want to be there even more. Oh, you're going to see me, man. Keep looking. Get used to it.

Despite the disappointing ending, the campaign was a huge success. I came home with my experience and to a finished practicum project and a Leafs TV internship.

A few weeks later, Nike called again.

"We need you to fly to Calgary. You're going to be interviewing Gillian Apps, Jayna Hefford, and Jennifer Botterill from the Canadian women's hockey team, as well as Jarome Iginla.

Holy crap.

I went to tell Clarkey, thinking getting the day off would be no problem. Think again, kid.

I didn't keep any secrets from Leafs TV when it came to Nike. I told them about the World Juniors, which they were cool with. I told them I might be going to the Olympics, which they were also cool with since the Leafs didn't have any games. This day trip, for whatever reason, was a sticking point.

He wanted to make sure my head and heart were still with Leafs TV and that I was taking my internship seriously. After all, Leafs TV had let me on their televised pregame shows as well.

It's also entirely possible he wanted to keep my head from getting too big. This was a lot for me in a very short time, fairly early in my career. I often lacked confidence and second-guessed myself, but I was definitely starting to get a little cocky. Mean YouTube comment? Kiss my ass, buddy. I'm on TV and going to the Olympics and I haven't even graduated.

"Clarkey, if you were me, you would be going," I told him.

"I know," he nodded.

"I'm going," I said with a lot more authority than I should have.

I was so sick in Calgary. With all the congestion in my sinuses, I thought my brain was going to blow out of my ears on the descent into the city.

I powered through the Apps and Hefford interviews, which were over half an hour each. Corporate interviews, man. They're a different beast. This wasn't a short scrum where I might get a question or two in. I needed at least 20 questions ready, and once I exhausted those, Nike reps threw in another 10.

The Botterill interview was a cringe-fest on my part. I tried to ask something about Harvard, Botterill's school, and how it was a lot more famous for things that weren't hockey. The question came out totally wrong and let's just say she didn't like some little boy chirping her hockey team. I corrected myself and she laughed it off, but wow was it bad.

Then Iginla walked in. I thought my days of getting star-struck were over, but nope, that's Jarome-fricking-Iginla walking into the room right now, and I'm pretty sure he has wings.

I had been struggling to hear all day because of what the flight did to my sinuses. Out of nowhere, I heard a deafening squeal in one ear and jumped.

Everyone turned and looked at me.

"Did anyone else hear that?" I asked. Apparently a bunch of pressure burst out of my ear and I could hear again. *Great first impression with Iggy, Steve.*

A few weeks shy of the Vancouver Olympics, I got word: I was going.

I could have written an entire book about just my Olympic experience. It was the time of my life. These 17 days living away from home were, in some ways, the college experience I never got as a commuter.

Laura, Darryl, Mark, and I rented a house from a family in the city. When we walked out the front door, we could see mountains to our right.

My favourite non-hockey experience was easily my Alex Bilodeau interview. A few days into the Olympics, Bilodeau, who was a Nike athlete, won Canada's first-ever gold medal on home soil in moguls. Nike had clamped down even harder on messaging, and getting them to approve jokes, random lines, and ideas was a struggle. One day, mostly as a joke, Mark, Darryl, and I brainstormed a ridiculous Bilodeau video idea. We would use effects to make it look like we turned a van into a gold Cadillac and then we'd drive around Vancouver. And while in the car, we'd pull up to Japadog, the gourmet hot dog stand in Vancouver with 40-minute lines, and get hot dogs together.

To our shock, Nike approved everything. It's still one of the coolest videos I've ever done.

I also got to reunite with Apps, Hefford, and Botterill for a video where they took shots on me and I tried to stop them. We gave them these crappy little mini-sticks with no curve and they still murdered me. We shot two takes: one where I flailed around and let them score so that the video would be funny and another where I tried my absolute hardest. I can't emphasize enough how little of a difference it made.

For some reason, I got to talk to Canadian rapper and producer Kardinal Offishall. That was actually quite difficult. We were on our bright red Canada couch in front of the Nike store by Robson Square.

The couch was awesome. It was just a simple IKEA couch with a red cover on it. Then, we gave the couch stripes, and, I'm ashamed to say, we cut up a Canada jersey and stuck Canada's Olympic leaf logo right in the middle. We used that couch to shoot all our post-game videos, and on a couple nights, people slept on it.

I had never interviewed a musician before, and when I spoke into the microphone, I heard my own voice echo across the street. They had fed the audio through the store's outdoor speakers without me knowing.

I asked him about Baby Blue Soundcrew, a group he had collaborated with when I was just getting into rap. They had a hit in Canada called "Money Jane," with Kardinal and Sean Paul on it, as well as Jully Black singing the chorus. He seemed pleasantly surprised I even knew about that, and it made the rest of the interview more comfortable. We ended up holding a push-up contest for fans to win a Team Canada jersey. It was all so surreal.

And it was just getting started.

STOLEN
COUCH

While in Vancouver for the 2010 Winter Olympics, I almost got myself arrested. Twice.

It was the tail end of the games. We'd been away from home for over two weeks, so everyone was tired and a little punchy but energized by the ridiculous medal haul from the past few days.

February 24 was an enormous day for Canada's women. Clara Hughes won bronze in the 5,000-metre speed skating. Canada's women also won a silver medal in the 3,000-metre relay. The two-women bobsleigh was the moneymaker, though; Shelley-Ann Brown and Helen Upperton captured silver, while Kaillie Humphries and Heather Moyse brought home the gold. The next day, February 25, saw only two medals, but they were both emotional. Joannie Rochette brought home a bronze medal in figure skating. Rochette was a huge story, tragically losing her mother to a heart attack just four days prior. Everybody, not just Canadians, wanted her to succeed, and she did.

It was also the day of the gold medal game in women's hockey. It was the classic Canada versus USA matchup that everyone wanted. Everybody remembers Marie-Philip Poulin, who was just 18 years old at the time, scoring both of Canada's goals in the game. She was dynamite. The performance that gets overshadowed a bit, however, is from Canadian goalie

Shannon Szabados. She stopped all 28 of America's shots, en route to a shutout in the gold medal game at the Olympics. How do you top that?

One little aside: before the game, Laura gave me a small plastic shopping bag and looked me in the eye.

"Do *not* open this unless Canada wins," she told me.

When the final horn went, I reached under my seat and opened the bag to reveal a red t-shirt commemorating Canada's gold medal win in women's hockey. What would have happened to the shirt if Canada lost? I guess we'll never know.

The players went bananas. You might remember that after the game, the team notoriously brought beer cans and cigars onto the ice. For the briefest of moments, there was talk about stripping them of their medals, until Canada, and most of the rest of the world, said shut the hell up.

At some point during the gold medal celebration, the jumbotron showed Canada's men's hockey team all sitting in a box together. The crowd was freaking out already and then they started cheering on the men ahead of their own gold medal game. All the men were either stoned-faced or wearing nervous smirks. I know the crowd was being supportive, but that couldn't have been a great feeling. No pressure, boys . . .

February 26 kicked everything up yet another notch. Canada won a bronze in the men's short track speed skating, and Canada's women brought home a silver in curling. But the star of the day was Charles Hamelin.

Hamelin won gold in the 500-metre short track. Find that race on YouTube — it's crazy. Hamelin has the lead, loses it, and on the final turn, the leader trips and falls, almost taking Hamelin with him. Hamelin barely manages to stay upright as he crosses the finish line first by a fraction of a second. On the very same day, Hamelin won gold again, this time in the men's 5,000-metre relay with four other skaters, including his brother, François.

And because Charles and François were both Nike athletes, we got to interview them.

The next day, we rented a van and brought our big red Canada Couch down to a TV set at Robson Square. I was about to interview both Hamelin brothers while the whole country was buzzing about them.

I was incredibly nervous. The Hamelin brothers would be wearing their gold medals, and we would be outside in the open for everyone to see. Everybody would be watching and wondering who the hell the child sitting with them was. Their frumpy little brother?

It wasn't just the fact that people would be watching. Almost every athlete I had ever interviewed in my entire life up to that point had been a hockey player. I had spoken to a few baseball players as an intern but not one-on-one. The only non-hockey athlete I had ever interviewed before this was Alex Bilodeau, and that was just a week earlier. What if I sound like an idiot?

After we unloaded the couch onto the set, we sat and we waited. The appointed time had finally come for the Hamelin brothers to arrive, but they still weren't there. This did nothing to calm my nerves — although it did give me a little extra time to cram some phone research in.

We waited. And we waited. And we waited. Finally, after about two hours, we got the call that Charles and François had to reschedule. It sucked for us, but it's hard to really blame them. First of all, they're gold medal–winning athletes at the Olympics, so they probably have someone else managing their schedule for them. They might have been booked for an interview with someone who had a bit more clout than a YouTube blogger. And lastly, and I don't know this to be true, it's just a theory . . . they may have been a little banged up.

Canadians were literally handing Jon Montgomery beer in the street after he won gold in skeleton. Who wouldn't want to treat these guys to more of the same?

We started to pack up our equipment and, of course, the Canada Couch.

"Hey!" someone shouted.

A guy, probably in his late 20s, with a bright vest and some kind of credentials around his neck, started walking up to us all fast and authoritative.

"What are you doing?" he asked.

Mark, Darryl, and I just kind of looked at each other.

"You can't just take that!" he told us.

Whoa, whoa, whoa. Take?

"The couch?" we asked.

"Yes!" he said. "This is a CTV set. Everything on here is CTV property."

We were still super confused.

"Actually man, um, this is our couch," we explained.

He started to get angry.

"No, it isn't," he told us. "I saw you. You guys just showed up and started making off with it."

What the hell was this guy talking about?

We explained exactly what we were there for, that we were supposed to interview the Hamelin brothers, and that we had already been there for about two hours.

"Two hours?" he asked.

"Yeah," we told him. "At least."

Now it was his turn to look confused. It's a face I wear often, so I recognized it right away.

This guy was clearly supposed to be in charge of watching over this set. That makes sense, right? There was expensive equipment, it was all outdoors, and the streets had been crawling with people for over two weeks.

I don't know what buddy was off doing, but he obviously wasn't keeping a close eye on the set. We had time to bring all our camera stuff, unload a bright red couch onto the stage, and hang out for two hours. And it's not like I'm the quietest guy. How did he not see or hear us?

You could tell what he was thinking: *Uh oh. I messed up.*

"Wait here," he told us before taking off.

A moment later, the security guard returned, only this time it was with two other guys. The men were older and had much more official-looking uniforms. I wondered who they were. Maybe they were his bosses or somethi— oh boy, those are cops.

Five minutes ago, we were supposed to be interviewing Olympic gold medalists and now we were getting interrogated by the police.

We tried to explain ourselves all at once, like a bunch of scared third-graders trying to explain who pushed who first, which didn't help our case.

Between us talking like we had just been caught red-handed and the fact that it was our word against the security guard's, the cops took it to the next level and separated us to ask us more questions.

One officer took Mark and me, and, being the youngest member of our group, I mostly just kept my mouth shut. I kept looking over at the conversation our cameraman, Darryl, was having with the other officer. Picking up on that pretty quickly because, you know, he's a cop, the officer we were speaking to got annoyed and walked us farther away, out from beneath the nice, dry awning we were standing under and into the cold Vancouver drizzle.

"This is fucking ridiculous," Mark muttered, not so quietly.

"Watch it," the cop barked. "Your job here is to tell me what happened. That's it."

I turned into my mother right away. *Please just do what the man says*, I thought. I even grabbed Mark's arm and looked at him pleadingly.

An idea dawned on me.

"Look, officer," I tried to say in the politest way possible. "I can prove this is our couch. I can actually show you a video on my phone of us building it."

I reached into my pocket to grab my phone, which, looking back, was a pretty dumb thing to do.

"That doesn't matter," the cop said dismissively. "Put that away. I don't need to see that."

That doesn't matter? I have a video on my phone where you can literally watch us building the couch we're currently being accused of stealing!

After a few minutes of interrogation — I mean, that's what it felt like — the cop left to go discuss things with the security guard.

Mark and I were just standing there. We kept looking over at Darryl and he kept looking over at us. Were we allowed to talk to each other now? Can we get out of the rain? Should I call my parents for bail money? We tried phoning Laura and others with Nike a few times, but nobody picked up.

Finally, after a few minutes, the officer informed us we were free to go.

We loaded up the Canada Couch and went on our merry way. Did that really just happen? Of all the things I thought I'd be getting up to at the Olympics, being accused of stealing a couch was not on that list.

Night fell and we were starving. We went to a little Japanese place for the 100th time because that's what you do in Vancouver. I ate a bunch of edamame without even taking them out of the pods. After watching me slowly erode my jaw for a while, my friends told me you were supposed to take the beans out first. Thanks, guys. We were tired but undefeated. The incident at Robson Square was pretty annoying when it happened, but as our stomachs became fuller, the story became funnier. But with the men's gold medal hockey game looming, we knew our biggest adventure was yet to come.

Little did I know, the theft of the Canada Couch wouldn't be my last encounter with the Vancouver PD.

THE GOLDEN DAY

There are only two days in my life I remember from start to finish.

One is my wedding day. The other is the day of the 2010 Olympic men's hockey gold medal game.

When we woke up on the morning of February 28, we essentially had two plans. We were going to interview the Hamelin brothers first thing, no matter what. Then we had to find a bar to watch the game in. After that, it was a toss-up. Either Canada would lose and we'd have to figure out how to carefully word a super sombre video and maybe get a quiet dinner, or Canada would win, I'd go berserk on camera, and we'd party all night long.

The delay of our previous day's plans to interview the Hamelin brothers turned out to be a blessing in disguise — if you ignore our brief stints as couch thieves. We would go back to the same spot in Robson Square to interview Charles and François on the Canada Couch, only this time, the plan was to go zip lining with them afterward.

I was still scared I would bomb my public interview with these guys. On top of that, I'm afraid of heights, so the prospect of zip lining, let alone on camera, had me even more nervous. Then there was the issue of the gold medal game.

From day one, my biggest fear was that Canada would lose.

Nike's "Force Fate" campaign for the 2010 Olympics was built around creating your own destiny and finding a way to win.

But what if Canada lost?

I like making happy videos where I get to crack jokes and talk about my favourite team winning. Who wants to make a sad video after a devastating defeat? Nike was already hyper-sensitive about wording and messaging; imagine how bad they'll be after a loss. Actually, I didn't have to imagine. Canada had lost at the World Juniors — to the States, no less — less than two months earlier. Plus, who wants to watch a sad video? When the Leafs lost, I could yell and scream and lose my mind to my heart's content. I could even swear if I wanted. But that was my own personal channel. Something tells me Nike wouldn't appreciate a screaming "This team is ruining my life!" tirade.

Canada has to win, I thought.

Of course, I had zero influence in the outcome of this game, so that didn't help my anxiety. In fact, I wasn't even going to this game — which was strange.

I had seen a bunch of Team Canada's games in women's hockey, including the gold medal game. For the men, I had been to every single game so far, except for their round robin shootout win over Switzerland. (Shout-out to Sidney Crosby for helping with the win on that one, or Canada might have been in real trouble.)

It's obviously way more fun to go to the games, but that wasn't the only thing on my mind. If we had to watch this game at a bar, how were we ever going to shoot a video? Bars are covered wall-to-ceiling in logos. For example, if we captured a shot at a bar and there was a Canucks jersey hanging in the background, as in a Reebok jersey, we wouldn't have been able to use the footage.

And besides all that, how were we even gonna get into a bar? We weren't going to be wrapping up this interview until there was less than an hour before game time, which was noon locally. This was the most highly anticipated tilt in Canadian hockey history. Not to mention camera equipment scares the living daylights out of a lot of people, especially bouncers and restaurant owners. Everyone thinks you're doing some giant exposé, trying to catch someone doing something illegal or a rat crawling across the floor. Even if we did get in, we're not even going to be able to move, let alone shoot a video.

While my mind was focused on the million foolish hypotheticals, Charles and François Hamelin showed up, gold medals and all. They looked exhausted, but the good kind of exhausted. Their eyes had the kind of sleepy but happy look you get when you've just been having too much fun to go to bed.

I was tired, too. Looking back at the video of the interview, I realized I might not have looked so tired if I actually used hair gel back then.

The two brothers sat on either side of me. If you want a great example of why you shouldn't sit between two interview subjects, go watch this video, if you can stomach it. It always seems like a good idea at first. In reality, however, you always have your back turned to one of your subjects, and they're just sitting there twiddling their thumbs. If you sit on one side, you're actually facing the people you're talking to and you're making the subject of your interview the focal point, which is how any good interview should go. Luckily, these guys didn't seem to care.

Their relaxed nature put me at ease right away. Charles and François were 25 and 23, respectively, and I was only 21. Instead of an interviewer and two interviewees, we were just three young guys talking about sports.

"Guys, there is twenty-four grams of gold sitting on this couch right now," I began for the camera. "I'm sitting here with gold medalists and brothers Charles and François Hamelin." I completely butchered their names. It was pronounced "Sharl" not "Charles" and the *H* in Hamelin is silent. It wasn't the first time some goof from Ontario had destroyed their names on camera, so they took it in stride.

"How has the last twenty-four hours been for you guys?" I asked.

"Not a lot of sleep," Charles answered, rubbing his head.

After a few agonizing questions — seriously, why didn't I gel my hair — we went into the sketch portion of the video.

"Alex Bilodeau, with his gold medal, turned my mom's minivan into a golden Cadillac," I started. "What can your gold medals do?"

Then I grabbed one of Charles's two gold medals and looked at the camera. In the video, we disappear in beams of blue light and magically reappear at the top of the zip line. Again, I was sitting in the middle, so with my attention on Charles, François had to improvise and just hold up his own gold medal while posing for the camera. Thank God he did, too. Man, I sucked so bad.

After our incredible CGI effects, we got up from the Canada Couch and started making our way to the zip line setup, which was only a short walk away.

The lineup for the zip line was absolutely massive. It was one of a few tourist attractions set up during the games and it spanned across what must have been at least a couple hundred feet and an intersection. Everybody seemed to have the same plan: *Let's all go do that zip line thing we've been ignoring for the past two-and-a-half weeks and then go watch the game somewhere.*

The line went around the block and over a small hill. We had heard that the lineup was over an hour long. The gold medal game was set to begin in about an hour, so some people were looking pretty tired and cranky about it.

For a minute I was worried we'd have to wait in the line, too. *I am* not *missing this game*, I thought.

Nope. Arrangements had been made for us to completely bypass the line for the purpose of this video. That was a huge relief, until I started worrying about walking past all these people who had been waiting since earlier in the morning just to go on an eight-second zip line.

They might not have liked me butting in line, but thankfully I wasn't alone.

As the Hamelin brothers, the camera crew, and I began walking by the line, I saw the crowd light up. Some people looked annoyed for a fraction of a second until they realized who they were looking at.

Once everyone saw the gold medals around Charles's and François's necks, whispers turned into cheers which turned into an actual standing applause out in public.

I knew none of it was for me, but it was hard not to glow in that moment. It's the kind of surreal experience you think exists only in movies, but I was actually living in the middle of it. I'm not kidding, man — Canadian medals in Vancouver, especially the gold ones, were literally a golden ticket. There's no way any Canadian Olympian wearing one paid for a damn thing any time they went out in public. They had rock star fame with the added elements of pride and patriotism. I swear, if one of the Hamelin brothers shouted, "Beer me!" right then and there, they'd have one in each hand within a couple of minutes. Hell, a cop might have even delivered it to them.

All geared up, we began climbing up the staircase to the top of the zip line, exchanging a few nervous laughs on the way. Luckily, a couple little kids up at the top helped break the tension by goofing on us. There's nothing like being put in your place by actual children when you're too scared to do the exact same thing as them.

Someone working with Nike was up there, talking on her phone and sounding stressed. Somebody who either managed the Hamelin brothers or was supposed to get them next was raging over the phone, demanding that she hurry up the process. What did they want her to do? Shove the kids off the platform? What if we rushed it and the safety guy didn't clip me in properly and I splattered all over Robson Street? Can you imagine? Sidney Crosby scored the golden goal later that day; I wouldn't have even been in the newspaper. I'll take my time, thanks.

When it was my turn to go, François gave me a shove. I would have usually closed my eyes at that height, but they wanted to film the whole thing and I knew what a rare opportunity it was to zip line across a busy city street at the Olympics.

Once I got to the end, I started getting unbuckled. I heard a roar behind me. Charles and François were flying down the zip line and everybody was watching and cheering them on. Instead of holding on for dear life like I did, they were going no-hands, spinning around. They looked infinitely cooler than me.

When they got to the end, even more handlers were there, urging us to hurry up. We shot a quick outro for the video where I gave Charles an imaginary third gold medal for arriving first.

As soon as we stopped filming, I barely had the chance to say goodbye. Unbuckle, yep, OK, thanks, bye — they were whisked away. By then, it was less than an hour until game time. They probably had to go do something else before the game began. I'm telling you — if you had a medal, everybody wanted a piece of you.

We got down to our van and stashed all of our camera equipment. It was the full crew, a Nike rep or two, and myself.

"Alright," I said. "Where are we gonna watch the game, guys?"

They didn't say anything.

I turned to the Nike folks. "I mean, sorry, I assume you guys are going to the game, right?" I turned back to the crew. "Where should we watch it then? Did you want to try to find somewhere we can grab footage? We'll have a tough time with logos, but we can probably get some cool reactions."

Still, nobody said anything. Everyone just smirked at each other.

Was it something I did? Did I offend them? Am I fired?

One of the Nike reps reached her hand into her coat pocket, pulled something out, and slowly extended it to me.

"We got one ticket," she said.

The words left her mouth like I was watching a movie; it wasn't even real. *Oh cool,* I thought. *I wonder how the main character will respond to this news.*

But it was real. Man, I wish somebody filmed it. I'd love to relive that moment. I was too stunned to properly live it the first time.

"We managed to find one ticket for you," she repeated. "You're going to be sitting alone. I hope that's OK."

Can you imagine if I was like, "Actually, no. I don't like sitting next to strangers. I find them to be very common and smelly. Kindly give your pauper ticket to some other rube."

I reached out my hand and held the ticket. Everything was in slow motion. I looked down at the ticket and thought, *I'm going to the gold medal game. I'm actually going to be there.*

When she let go of the ticket, I suddenly realized exactly what I was holding. Honestly it might have been the most expensive thing I had ever held. *If I lost this, I'd probably get deported and have to retire from earth.*

While I'm sure the silent conversation I was having with myself was fascinating to everyone around me, they woke me up out of my hockey nirvana.

"The game starts in half an hour," she said, snapping me back to reality.

"Oh," I jumped. "How far away is the arena?"

"I'm not sure. Half an hour?"

"Oh God!"

Laura and I literally ran to the arena. It would've taken less than 15 minutes if the streets weren't so packed. I'm lucky I didn't trample anybody on the way there. I was still in such shock that my eyes were open but nobody was home. It was like my foot was operating the gas but some ancient override in my brain whose sole purpose was just to keep me alive was working the brakes and steering.

As we got closer to the arena, I took in the scene a bit more. The streets were absolutely buzzing.

Scalpers were shouting out to passers-by.

Guess how much they were asking for.

Three. Thousand. Dollars.

I don't know if that was for a pair or a single ticket, but either way, holy hot damn!

Consider this: my ticket was way up in section 322, row 11, seat 11. The printed price on my ticket was $550. That's just the printed price. Imagine what a scalper could sell lower bowl seats for less than an hour before the actual game.

For a split second, one of the dumbest thoughts I've ever had crossed my mind: *What if I sold this ticket?*

I know, I know. But I was a student! Getting a couple grand just for a ticket? Maybe if I sell this, I can get a real camera and stop using the one in my laptop.

You ever wish you could slap your own thoughts in the face?

Ignoring the fact that Nike would have never worked with me again, knowing what happened in that game, can you imagine if I had sold that ticket?

My parents would never look at me the same. Maybe my girlfriend would have dumped me. I probably would have dropped out of school, locked myself in my room, and eaten Doritos until I turned into an orange paste of jalapeño cheddar-flavoured sadness.

Luckily, even I am not that stupid.

Before we walked into the arena, she handed me another small plastic bag, just like for the women's gold medal game, only this time I knew exactly what was inside.

"Same deal as last time," she said.

With a silent nod, I took the bag and went on my way.

The game was packed before game time. Nobody was gonna be late for this thing.

My seat was in the middle of a row. Sitting on my left was an older man and woman in Team USA jerseys. On my right was a trio of friends. Three seats down was a guy in a Canada jersey. Beside him was a woman with short black hair and a red and black plaid shirt — supremely Canadian. Finally there was the woman with shoulder-length blonde hair sitting directly to my right. To me, this was the fanciest event I had ever been to — I figured I should introduce myself. I shook hands with all my seatmates and told them what I was doing with Nike and gave them a Cole's Notes version of my ridiculous morning.

The blonde woman, let's call her Beth because in my haze I heard her name but didn't comprehend it, said she was related to somebody who worked for Team Canada.

"Oh, yeah?" I asked. "Who's that?"

"He's in management. His name is Ken Holland."

Oh yeah, just the GM of the Detroit Red Wings, no big deal. His team just played in back-to-back Stanley Cup Finals and won the first one. That guy.

This game really was the event of the season. If you look at any pictures from inside the arena, you'll notice a lot of fans are wearing lanyards. Some of them bought them at the game in order to preserve their ticket, but many others were there with some kind of a credential. You either had to be working the game, have a lot of money, or know someone. I was sitting next to a family member of Team Canada's management, and we were in the nosebleeds. Being there was a big deal.

I remembered that I still had a job to do. I had to tweet from Nike's account throughout the game. Before the puck even dropped, I had made up my mind that I was going to keep the tweets to a minimum and actually watch the game. I was just picturing my future.

"Daddy, what was it like when Canada won gold?"

"Well, son or daughter, I was looking down at a screen. I just remember it being really loud."

I didn't want to be that guy.

In case you don't remember what happened in that game, let's take a trip down memory lane, shall we?

With about seven minutes left in the first period, there is a faceoff in the American zone to Ryan Miller's blocker side. American forward Jamie Langenbrunner flicks the puck behind the net on his backhand before Erik Johnson takes possession in his own end, now in the corner to Ryan Miller's glove side. Mike Richards flies in to apply pressure, causing Johnson to spin around and send a short pass to fellow defenceman Brian Rafalski. With Jonathan Toews in his way, Rafalski doesn't have much room to play with. Richards turns around, does a quick stick lift, steals the puck, and makes a tiny pass to himself. Completely uncontested in front, he loads up a wrist shot and fires. As Richards shoots, Toews scrambles to the net in case of a rebound. That rebound came after the initial Miller save. As CTV's play-by-play announcer Chris Cuthbert put it: "A tazer from Jonathan Toews! His first Olympic goal!" Rick Nash jumps into Toews's arms to celebrate and it's 1–0 Canada.

First intermission, I might have been feeling even worse than if it were simply a 0–0 tie. The shirt in the bag under my seat made me feel like I was smuggling drugs through an airport.

Second period.

Just over seven minutes in, Duncan Keith is handling the puck in his own zone, skating backward toward the corner on Roberto Luongo's glove side. Phil Kessel turns on the speed burst, forcing Keith to circle behind the net. With right-handed Drew Doughty crossing over to the left side, Keith runs into trouble. Joe Pavelski barrels down on him. At the very last second as Keith is losing an edge, he backhands it right up the centre of the ice. An inch here or there and that puck might have been a big dirty grenade. Luckily, Ryan Getzlaf comes up with it for Canada and he charges full-speed up the left wing. Corey Perry takes a slow approach up the middle of the ice while Patrick Marleau dashes toward the net on the right wing. Getzlaf switches from his forehand to his backhand to pass the puck around American defender Brooks Orpik. The pass nearly gets through to Marleau, but Ryan Whitney is there to bat the pass away. Unfortunately for the Americans, the puck goes right into the slot where Corey Perry is lurking. Nobody picks him up and he snipes it glove-side on Ryan Miller. "Corey Perry's fourth of the tournament," Cuthbert exclaimed. "Two to zero, Team Canada!"

With about seven-and-a-half minutes to go in the second, I hear it.

"MILL-ER! MILL-ER!"

Rogers Arena is chanting Miller's name from the top of its lungs and I might have been the only Canadian not participating. You see, during Canada's round robin game against the Americans, I started chanting "MILL-ER!" after a Canadian goal. I got my whole section to do it. As we were chanting, however, the Americans scored. I took that as a queue to sit my ass down, as a solid chunk of my section told me to shut up and stop being such a jinx. The Dangle Jinx is a powerful one.

Fast forward to the gold medal game and the similarity was eerie.

Ryan Kesler leads the charge for the Americans through centre ice. Kesler dishes to Patrick Kane at the blue line before barging through the Canadian zone and toward the net. Kesler streaks right through Canadian forwards Perry and Brenden Morrow while Scott Niedermayer was preoccupied with Kane. Shea Weber figures out what the Americans were trying, but he couldn't get to Kesler quickly enough. Kane lobs a shot on goal, and Kesler gets his stick on it for the tip. The puck just barely squeezes through the blocker arm of Luongo, Kesler's Vancouver Canucks teammate, and bounces on the goal line before hitting the back of the net. "It got through," Cuthbert yelled. "And the United States are on the board."

It's an absolute barn-burner of a period. The Americans

have several more Grade A chances almost immediately following their goal. Canada has a few of their own, including a last-minute breakaway from Eric Staal. Luongo and Miller are fantastic, facing 15 shots apiece in the second period alone.

Though Canada held the lead after 40 minutes, I could've barfed. *Oh God*, I thought. *Canada was up 2–0. If the States pull this off, it's going to be a choke for the ages.* Look, in 2010 the Leafs were about to finish second-last in the NHL, and they didn't even have their first-round pick that year. Pessimism was second nature to me.

Oh man. What am I even going to do with the shirt if they lose? No! Bad Steven! They're winning. Shut up and try to enjoy the game.

Third period.

Canada came out of the gate firing everything on net but just couldn't seem to beat Ryan Miller, who was dynamite all tournament long.

As the period wore on, momentum began to swing the Americans' way. Luongo, however, was up to the task.

Come on, you got this.

Sidney Crosby is sprung on a breakaway with about three minutes left. With Ryan Miller sprawled on the ice, Crosby has the entire upper half of the net to shoot at, but Kane gets back just in time to clip Crosby's stick, causing him to fan on the shot.

Just hold on a little longer.

There's just over 30 seconds remaining. The American net is empty. I am absolutely beside myself.

Ryan Suter rings it around the boards to Pavelski. Twenty-nine seconds left.

Pavelski tries to throw it in front but his pass is deflected by Getzlaf. Twenty-seven seconds left.

Kane comes up with the puck, spins, and fires from the right faceoff dot. It hits Langenbrunner in front. Twenty-six seconds left.

The puck is loose in front and both Langenbrunner and

Zach Parise have found a way past every Canadian defender. Luongo can't pick up the puck in time, and with just over 25 seconds remaining, the Americans tied it.

It was the least welcomed goal-horn in Canadian hockey history.

That was a weird aspect of how traumatic the American comeback was. Because this was the Olympics and we were in what was supposed to be an impartial arena, I guess, they blared the goal horn whenever either team scored.

Devastation.

The anxiety I felt during this overtime intermission was ten times worse than what I felt in Saskatchewan just two months before. It felt like the shirt under my seat was screaming at me, beating hauntingly and relentlessly, threatening to burst out of the earth like a zombie.

I made up my mind: I'm not tweeting in overtime. No way. I'll say my phone died. I'll flush it down the toilet if I have to. There's no way I'm missing a single second of this.

I tweeted a bunch from NikeTraining's Twitter during the intermission to ease the stress.

"Overtime? Seriously? 15-minute intermission? Seriously? My heart! #TeamCanada," I tweeted.

"New game. One goal. One gold," I sent in another tweet, trying to sound tough and not like I was totally hyperventilating.

After Canada has a few chances to win it, the Americans go on the attack. Pavelski charges right at Niedermayer who has Weber with him. They're able to easily strip Pavelski of the puck and Niedermayer takes it behind his own net. As he emerges out of Luongo's glove side corner with Pavelski in tow, Niedermayer decides to throw a pass, just an absolute muffin, through the middle of the ice. The puck lands right on Pavelski's stick.

Ahhhhh! That's all I could think. I couldn't even think words. Just screams.

Pavelski slams on the breaks, spins, and fires it. Luongo drops down to the butterfly and gets a piece of the puck with his glove arm. The arena bursts into the loudest "LUUU" of the whole tournament, except for me, of course, as I was halfway through eating my own jersey.

In the whole golden-goal conversation, that play doesn't get brought up enough. Imagine if that puck had gone in.

Scott Niedermayer retired as a four-time Stanley Cup champion and won an Olympic gold medal with Team Canada at the 2002 Olympics in Salt Lake. But if he, the captain of Team Canada, gave the puck away, in overtime, for the goal that lost Canada the gold medal, on home ice, in front of the entire world? Imagine how completely different we would view his legacy. No, you could never take away any of his accomplishments, but you can't tell me that wouldn't have followed him forever.

For decades, all American hockey fans would have to say to piss Canadian fans off would be "Niedermayer" or "Pavelski." After NBC decided to bail on Conan O'Brien, Jay Leno's return to *The Tonight Show* was March 1, 2010, the day after the gold medal game. In some alternate reality, in addition to having Jamie Foxx and Olympic gold medalist skier Lindsey Vonn, Leno invites out a gold medal–wearing Joe Pavelski.

"They just did a scientific study, Joe. Have you seen this? Have you read about this? It says Canadians are the nicest people on the planet. Yeah. They're so nice that they just give gold medals away on home ice."

Joe gives a bashful smile and the crowd goes nuts.

"Tune in to tomorrow's show when we have Sarah Palin and Olympic gold medalist Shaun White on the show!" That last thing actually happened, by the way. Hey, maybe his flight would have gotten delayed and Pavelski would have been on *The Tonight Show* with Sarah Palin, instead.

We'll never know, because, luckily, Niedermayer has to pay for Luongo's food and beer for the rest of his life.

Niedermayer takes the puck around the Canadian net like nothing ever happened and the Americans retreat for a change. Niedermayer passes it to a streaking Sidney Crosby along the right boards at the Canadian blue line. Both of Canada's other forwards are changing, so Crosby cuts to the middle and attacks all by himself, one-on-four. He's stopped in his tracks by the duo of Ryan Suter and Brian Rafalski but the puck isn't. It finds its way to Miller who directs it right into his blocker-side corner.

This was the beginning of the end.

Even though the Americans had numbers, they were never going to get to that puck first. With his momentum carrying him, Crosby is first into the corner. Jarome Iginla, who had just come off the bench, comes in, too.

I didn't have a great view of what happened next because it happened right along the boards on my side of the ice. I saw Iginla get knocked down, but once he was beneath the boards, that was it. The next thing I knew, Crosby had the puck.

What had actually happened is Iginla went into the corner while Crosby took the puck up the half boards. An official was standing in the way and Crosby momentarily lost the puck in the official's skates. With Rafalski charging in, Crosby slams on the breaks and knifes the puck into the corner to Iginla.

With Rafalski's momentum still carrying him toward the blue line, and seeing that Iginla was going to safely receive the pass, Crosby dashes toward the net.

"Iggy!"

Suter knocks Iginla down. As he's falling, however, Iginla is barely able to get a pass off, right underneath a retreating Rafalski's stick, while neither of his skate blades are even on the ice.

But again, I didn't see all those little details. All I saw was a Canadian player with the . . .

It's the loudest ovation I've ever heard in my entire life.

It was so stunning, so unexpected. The shot seemed so benign compared to so many of the chances Canada had throughout the game. I was so sure that Miller would be the death of Team Canada.

American fans are going to hate this, but my first thought was *That was it?* But then, amid the chaos, I looked down at the players celebrating, and I thought, *Oh my God, was that seriously Sidney Crosby?*

That's the beauty of Sidney Crosby's game, though. He can be fancy when he wants to be, but for the most part, it's precision, timing, and hustle. Miller went for the poke check, Crosby shoots, and there you have one of the most iconic moments in the sport.

It was perfect. It was just too damn perfect. The best player in the world scores the overtime winner for Canada on home ice? That's fairytale Disney movie stuff.

I was jumping up and down. Maybe I had been standing the entire time. I grabbed my three new Canadian friends. We hugged and went completely insane.

Then just like that, I completely shut it off and turned to the Americans on my left. They were still sitting, but to my surprise, they were smiling. Maybe it was just out of politeness, but it's something I'll never forget. If Canada had lost, I would have been crying in the fetal position until security dragged me out.

It's also a scenario I specifically asked about before we had even left for Vancouver.

Because this was a Nike thing, we wanted to keep mentions of certain players to a minimum in my videos. Crosby was the poster boy of Reebok, so his name was brought up specifically.

"What if Crosby scores the gold medal–winning goal?" I swear I said that. Those. Exact. Words.

"We'll cross that bridge when we get there," I was told.

Two-and-a-half weeks later, and the entire country is partying on that bridge.

"SAY IT WITH ME CANADA: #canadawinsgold," I tweeted from Nike's account after I remembered I was supposed to be working.

Equipment was tossed all over the ice, and after watching the women win gold, I knew it would be at least a few minutes before the ceremony started. I reached under my seat, grabbed the little golden shopping bag, and darted for the concourse.

I don't even think I made it to the washroom; I just changed right there in the open. It was a bright Canada-red shirt with a golden leaf on it. At that moment, it was the best shirt I owned.

When I got back to my seat, everyone started asking right away, "Where did you get that?" Oh Nike, you clever cookie.

There were no lip-syncers in the stands. Everybody sang "O Canada" loud and proud. I think the American couple next to me might have even joined in.

On my way out of the arena, a whole bunch of people asked me where I got my shirt. It's said that when you wear a company's logo, it's like you're a walking billboard for them, and I literally was. I'd probably sold a lot of shirts that day.

The scene outside of Rogers Arena was surreal. I remember it vividly. It was still broad daylight. People who were out east forget, it was like three in the afternoon when the game ended in Vancouver. Fans poured onto the streets by the thousands, myself among them as I struggled to look for my work friends.

Several cars were already stuck because people simply flooded the street. I'd love to know what percent of the country, let alone Vancouver, was behind the wheel at that very moment. It couldn't have been many. Did these guys not have a radio? Sometimes I like to think that they had no idea a game was even happening. Imagine how freaked out you'd be by thousands of people suddenly surrounding your car for no good reason.

As the mass of humanity approached the vehicle, I thought, *Oh buddy. You're going to be here awhile.* Just as I was passing the car at the front of the line of three or four, a police officer stepped in front of the car. One step at a time, he slowly guided the car through the crowd by himself. It was the only way they were ever going to get out of there. The cop was even smiling because of how ridiculous it must have looked. I wonder if he had to take care of each car one at a time or if he called for backup.

Maybe I had been caught up in the euphoria of the golden goal, but the farther I got from the arena, the more the reality of the situation I was in took hold of me. *This is a crazy amount of people*, I thought. *This could get really bad really quickly.*

Just then, from out of the enormous crowd on a packed street corner, some big dude began chanting, "Fuck the States!"

Come on, Brad — let's be honest, his name was probably Brad — your team won, dude.

Almost as soon as Brad began chanting, however, the entire crowd, I'm talking hundreds of people surrounding this guy, started booing the crap out of him, and there was at least one distinct and clearly annunciated, "Shut the fuck up!"

Serves you right, Brad. You proud of yourself? The crowd of people was so thick that he couldn't even go anywhere. He just had to silently penguin-walk in an ocean of people who just called him out for being a dick. Out of all the "Man, I wished I filmed that" moments I've ever experienced — man, I wish I filmed that.

People sang "O Canada" in the streets. People sang "O Canada" on the SkyTrain. To this day, I don't think I've ever seen any group of people that happy en masse. I tried my hardest to concentrate on what I was going to say in the video, but there was just too much happiness to look at.

One question I often get asked is what do you think will be better: the golden goal celebration or when the Leafs finally win the Cup? For me, personally, the Leafs finally winning will be more gratifying. Canada winning in 2010 was pure euphoria, but I honestly think if the Leafs win, it'll just be a crowd literally weeping with tears of joy, myself included. Knowing what the golden goal celebration was like first-hand only makes me hungrier for the blue and white celebration to come. You know, whenever that'll be.

When the whole crew finally reunited at the house, we all had the same stupid smiles on our faces. Honestly, it was the happiest I think we had all been the entire time we were there. Again, Nike had built an entire campaign about Canada winning. We all wanted Canada to win anyway, but a Canada win was going to make everything a thousand times easier for us. All our stress melted away. Let's make a happy video, go out for a little fun, then finally go home.

While we were setting up for the video, Darryl told us he had watched the game at the Molson Canada Hockey House. It was a brilliant idea. After all, it had to be the biggest gathering of fans watching the game in the city, outside of the game itself.

The footage was pure gold, no pun intended. The place went off like a cannon when Crosby scored, Darryl's camera was shaking, and confetti poured from the ceiling. We had to start the video with it.

The terrified anxiety I had for almost three weeks had turned into happy anxiety. I wasn't worried about the outcome of anything I couldn't control anymore. All I was nervous about was doing a good job on the video I had been dreaming of making since I was first approached by Nike almost a year ago.

For the first time since we had arrived, everyone in the house was watching me. And for the first time, I didn't mind. Seriously, we were all so damn happy.

I talked about the suspense of heading into overtime, about the celebrations happening all over Canada — we could actually hear cars honking outside as we filmed — and about the juxtaposition between Canada's crushing defeat at the hands of the U.S. at the World Juniors and this glorious, golden redemption.

After we shot the video, we took a minute to relax, have a beer, and watch the closing ceremonies. I can't even tell you how many texts I had to respond to. Most of them were simply: "HOLY SHIT, YOU'RE THERE!"

Once the video was edited and uploaded, we had one more bit of work to do.

We decided the Molson Hockey House was probably one of the best places to be anyway. Why not go there and see if we can get one last interview with Jarome Iginla?

It was rumoured that he was going to be there and it would be absolutely perfect. I didn't realize how crystal clear Crosby's "Iggy" scream had been until I saw the highlights.

With a backpack full of Nike clothes, just in case, we went to Molson Hockey House. The building was packed. If it weren't for our credentials, there's no way we would have gotten in.

After about half an hour of searching, we were told we couldn't secure an interview. We were disappointed for about two seconds, until we realized this meant it was party time.

Where should we go? Every place is going to be packed by now. Oh, wait a sec, we're in a building with a beer logo on it. Let's stay here.

I tried to mingle with the other Nike folks I could find, especially the big wigs. They were all tickled pink with the win and had probably had a few, so I figured this would be a good time to show face. Like, "Hey, guys, it's me, the wacky YouTube kid. Canada won! How cool is that? So, anyway, please hire me to do more stuff like this!"

We were standing next to a roped-off section. Mark was leaning on one of the poles, and this big security guard walked up and put his hand on Mark.

"I need you to step away, please," he said authoritatively.

"Why? What am I doing?" Mark shot back.

"Step away from Corey Perry, sir." Apparently Corey Perry was there.

It was the stolen couch incident all over again.

"I don't even know who the hell Corey Perry is," Mark told the security guard, exasperated.

What's hilarious is Mark was telling the God's honest truth. He liked hockey, but he wasn't big on names. I 100 percent believe that he had no idea who Corey Perry was, regardless of the fact that Perry had scored Canada's 2–0 goal mere hours ago.

"Yeah, right, you don't know who Corey Perry is," the security guard smirked.

"I don't! Who is he?"

Mark is priceless, man.

We eventually left and found a few other friends.

We had just been in a beer tent for a couple of hours, so I don't remember exactly where we ended up. Whatever street we were on, however, was absolutely flooded with people. Hell, every street in Vancouver was flooded with people, some until sunrise. Mark and Darryl went back to the house to work on a few of the last remaining unedited things while others went off to do their own thing. Before long, it was just me and one other guy we'll call Bill.

We just walked around town and joined the hordes still cheering in the streets, high-fiving strangers, and singing drunken renditions of "O Canada."

"Let's find somewhere to hang out," Bill said after a while. "I'll call my wife." His wife was my boss for all things Nike.

"Hey, honey? Honey, it's me! We were just wondering where you were. I'm here with Dangle."

I gave him an enthusiastic drunk wave.

"Where are you right now?" he continued. "Where? OK, cool. We'll be right there. Love you!"

He hung up.

"She said she's at this place called P.J.'s," he told me.

"Let's hit up P.J.'s!" I shouted.

We tried looking it up on his phone but for some reason we couldn't find anything. Looking it up now, Vancouver has a PJ Cabinets Ltd., a PJ White Hardwoods, but no bar called P.J.'s.

I think he tried to call his wife again, but she didn't answer.

"Alright," he started. "She probably went somewhere close to the hotel. So let's just start walking back to the hotel and keep an eye out for P.J.'s."

"Sounds cool to me, man!" I told him.

We stumbled through the streets of Vancouver, and I swear

everybody else was stumbling, too. The cops were out in full force and rightfully prepared for it to get out of hand, but honestly, it was all love. I didn't see any fights or even arguments — just people celebrating together. Hell, people were even high-fiving the cops. I was one of them.

Every now and then, we would poke our head in a random pub and ask if they were P.J.'s. We probably walked for an hour before we finally arrived back at the hotel.

"Hey, what if the hotel bar is called P.J.'s?" I asked.

That must be it. That would explain why we couldn't find it on Google Maps. Let's ask.

The hotel bar didn't have any signage indicating that it was P.J.'s. In fact, the place was empty. I had no idea what time it was. The city was still buzzing, but they had clearly started shutting it down. It must be getting late.

Bill approached the clerk standing behind a little podium at the front of the bar.

"Hey, man," Bill began. "Is this P.J.'s?"

The young clerk look so confused.

"Is this bar P.J.'s?" he asked again. "We were looking for a place called P.J.'s."

The clerk told us no.

"Oh, OK. Do you know where P.J.'s is?"

No idea.

"Alright," Bill turned to me. "I'm going to try my wife again."

He called her a few times until she finally answered. The following is a rough synopsis of what I heard.

"Hey, honey, I . . . you alright? Everything OK? No, no — I'm OK. Look, uh, we're still out here looking for P.J.'s and we can't find it. We thought it might be the hotel bar, but — huh? P.J.'s, the place you said you — what's that? Oh . . . OK. Sorry, honey. OK, I'll be right up. Love you."

He hung up and looked at me.

"She said she's in her P.J.s and wants to go to sleep."

At the time, I was super bummed because I really wanted

to party at P.J.'s. Today, it's one of my favourite stories. This man's wife told him she was in her pajamas and just wanted to go to bed, so Drunk Batman and Drunk Robin wander around town for over an hour looking for a bar that doesn't exist.

My friend went to bed. Not me, though. I'm 21; I'm in a good mood; I'm still up. I wanted to keep the party going.

I called John, one of the younger producers from when I was an intern at the Fan, who I knew was in town. I just didn't want the gold medal day to end. Past midnight? Don't care! As long as I stay awake, it's still gold medal day.

We linked up for a few drinks at a bar and exchanged Olympic stories. John had a few adventures of his own. He showed me this great picture of him in a Team Canada jersey on the left, David Alter, another friend I had met at the Fan, wearing a toque on the right. In the middle? None other than famous Vancouverite actor Joshua Jackson. Many of you probably remember him as Pacey Witter from *Dawson's Creek*. What you should remember him as, however, is none other than Charlie Conway from *The Mighty Ducks*. I had some cool Olympic moments but, man, *the* Charlie Conway? This guy scored the game-winner on a penalty shot, no bucket!

After a few drinks, we went back out on the town. I don't even know where we were going. It was past 2 a.m. and the streets were still swamped. Despite the alcohol, everyone still seemed perfectly friendly and cops were still high-fiving them.

An absolutely delicious smell danced right under my nose. You know the feeling. It's the end of the night, you've had some drinks, you have to shut it down at some point. What do you do before you shut it down? Drunk snack. And I was very drunk hungry. Drungry, if you will.

What is that? It's got to be some kind of meat. It's so familiar. Wait . . .

"Bacon!" I yelled.

I turned to John who was standing on my right.

"Do you smell that?" I asked.

I don't think I even waited for him to answer. I blindly turned to my left and shouted: "Where is that bacon smell is coming from?"

Staring me dead in the eyes was a short and alarmed-looking police officer.

Barely a second later, I was on my ass.

It felt like I had been sucked into another dimension. Something pulled me right off my feet.

It took me a second to figure it out what happened. I was still wearing my backpack full of clothes. Whoever was standing behind me must have grabbed my backpack, yanked on it as hard as they could, and completely laid me out.

I looked up at the culprit.

It was a much taller, thicker, angrier police officer.

"You're being a drunk asshole," he started. "We're going to search you; I have suspicion you have alcohol on you; we're going to drag you in and make you fill out all kinds of paperwork; we're going to take up hours of your night."

I swear he said all of this in one breath.

"What?" I asked feebly. That was all I could think to say. I had no idea what I had done. "It's just clothes, that's all I have," I tried to explain.

"I don't care!" the cop yelled at me. "You need to apologize for the bacon comment."

The bacon comment? What the hell is he talking abo— oh! *Oh no!*

Here's a little lesson for you. Hopefully you'll never need it, but it might come in handy if you're ever wasted at the Olympics: "pig" is a derogatory term for a police officer. They don't like it.

"Bacon" is a worse version of that. They like it much less.

All this officer saw was some drunk idiot shout "bacon" at his partner.

"You need to apologize for the bacon comment right now," he repeated.

You know how drunk people like to over-explain things? That's what I was on the verge of doing. In my stupid mind, I was going to calmly explain, "Dreadfully sorry for the mix-up. You see, my friend and I we merely gallivanting along when we smelled the most delightful aroma. We thought, *We must find whatever delightful dish was the cause of it.* I say, my good chap, might you point us in the direction of the Bacon Shoppe?"

But the last sliver of sober in me reached up all the way from my liver, grabbed me by the collar, and screamed, "Just apologize, you idiot!"

I opened my mouth to explain myself.

"I . . . uh . . . I'm sorry."

The cop shoved me in the back and told me to go home.

I just nodded, and John and I started walking away.

After a few seconds of awkward silence, I turned, looked to make sure the cop wasn't within ear shot, and started talking about how he wasn't so big and tough.

That's what you say when you're drunk and embarrassed. Now, I'm sober and embarrassed and can say that cop was 200 percent right. It was time to go home.

When I got home, Darryl was still working and Mark had only just gone to bed.

I still think about that. That's the kind of dedication you have to have in your work. Sure, it was all fun and games for the YouTube kid that Nike took a blind chance on. Everyone else was working at the Olympics because they were the cream of the crop. They had resumes and years of experience. They had talent that they had accumulated through years of dedication. He wasn't working until 3 a.m. because he had to. He was up that late because he cared.

I threw my things haphazardly into my bags and went to bed. I turned over to my phone and begrudgingly set my alarm for 6 a.m. — just three hours later.

My alarm went off, my Frankenstein body reanimated, and I loaded my stuff into the cab.

Hey, you ever go on a cross-country flight that's over five hours long? Not the best experience, is it? OK, how about this: you ever go on a five-hour cross-country flight after an all-night gold medal bender? Less fun.

Once again, while I was nursing my hangover, Darryl was going through footage on his computer. Darryls make the world go round. A smarter version of 21-year-old me would have asked himself, *How can I be a little more like Darryl?*

When I got home to my parents' house, I star-fished on the living room floor. I shovelled in some dinner while my mom bombarded me with questions. I did my best to answer as many as I could. Luckily my dad, who was once a 21-year-old knucklehead himself, sensed his son's condition and slowed down the interrogation.

So much had happened over those 17 days that it was impossible to recount it all at once. I was still remembering and telling new stories at the dinner table for months after the Olympics. The party after the gold medal game, though? My parents didn't have to hear about that right away. Besides, I figured it would sound pretty good in a book one day.

UNTIL
THE FINAL
BUZZER

Never leave a game early.

The last game I ever saw at Maple Leaf Gardens on January 4, 1999, was an absolute barn-burner against the Tampa Bay Lightning.

My uncle Anthony and aunt Sharon gave me a pair of tickets to the game. For some reason, presumably because I was just a stupid kid, I thought these were tickets to the Leafs' last game at the Garden. I don't know why I thought that. I had no idea it was scheduled to be against the Chicago Blackhawks.

Everyone wanted to see one last game at the Garden. It also helped that the Leafs were doing pretty well that season. My dad and I went to this game together. Awesome seats: lower bowl, not too high up, and dead centre. Shutout to Uncle Anthony for not ripping up his bratty nephew's tickets for whining about it not being the last game.

Tampa, who completely sucked that season and still didn't even have 10 wins by New Year's, scored a goal past Curtis Joseph just 35 seconds into the game. The goal was by some guy named Darcy Tucker. There was one assist: Wendel Clark. What a gut punch.

Late in the period, some rookie named Vincent Lecavalier scored his seventh goal of the season and seventh goal of his career. 2–0, Bolts.

Early in the second, Wendel Clark got the lone assist again as Alex Selivanov scored. Now 3–0 for smelly, stinky, barely even a team Tampa.

Alright, I changed my mind, Uncle Anthony. Blow your nose with these tickets.

When it comes to sports, I definitely get some of my attitude and, let's gently say, temper from my dad.

"B'oh!" he shouted at the Lightning's third goal. "They're sucking!" He slouched into his chair.

This was a disaster. My Leafs were getting murdered right in front of my eyes. The game isn't even half over and I'm 10 years old so the rest of the game is going to feel like an eternity.

Finally, Sergei Berezin scored to get the Leafs on the board, 3–1 now. Alright, so that's something.

Two minutes later, the comeback began. Mats Sundin bagged a goal to bring the Leafs within one, 3–2. We've got a hockey game, people!

Later in the period, although it might be hard for Leafs fans to picture today, Tucker got in Sundin's face. Sundin gave Tucker a little shove before Sundin's linemate Steve Thomas swooped in and completely gooned Tucker, catching him off guard and slamming him into the boards.

Tucker bounced up instantly and gloves flew all over the place like confetti. Imagine that: Steve Thomas fighting Darcy Tucker. Well, it happened. I saw it!

Tucker had on his patented psychopathic "I will murder you and eat your flesh" smile on. What a mad man. Happier than a pig in poo. Both he and Thomas had those fast fists, performing a mutual knuckle Riverdance on each other's faces.

Just 35 seconds later, Mikael Andersson scored to give the Lightning a 4–2 lead, but that didn't matter. There was genuine hate in the air now. The entire Garden, including one rabid 10-year-old boy in particular, wanted blood. It's hard to imagine Darcy Tucker as enemy number one in Toronto.

Less than five minutes into the third, Steve Thomas scored

to cut the lead to one. Sweet justice! Three minutes later, Scarborough native Mike Johnson scored for the Leafs, tying the game at four. It was a good thing the Leafs were moving because we blew the roof off the Garden that night. The Leafs came back from a 3–0 and then 4–2 deficit to force overtime.

Then a moment I'll never forget.

My dad is a commuter. Like, a real morning commuter. Getting to the train to either go to or from downtown Toronto was a down-to-the-second art form for him.

Between the third period and overtime, he actually asked this question: "Do you want to go catch the train?"

I still remember the look I gave him — just utter mutiny — and the look he gave me back.

"Dad," I said, with surprise, "it's overtime."

"Yeah," he started. "Yeah, uh, right. You're right. OK."

It was a bizarre benchmark moment in life. Without saying the words, my face said, *That was a really stupid question*, while his face silently responded, *You're right, that was a stupid question and I'm sorry I even asked it.*

I still rip on him for it today. "Do you want to catch the train?" Before overtime. Honestly.

"We'll leave right away, when the game's done," I said, momentarily assuming the role of dad, apparently.

Thank goodness we didn't leave, too. With less than two minutes to go in overtime, Freddy Modin beat Tampa Bay goalie Bill Ranford to give the Leafs a thrilling comeback win in overtime on home ice.

I barely knew it was Modin, though. Everyone jumped out of their seat when he scored, and my little head wasn't up high enough to catch a number. We were up and out of there like lightning, ironically. Dad's commuter instincts kicked in, shifting in and out of the crowd like he was made of water. I just did my best to keep up.

And that was the last game I ever saw at Maple Leaf Gardens. I couldn't even imagine Tucker and Thomas as teammates after that brawl. And 10-year-old me would never have believed that many years later, while working for Sportsnet, I would snap a photo with both of them along with Curtis Joseph.

I should mention that I did leave the game with one souvenir that night: a navy blue baseball cap with "Memories and Dreams" written on the front and a little Leafs logo on the temple.

The game's not over until it's over. Never leave early.

ROOKIE SEASON

After my Olympic adventure, it was back to reality.

The zoo finally removed the simulator ride. It was replaced with a giant colourful carousel full of hand-carved wooden animals. The zoo wanted to post a big video on their YouTube channel to promote it, so they got yours truly to host it.

I got to interview zookeepers, pet an elephant, and I even fed a giraffe. I still hadn't discovered hair gel, though . . .

Nike signed me to keep making videos. One of the ways they paid me was with credit at the Nike store. The first time I used it, I went with my mom. I told the people at the store that I had no idea how to spend it.

They were clearly used to fancier folks than me, buying whatever they wanted without thinking about it. Meanwhile, I'm walking around with free made-up money and I'm too afraid to spend it.

"What exactly are you looking for?" a store rep asked.

I looked at my mom and thought of my sister.

"Socks," I said. "My sister goes through a lot of socks."

I didn't get down on myself like the previous summer. It helped that I had my job at Leafs TV to look forward to. Not an internship anymore — an actual job. They hired me!

My job would be a little different this year. I'd be hosting the Leafs' live chats from MLSE's brand-new giant sports bar, Real

Sports, which just so happened to be across the street from the ACC and had almost 200 TV screens, including one that was 39 feet wide.

They positioned me in the DJ booth at Real Sports for my chats, and that became my office.

The buzz around the beginning of the 2010–11 season was great. Fans were rejuvenated, feeling that after last season, well, there's nowhere to go but up. (You may recall the Leafs finished last in the Eastern Conference for the 2009–10 season.) It also helped that the Leafs beat Montreal 3–2 in the home opener.

I'll never forget the second game, though.

I was walking around Real Sports and this very familiar-looking man was walking in front of me. He glanced back and we locked eyes. To my surprise, he stopped.

"Steve," he began. "Good to meet you. Tom Anselmi."

Oh. Holy crap. Yeah, this guy's a bigwig at MLSE.

He told me he had seen my videos on TV and that I was doing a great job. We spoke for a minute while walking out of the building and into the square.

As fate would have it, we bumped into my parents, who were both in Canadian tuxedos.

"Hi, Steven!" my mom said, waving way too enthusiastically as I stood there with my boss's boss's boss.

"Mr. Anselmi," I said, "these are my parents." He shook their hands.

"Mom, Dad, this is Tom Anselmi. He's, uh, what's your exact title again?" I asked.

His smile dropped a bit. "Chief operating officer," he said.

Way to remember the COO of the company you work for, Steve.

"Where are you sitting tonight?" Tom asked my parents.

They told him they were just checking out the new square.

"You didn't get them tickets?" Tom asked me surprised.

I just laughed. "I'm a part-time highlight editor, sir."

He paused. "Wait here for ten minutes," he said. He turned around and took off.

We waited there and, sure enough, he came back and gave my parents two tickets, nice and low in the reds. The Leafs wiped the floor with Ottawa that night, 5–1. My mom stayed undefeated at Leafs games.

The Leafs won their first four games that season, with new-signing Clarke MacArthur scoring in each of those games. One day, when my dad was bored at work, he had made a prop sword out of wood and metal. I used it as a prop for my videos, calling him King MacArthur and his stick the sword Excalibur.

During that hot early season run, I was walking out of Real Sports when Clarke MacArthur, his wife, and his agent walked in. Surprisingly, he stopped me.

"We've seen your videos," MacArthur said. "We love the sword thing."

Between that, the Leafs' early success, increased TV appearances, an actual salary covering hockey, and continuing to do Nike videos part-time, I was feeling pretty good about myself. Still, there were a couple of hard lessons I learned that season, too.

They gave me this LG laptop to use for the MapleLeafs.com chats. We usually had somewhere between 500 and 2,000 people in the chat, and I had to approve every single message in order for it to get displayed. For chats after a trade, we had over 20,000.

The reason they occasionally let me on the Leafs' TV pregame show, and often the postgame show, was to talk about the chat. I relayed fan questions to our amazing host Andi Petrillo, and she would ask the questions to one of our panelists, usually former Leafs Bob McGill, Mark Osborne, and Brad May, who would answer live. It was a cool, interactive idea for that time.

But on one occasion, I wanted to leave quickly after a game. I put the laptop in a bag and went to the floor director and asked her if she could put the laptop away, so I could run to the train. She briefly paused to smile and nod before leaving to do something else. A few days later, I discovered that the laptop was gone. Apparently, the floor director, who was wearing big head-phones when I spoke to her before rushing out, thought I was just saying bye. The laptop got left out and somebody obviously stole it. I searched high and low for the thing, but it was gone.

Whose fault was that? Mine.

First of all, I shouldn't have been rushing out the door. Need to get home to make a video? Who cares. My job was to be in charge of the Maple Leafs chat, and that included not losing the damn laptop I needed to do my job. Even if she wasn't wearing headphones and heard me, it wouldn't have been fair to put that on her. Any way you slice it, I was wrong to pawn my job off on somebody else. The laptop was my responsibility. I could have even brought the thing home!

I got chewed out for that one. Clarkey had to make an embarrassing phone call to ask LG for a new one because some 22-year-old idiot he hired out of school decided he wanted to catch a train home instead of waiting half an hour for the next one.

Now, let's take stock of what Leafs TV had in me as an employee:

I had a YouTube channel and my videos were getting maybe 4,000 views each at the time, which isn't enough to go around acting like a big shot who can cut corners.

I had 5,000 Twitter followers, maybe less.

I was a below average cameraman.

I was a mediocre video editor.

I was also mediocre on live television.

I was just 22.

I'd lost their laptop.

Put yourself in Clarkey's shoes. Do you really need this?

At one point, in the middle of a casual conversation, Clarkey had mentioned that he didn't like hiring Ryerson students.

"They're very entitled," he told me. You know, if I didn't know any better, I could swear he was trying to tell me something.

Brocky, Leafs TV producer and resident good cop, instilled a simple concept in me that everyone should know: the tool belt.

Basically, your tool belt is this invisible thing that holds all of your skills and things you know how to do. I kind of hated my tool belt when Brocky first told me about it, but that was because I didn't have much in it. As the weeks and months passed, however, I realized it was starting to fill up!

In media, whether it's in the studio or the field, it's so important to know what's involved in various roles. I edit my Leafs videos myself, but for the videos that I'm not editing, I know what the editors need, what challenges they have, and so on. Pro tip: never tell an editor how long you think something takes to edit. Just because you want something done by a certain time doesn't mean it's going to happen. You'll either have to sacrifice quality to get it quickly, or have it done well and wait. There's no such thing as the content fairy, a magical pixie that leaves well-produced videos under your pillow every time you ask for one.

Similarly, I suck at using the camera, but I at least have some idea about camera angles, framing, lighting challenges, and so on.

No matter what your specialty is, it's worthwhile to know the intricacies of the other roles around you. It'll make you better at what you do and a better coworker.

The Leafs crashed back to reality and totally sucked, yet again, missing the 2011 playoffs. One cool thing did happen, though: the team called up James Reimer, whose first AHL game I had covered years before. Turns out, he was pretty good. Really good, actually. He almost single-handedly dragged the Leafs, kicking and screaming, into the playoffs.

At one point that year, I got to watch Reimer and the Leafs on the road in Boston. The station sent me there with four contest winners; I was supposed to shoot and edit the entire thing myself.

I remember asking Brocky why they wanted me to do that.

"Sometimes they just want to see if you sink or swim," he said. This was a test.

It was a blast. Jay Rosehill fought Milan Lucic, Nazem Kadri scored a wicked shootout goal against Tim Thomas, and James Reimer sealed the win in the shootout, his gloves shaking with joy.

The Leafs ended up falling short that season, but Reimer made it fun. To make things even more special, the Leafspace episode that I shot and edited myself actually turned out pretty well.

After an up-and-down season in what was technically my first as a full-time media professional, I ended strong. But the deeper I got into that world, the weirder things got.

HEADLOCK

One of the biggest "How the hell did I get myself into this?" moments of my life happened while I worked for Leafs TV. Somewhere toward the end of the 2010–11 season, I was out in downtown Toronto with Justin Fisher and this guy I'll call Dylan.

He wanted us to go to a very specific bar. The name sounded familiar, but I hadn't been there before. But if Dylan says it's the place to be right now, then I guess that's what it is.

We got inside, and right away, something seemed a little strange. The first thing I noticed was that the clientele was 90 percent dudes. The second thing I noticed was that 100 percent of those dudes looked like they could kick my ass.

Wait a second — that guy looks familiar. So does that guy. And that guy.

Dude, are these the Toronto Marlies?

Turns out, Dylan had brought us to what was apparently the Marlies' end-of-season party. My naïve 23-year-old self was very impressed. I had done occasional post-game interviews with a few of the Marlies, but somehow Dylan knew them much better. I got to meet captain Ryan Hamilton and his wife, Alexa. I also got to meet this goalie the Marlies had, some AHL rookie who was called up from the ECHL named Ben Scrivens, along with his then girlfriend, now wife, Jenny.

It wasn't just players at the bar, either. There were a few

familiar faces from the media, too. One particular guy was serving drinks behind the bar and I'm pretty damn sure he didn't work there.

It was incredible. It was like I was in a scene from *Wolf of Wall Street*. I watched these guys all the time. I was always talking about who the Leafs should call up from the Marlies in my videos because lord knows the NHL team sucked. And here I am just hanging out, having beers with them.

I was having a great time, just soaking up the scene, meeting a few folks, and shooting the shit with a couple of friends. And then everything went black.

A giant, meaty arm wrapped itself around my head and put me in a tight headlock. Remember when I said that everybody in the bar looked like they could kick my ass? This arm felt like it could beat me up by itself, without the rest of the body. *It's OK, Steve. You brought friends, remember!* No, no. The arm could've kicked their asses, too.

Whoever that arm was attached to pulled me in tight. A gruff, boozy voice said something right in my ear.

"You better not write anything about me, fuckin' Dangles."

I wriggled free a bit, so I could turn to see who it was. And also breathe. I won't say who it was because I'm sure they don't remember doing this and I'm not trying to get sued, but let's put it this way: when I saw who had put me in a headlock, it was the absolute last person on that team who I would want to put me in a headlock.

This is it, I thought. *You knew this day would come. All you do is talk crap about players in your videos, one of them finally saw, and now one of those players is about to beat you into a crater.*

Just then, he loosened the grip. The player still had his hands on my shoulders to hold himself upright as he stumbled. This guy wasn't just drunk, he was blackout drunk.

"I'm just kiddin', man," he slurred. "It's OK. I know I'm a fuckin' plug."

"Nah, come on. That's not true," I tried to reassure him.

Sage advice, I know. Look, only a few seconds before that, I thought a professional athlete was about to kick my ass. Forgive me for not being the greatest motivational speaker in that moment.

We ended up talking for a few minutes. You ever try to make somebody who's completely hammered feel better about themselves? Yeah, it was pretty much exactly that, except with a professional hockey player.

When the player finally walked away, Fisher and I exchanged wide-eyed glances. *Did that really just happen?* The next time I saw Andre the Giant, he was on his knees in the middle of the bar ripping the hardest air guitar solo I've ever seen. He was definitely feeling no pain.

Fisher and I were hanging out in a corner by ourselves while Dylan talked to his Marlies pals. We were just minding our business when the same plastered player walked up to me again. He grabbed the nearly full pint of beer out of my hand, took a slow sip while staring me dead in the eyes, and then just walked away.

Pro tip: When somebody way bigger, stronger, tougher, and meaner than you takes your beer, just let them. Beer is cheap; facial reconstruction surgery is expensive.

The night passed, and I lived to drink another day.

Months later, I had the opportunity to cover a Leafs game at the Air Canada Centre. I walked into Gate 2, got in the elevator, and a few Leafs were in there, and, sure enough, one of them was none other than the guy who had put me in a headlock and drank my beer.

Do you know what he said to me? Nothing. Not a single word the entire way up. As a matter of fact, he didn't even look at me.

There's no way he even remembered.

In retrospect, I took away a few things from the experience.

It's possible that this player had never actually seen anything that I had ever made, but he did, at the very least, know that I was in the media. One thing you're going to have to keep in mind if you want to get into any kind of media, especially reporting, is that a lot of people are going to paint you and everybody else in the media with the same brush. If one person wrote a negative article about them, then *everybody* has written something negative about them. To some, "the media" is one massive gelatinous blob.

Whether it's hockey or politics, a lot of people automatically think that the media are just a bunch of frothing, agenda-driven hacks, hell-bent on lying and making things up to suit their needs. Picture something like J. Jonah Jameson trying to frame Spiderman. So if you're trying to talk to a player, or any subject, and it's obvious that they don't trust you — even though they just met you — don't take it personally.

On that note, if this guy was sober that night, he might not have said anything. As fate would have it, however, he was completely plowed when I walked in the door. It's amazing what can happen when you mix inherent distrust and alcohol.

Let's assume that this player had in fact seen videos where I had talked about him. Let's also assume that the things I said were negative. That certainly wouldn't give that player any right to hit me, but, unfortunately, a lot of angry people don't really think about legal repercussions until after they've punched you in the mouth.

What are you going to do, though? Not speak your mind? Not talk about your perspective on things? Of course not. So when you speak your mind, speak the truth. Think before you speak, have purpose and evidence to support what you say, and be confident in your words, even if somebody gets in your face.

A drunk hockey player might take your beer, but your words will buy you others.

DOUGIE EFFING HAMILTON

In June 2011, the Boston Bruins were the reigning Stanley Cup champions. They had just beaten the Vancouver Canucks in a gruelling seven-game series. After the Cup win, the party became the stuff of legend.

A picture showing the Bruins' alleged bar tab from the night they won the Cup went viral: $156,679.74. But the real gift that kept on giving was the dynamic duo of Brad Marchand and Tyler Seguin, two Bruins rookies who were living large and boycotting shirts.

For a few days running, it was "Oh, look, here's Marchand and Seguin and, oh, they don't have shirts on again." They appeared to even get matching rib tattoos to commemorate the championship.

Seeing Seguin succeed like that was a bitter pill for Leafs fans to swallow. After all, Leafs GM Brian Burke had traded three picks to the Bruins, including two first-rounders, in exchange for Phil Kessel.

Sure enough, the Leafs had sucked (despite how good Kessel was) and finished second-last, giving the Bruins the second overall pick, which they used to select Tyler Seguin.

Early in the 2010–11 season, Seguin had scored against the Leafs in Boston. The fans at the TD Garden greeted that with a loud chant: "Thank you, Kessel!"

A few months later, and now Seguin was a Stanley Cup champion and not with the Leafs.

Fast forward a couple of weeks, and I was sitting in the VIP section of Real Sports. No, I'm not important, it was the day of the 2011 NHL Draft and I was working.

The Leafs did have two first-round picks that year, just not their own. Their original 2011 pick, however, the ninth overall pick, belonged to Boston.

Shortly before the first round began, two familiar faces walked by: Leafs prospect Jesse Blacker and none other than Tyler Seguin. I had met both of them before, so I said hi.

"Who are you hoping the Leafs get?" Seguin asked.

"I know it's unrealistic," I began, "but I want them to get Dougie Hamilton somehow. I think he's going to be great."

With the seventh overall pick, the Winnipeg Jets select Mark Scheifele. OK, cool. Hamilton's still there.

With the eighth overall pick, the Philadelphia Flyers select Sean Couturier. Hey, that's a steal for them! He was supposed to go first overall at one point.

And now, with the ninth overall pick, the Boston Bruins select . . . Dougie Hamilton.

I immediately put my head in my hands.

Why? It could have been anybody. Why did it have to be him?

Just then, I felt a tap on my shoulder. I looked up from my Leafs-fan misery, and Tyler Seguin was standing in front of me.

He looked me dead in the eyes and said, "Thank you, Kessel?"

Then he smiled and walked away.

Cold, Tyler. Cold.

On the bright side, I never thought that I'd be getting chirped by up-and-coming NHL stars when I was making video rants high off dental drugs. And I'll take a playful chirp over a headlock any day, as long as I'm on the radar.

Man, that trade sucked.

CABBIE

One of the best job interviews I've ever had was also easily my worst.

For a few years, pretty much all I did was hustle to get work. The more phone numbers and email addresses I had, the better. Every single one of them was a potential job and chance to move out of my parents' house before my 40th birthday.

One day, in summer 2011, I managed to wrangle a "chat" with Sportsnet. I considered these chats as job interviews. There are jobs you apply for and there are jobs you get through these "chats." Here's the difference: a posted job is limited to the description; the job you get from a chat is up to the imagination.

There's a certain flexibility you get from a job interview that isn't actually a job interview. Besides the freedom of not having to apply through a soulless online HR robot, there's also a freedom to the conversation. Based on the questions and answers you have, maybe they'll realize your skillset matches a job opening within the company you hadn't even heard about. Even better, maybe the wheels will start turning and they'll invent a job specifically for you.

It sounds ridiculous, but certain employers get excited when they see an opportunity to create a new position. Don't believe me? How many of you reading this right now are expected to do things that have nothing to do with your job description? Exactly.

In an ever-evolving and hard-to-predict technological landscape, especially in media, a lot of boss and middle management types get excited when they see an opportunity to evolve their business. Just the same, those types get excited when you sound like you could take on a bunch of work that they barely understand.

Odds are your boss is in their 40s or 50s. Trust me, they don't want to be worrying about what the newest trend on Snapchat is. "Instagram stories? I just figured out what Instagram is and now they've basically made it Snapchat?"

These days, managers and companies are a little more savvy than they were in 2011, but there are still many companies that will give you a job because you're young and seem like you have a decent idea of how the internet works.

When "chat day" came, I went to the Sportsnet studios with my "get a job" shirt on, which looked an awful lot like the dress shirt I wore to my high school graduation.

Two men, we'll call them Marc and Ryan, came to greet me. *Firm handshake*, I thought. *Not too firm, though. This isn't a mugging. Just firm enough to establish that yes, they're in charge for now, but one day you won't be 23 anymore and it'll be your time to . . . wait, what'd they say?*

They brought me into a large dimly lit boardroom with a long table. I sat in the middle on one side and they both sat across from me.

Why are we sitting in the middle? Well, why wouldn't we? What were we supposed to do? Sit at opposite ends of the table like we're having dinner at Mr. Burns's house? That's insane. Middle works. Middle is good. (This is what goes on in my head.)

Anyway, we start talking. I tell them about what I know how to do professionally, which is edit highlights until my hands fall off. What they were more interested in, however, was what I did online. I went through my YouTube videos, my story, my

Twitter followers, my Nike adventures. I was tap-dancing. Marc and Ryan seemed impressed, too. More than impressed — dare I say, interested. I could see the wheels turning in their heads, which is exactly what you want during a chat like this. If they weren't thinking about how to have me escorted out by security, they were thinking about how to give me a job.

We talked about a few things I could do for Sportsnet. Maybe videos for the site, a few interviews. One thing I specifically remember was a podcast pitch.

"Do you know Jeff Marek?" one of them asked.

"I do," I said. I told them about how Jeff had put me on *Hockey Night in Canada*'s playoff preview show in 2009 and had basically been in my corner since the beginning.

"Well, we've been talking about him doing this podcast," they explained. "Maybe it could be you who does the podcast with him."

For those of you who don't know, which I assume is approximately none of you, Jeff Marek was one of the hosts of the extremely popular *Marek vs. Wyshynski* podcast with Greg Wyshynski before it tragically came to an end in 2017 when Greg left Yahoo for ESPN. Of course, at the time of this story the podcast didn't exist yet.

By the end of our discussion, which lasted almost an hour, the guys told me they wanted me to meet their boss.

Meet their boss? Like, a second "chat"?

This was uncharted territory. I'd never been asked to have a second chat.

Oh, man — I got the job for sure! It didn't matter that there wasn't even "a job" yet.

The next week, I returned to Sportsnet, wearing my one other dress shirt, to meet Marc and Ryan and their boss. Let's call him Shawn. I shook Shawn's hand, put way too much thought into it, and we walked down the hall to his office.

The Sportsnet studios are very cool. There are huge sports murals and memorabilia everywhere, and one of the conference rooms has the old Sportsnet logo on the wall made up entirely of cut-in-half baseballs.

When we got to Shawn's office, we sat at a round table. I sat at six o'clock, Shawn sat at about 10, while Marc and Ryan sat at roughly one and four. Trust me, this is important . . .

"So, you can be, like, our Cabbie?" Shawn said.

His question, which sounded an awful lot like a statement, caught me off guard.

In case you don't know, Cabbie, or Cabral Richards, is somewhat of a pioneer in Canadian sports media and definitely somebody I looked up to growing up. Like me, Cabbie loves sports, and like me, Cabbie is freaking weird. From the moment I first saw him on TV, I loved him.

Cabbie would run up to athletes with this excited, wide-eyed face, like a kid who just saw the ice cream truck and couldn't wait to tell his friends. He would instantly disarm usually guarded personalities and get quotes out of them that seasoned journalists had been begging for, for decades.

He often brought props, conducted his interviews in unusual settings, and asked ridiculous questions. In 2009, Cabbie famously got to ride around with Kobe Bryant in his helicopter.

Here's how Cabbie described himself in a 2015 article written by Courtney Shea in the *Globe and Mail*: "I went to Ryerson for radio and TV and then my first internship was at a sports station. I was doing the usual stuff — gathering data and stats. Then I pitched this idea of being a man on the street. That was based on my big, silly personality. I've always been that guy in the group of friends, the one idiot who will go and lick the frozen pole. When I'm interviewing, I'm never going to ask those cliché questions. Instead, I'll ask Kobe Bryant if I can come and stay at his house. Being a little bit different makes people remember."

Cabbie's story is incredibly inspirational to me. We went to the same school, got a similar internship, and found a way to carve a niche for ourselves as the weird ones.

I've always looked at Cabbie as a guy who "got it." We're talking sports, here. It's supposed to be fun.

But getting compared to Cabbie really bothered me.

For starters, whenever I showed people my early videos they would say, "Oh, so you're trying to be Cabbie, right?" A few years later that evolved to sometimes include, "Oh, so you're trying to be Jay Onrait?"

Why? Because I'm making jokes? Because I'm actually trying to have fun with sports? Why should that make me an outlier?

Not to mention that even if I was trying to be Cabbie, I would fail. Only Cabbie can be Cabbie. I'm not trying to be a cheap knockoff of him or anybody else. Which is why this guy had thrown me off so badly.

In less than 30 seconds, this guy had met me, shaken my hand, sat down, and basically assumed I was just some knock-off gimmick — some Cabbie wannabe.

"Well, not exactly," I tried to explain.

As I continued my little rap about myself, Shawn was staring at the wall above my head. TV studios tend to have a lot of televisions in them. It just so happened that one of them was right above my head.

After about five minutes, Shawn knew last night's baseball scores a hell of a lot better than he knew me. I wish I was exaggerating when I say he must have watched the TV above my head the entire damn time. I glanced over at Marc and Ryan, who looked right back at me. You could see it on their faces. No smiles, no wheels turning — only pity. They felt bad for me. They even took over for me at certain points as they helped pitch me to their boss.

After only about five minutes, we were done. I don't think I even got a "We'll let you know" from Shawn.

Marc and Ryan led me outside while their boss stayed in his office, presumably to continue to watch the baseball highlights after I had rudely interrupted them. I'm dead serious: if he had hit me with his car later that day, he would've had no idea who I was.

"Well," one of them said, "sorry about that."

That's how bad it was. These guys actually apologized. You know what you never want a job interview to end with? An apology.

For the record, I like Cabbie. We got to work together in a little vignette with PK Subban for a Nike video once. When I worked at the NHL Network, which used to share its studios with TSN, I pestered him for wisdom a few times. We even text every so often.

I told Cabbie this story a while back. His response was enlightening.

"Sucks to be compared to someone else," he started. "I get the 'you'll never be as good as Nardwuar,' and I'm like, 'I know! He's a legend.' But also we're super different, much like you and me."

Nardwuar, by the way, is another guy who likes interviewing in a silly way — except he's way more over the top. He wears ridiculous outfits and hats to interview celebrities, usually musicians, and ends every interview with "Doo doodle doo doo . . ." in the hopes of getting the artist to say, "Doo doo."

It was annoying but comforting at the same time to hear that Cabbie had to deal with similar hurdles when it came to establishing himself. We both still hear it today.

After this experience, I could have applied a lesson every hockey player learns: no team ever goes undefeated.

The Pittsburgh Penguins won back-to-back Stanley Cups in 2016 and 2017. Between the regular season and playoffs, they lost 83 times over those years. As much as they have a reputation around the league and with some fans as being a bit too whiny, they definitely know how to rebound from a loss.

Well, I didn't bounce back from the loss at Sportsnet. I stewed.

I'd had a nice little winning streak going: an internship at the Fan 590 at 19; my first paid job in sports at 20; an internship at Leafs TV at 21; the Olympics at 21; a job at Leafs TV at 22. I thought I would walk into a job at Sportsnet, no problem.

Instead, I found out that I wasn't even interesting enough to capture the attention of somebody I was sitting across from.

After several months, Ryan told me they weren't able to figure anything out for me. I was both heartbroken and angry by the call. If I'm being honest, it soured me on Sportsnet for a while. I would try to rationalize it by saying if they employed guys like Shawn, I didn't want to work there anyway. All summer long, I pictured the look on that guy's face as he watched the TV above my head.

I was so damn close, I thought. *I'd be working for Sportsnet right now if that prick hadn't been watching TV. He's an idiot. Everyone in charge everywhere is an idiot. Nobody gets it. They're all dinosaurs. It's just because I'm on YouTube. They think I'm just some stupid kid. I'll show them.*

Then the self-sabotage began.

SUMMER SLUMP

The Toronto Zoo, the decent-paying, fun, and dependable job I had for six years wanted me to come back for a seventh summer. Instead of taking the offer, I told them no and that I wanted to dedicate my time to finding a job in my industry. I'm a graduate now, I want to move out at some point, and I really need to get my act together since Leafs TV had no summer work to offer. Thanks, but no thanks.

That was not smart. A few people tried to talk me out of it. My boss at the zoo, who had always been so good to me, asked if I was really sure. My friends mostly took my word for it, but I could tell they were skeptical. But looking back at that summer, what hurts the most is how my parents and my girlfriend, now wife, took it.

One thing I love about my parents is they give me the benefit of the doubt, and they especially did during high school and university. They didn't go over my grades with a fine-tooth comb. They made sure to ask me questions about how I was doing and what my goals were, and I was honest with them. Whenever I came home with good news, it validated their faith in me. I told them I wanted to get into broadcasting as a teenager, I figured out what I needed to do to start achieving that goal, and I got into university. The whole time, they only jumped in when needed and mostly stayed out of the way.

Once I was in university, I told them what courses I was taking, what I liked, what I didn't like, and what I struggled in but wanted to keep at because it was worth knowing. When I told them about getting involved with Nike, they were nervous for me, but they trusted that I knew what I was getting into.

Similarly, my future wife has always had faith in me and been supportive. After all, she didn't dump me when I started making YouTube videos, so that was a huge sign . . .

I had never given them a reason to doubt me before, so when I told them I wasn't going back to the zoo, they trusted that I was making the right decision. But I wasn't.

What broadcasting job did I actually think I was going to get during the summer? Covering the Blue Jays? My baseball knowledge sucked. Covering hockey? There is no hockey, unless I wanted to cover the Australian Ice Hockey League.

A few little victories did come my way, but they weren't enough to redeem that whole summer. I got a job as a volunteer at the NHL's 2011 Research and Development Camp. That's when they take all the players hoping to be drafted the following year and have them play scrimmages against each other to test out new rules or ideas.

I had the privilege of being the score announcer in the penalty box. Easy, right — no pressure? Sure, until I look behind me and realize half of the league's executives are there. *Whoa, that's Steve Yzerman! Whoa, that's Scotty Bowman!*

When there was a goal, the refs would come over to the box and say the jersey numbers of the players who scored. Outside of Nail Yakupov, there were maybe five names I actually recognized.

A goal got scored and the ref came over with the numbers. I looked at the page to match those numbers to names. After I announced the goal and both assists, I realized I was looking at the numbers for the wrong team. All three players were wrong. I tried to correct it, but it was too late, and mid-play . . . and, God, even writing this is making me cringe.

Derek, my fake lawyer, had started his own marketing company and gotten a few clients. He offered me a couple hundred bucks to work on a few things with him. I made a video talking about KFI butter chicken sauce. I went to a baseball game with some fans who won a contest with Alokozay Tea. Derek was helping me more than I was helping him, and I couldn't expect him to bankroll my entire summer.

A magazine called the *Maple Street Press* commissioned me to write about James Reimer's and Keith Aulie's great rookie seasons with the Leafs. I did long interviews with both of them — especially my James. (I know he's married, shut up.)

The interviews took forever to transcribe, but it was great practice, I had fun doing it, and they were going to pay me about $300. It was so cool seeing the magazine on sale. Hey, I've been published!

Then I got a letter saying the magazine had gone bankrupt.

I got a cheque for $28.

I was miserable. I would search the internet aimlessly and go to bed super late. I obsessed over my YouTube numbers, but because I was feeling so sorry for myself, I was barely making any content. A smarter Steve would have made a video about every Leaf and, once I was done with that, every Leafs prospect. Once I had exhausted that topic, I'd do a video about every other NHL team . . .

"You have a YouTube channel that people actually watch, you idiot! Use it!"

"Yeah, but my camera sucks . . ."

"Then buy a new camera!"

"Nah, I think I'll just drink with my friends instead."

I had a little bit of money in savings, desperately clinging to the hope that I would move out before we put a man on Mars. I saved a lot of my Nike money. Why I didn't spend that money on boosting my camera quality, which was a point of contention with Nike because my videos were starting to look like ass, I'll never know. I was being too much of a baby.

I hung out with my friends and drank like a fish. You don't really get judged too harshly for drinking during your university years. But when it keeps up a year or two after you've graduated, it's like, "Alright, are you OK, man? This isn't OK."

I started slowly eating away at my savings or, I guess, drinking it away. Then after going to bed at two or three in the morning, maybe even later, I would set my alarm for eight or nine. Why? Because, I don't know, I'm supposed to be awake or something. I set my alarm that whole summer because what if TSN called because Bob McKenzie was sick and they needed a replacement they were willing to pay in gold bricks?

I'd had a setback. I was bitter. I was angry. I was out of my mind with exhaustion, despite not having done anything. I was in terrible shape. In short, I was not living my best life.

Today I look back and I'm ashamed. I know things worked out, but I still look back at that summer and wonder what I was thinking.

My future wife must have been so embarrassed. For crying out loud, she was still working at the zoo while I refused to! And my loving, hard-working, trusting parents? You might wonder how they allowed it. What a lucky bastard I am that my parents even tolerated that nonsense. Until then, I had usually shown at least some responsibility and decent judgment when it came to my career. That summer, I let them down. Man, I'd love to go back in time and fight myself.

Unfortunately, things only got worse.

I had ended my first full year as an employee at Leafs TV strong. After my Sportsnet debacle, I had a meeting with Clarkey and John that went very well. "We've been talking about giving you more," I remember them saying. Lots of different ideas were proposed, but the primary one was doing more TV, including potentially co-hosting a show during the 2011–12 season. I left that meeting excited and full of confidence. And just one week later, they called me in for another meeting. I assumed it was to finalize the stuff we had just talked about.

Alright. I'm going to get a wicked job, get famous, and make NHL minimum salary. Throw in a free jersey and we've got a deal.

I would also take a part-time job paying $15,000 over the course of the season.

The second I walked into the office, everything seemed off. I closed the door and sat down.

"So," John began. He paused, then looked at me. "I got fucked by the budget committee."

Well, that's certainly a bad way to start a meeting.

The details are hazy because my mind was racing, but here was the general idea: the budget had just been slashed. That new idea they had for me? Yeah, no, that's gone. The job I did this past year? Yeah, that's gone, too.

"We want to start a blog on RealSports.ca," John told me. "We'd like you to write for it, if you're still interested. I'm asking them to set aside $3,000 for that. For the season."

When I left the Sportsnet office after my disastrous job interview, I was fuming, but at least I knew I had something to fall back on once the season began. When I left Leafs TV that day, I had lost that thing to fall back on. Even the Nike partnership had run its course. The whole reason I didn't return to my job at the zoo was to look for more work in sports media, and I ended that summer with fewer prospects than I started with.

OK, so $3,000 divided by twelve months. That's . . . $250 per month? Dude . . .

Now what?

KEEP YOUR HEAD IN YOUR OWN BOAT

During high school, I competed in dragon boat. If you don't know what that is, it's a long boat that fits 20 paddlers in it, 10 on each side. For whatever reason, it sort of became our school's thing, sometimes getting up to 100 students registering to fill five boats.

Our coach was a teacher named Scott Madill. He was one of the funny teachers, always clowning around, but our school won almost every year so he clearly knew what he was talking about. Please don't let him read this, his head might weigh down the boat, and I don't want to put students through that.

He always told us one thing: keep your head in your own boat.

This quote is a variation of "run your own race," which I also learned while running track. If you keep your head in your own boat, you will paddle better because you're more focused on your form and technique. If you're running, it's best to look straight ahead of you because looking to your sides slows you down. Well, unless you're Usain Bolt, then you can just do whatever you want.

"Keep your head in your own boat" is as true in athletics as it is in life.

When I was younger, I wasted a lot of time looking at my peers. I did it in school, always feeling inferior when people had an internship and I didn't. Then once I got an internship, I started sweating that other students had actually found money-making jobs in the industry while I had none.

Once I experienced some success — the YouTube channel, the Nike Olympic experience, Leafs TV, and so on — I became even more insecure. I wanted every day to be like the Olympics, and when it wasn't, I felt like I was falling off — like I was failing.

Sometimes I would look at my peers and wonder if I was being leapfrogged. I couldn't help but ask myself why I wasn't where they were. How come they can do this? How come they got this opportunity and I didn't?

I was asking all the wrong questions. That line of thinking made me resent others who I thought didn't deserve it and resent myself for being an idiot. I should have been asking myself, "How can *I* do better?"

You're in charge of what you can do. If you have a strength, you need to know how to best use that strength. If you have a weakness, identify it, acknowledge it, and figure out what you can do to make it better.

Sure, you can get advice and lessons from others. That's just smart; you should always be doing that. But never let the green-eyed monster steer your boat.

MY DAY AS A SENATOR

Summer 2011 was essentially one long epic fail, but I did make one decent career decision.

Justin Fisher and I covered the Mastercard Memorial Cup in Mississauga, Ontario, just prior to the summer. We managed to snag some press passes in part due to my time with *Junior Hockey Magazine*. We hung around three other people in particular.

One was Julie Stewart-Binks, who I had met as a Leafs TV intern. She was doing some reporting for CBC at the time. She's a huge deal in the States now, with a resume that includes FOX Sports, Barstool, and ESPN. Another was Cam Charron, a Vancouverite writing for a website I had never heard of called AllHockey.ru. Why had I never heard of it? It was a Russian hockey site.

Lastly, there was Andrey Osadchenko, who also wrote for AllHockey.ru. Cam and Andrey went to school together out west and Andrey got a budget from them to travel to the Memorial Cup and talk to the Russian players at the tournament, along with others.

Andrey approached me a while after to say we should make videos together. I wasn't sure about the idea. I had gotten a few requests like this before but they all sounded an awful lot like, "Hey, I'd really like to latch on to your audience."

When I first met Andrey, he was this quiet guy with a thick

Russian accent, who I knew very little about. *How is this going to work?* I thought.

Luckily (or unluckily) I had some free time that summer. Screw it, let's try it.

The videos were very strange, but I actually really liked doing them because of how different they were. We would talk about the NHL and also the Kontinental Hockey League, or KHL. Andrey even put Russian subtitles underneath so that people could follow along. Looking back, with all of the jump-cuts added, I can't believe anybody watched.

Andrey must have been shy at the World Juniors or something because I quickly realized he's one of the top five loudest, most talkative people I've ever met.

Making these videos was an interesting lesson in cultural difference. Andrey was a brilliant guy, who, while still discovering North American culture himself, actually understood many of the nuanced differences and similarities between the North American and Russian cultures. For example, when I would make a joke in a video, he'd laugh a little, but then he'd explain a way to do it better to make the joke funny to Russians but also keep it funny in English.

He was also way more connected in the Russian sports media world than I thought. Apart from having the inside scoop on stories with legitimate sources, he would tell me about Russian hockey news that nobody in Canada was even aware of.

We uploaded the videos to my own YouTube channel for a while. They weren't exactly a hit but some of them got some laughs and I started to get a lot more viewers from overseas.

At some point in the fall of 2011, Andrey asked me if I wanted to see a Senators game in Ottawa. My natural instinct was to say, "No, thanks." First of all, it wasn't a Leafs game and second, Ottawa was something like a four-hour drive away. This wasn't just any road trip, though.

You see, Andrey knew Nikita Filatov. For those of you who don't remember, the Columbus Blue Jackets picked Filatov sixth overall in the 2008 NHL Entry Draft. He had all the skill in the world, but things just didn't work out for him in Columbus. He was traded to Ottawa on June 25, 2011, for a third-round pick.

In late October 2011, Filatov and Andrey had been talking and, one way or another, Nikita was able to get us tickets for a game if we were willing to make the trip.

Of course I was willing to watch a *free* hockey game. As for the long drive, I actually didn't mind the idea because only about two months earlier, I had finally purchased my first car. Why not take it out for a spin, check out a game, and hang out with an NHL player?

Steve, didn't you just say you lost your job at Leafs TV? Yep, I didn't know that before I made that purchase, so there's a little extra incentive to polish the ol' resume.

We got tickets for the game on November 5, 2011, a matchup between the Sens and Buffalo Sabres. We made the trek up to Ottawa along with Andrey's girlfriend at the time, Lina. I liked her, but she was sick as a dog and should have never come. She sprawled out on the backseat the whole ride up.

For those of you who have never been, the Senators' arena is in a pretty sparse area on the outskirts of town. It's a bit better now, but back in 2011 it was basically in the middle of an empty field. We didn't even realize we were close to the arena until were figured out that the traffic we were sitting in was to get into the parking lot. Seriously, it was pretty much pitch black — no lights, no civilization. Like I said, it's a bit better now.

The Leafs were playing that night against the Boston Bruins, so I naturally put on my Leafs jersey to go to the game. Yes, I was *that* guy. I thought I was so funny until I got to the arena and immediately felt like a total moron.

To make matters worse, while the Senators and Sabres were playing an entertaining, closely matched game, the Leafs completely got their asses kicked by the Bruins, 7–0, while Tyler Seguin — why did it have to be Tyler Seguin — scored a hat-trick.

Meanwhile, in the arena we were actually in, we were hoping to see Filatov have a great game. Unfortunately, he played a team-low 8:51, spread over just 10 shifts.

After scoring a goal earlier in the night, Derek Roy won the game for the Sabres in the sixth round of the shootout in his hometown.

We all still had fun, though. A bunch of Sens fans were making fun of me for my Leafs jersey and how bad they'd lost that night. I took a picture with a Sens fan who had a Danny Heatley jersey on, but he put tape on a few of the letters so it just spelled "HATE."

When Filatov got to the restaurant after the game, he ate like a king. Even if he didn't play much, the guy had just played in an NHL game. Not to mention that coaches had been barking at Filatov to put on weight ever since he was drafted.

After dinner, it was time to hit the bar. When we got there, Filatov led us through the main floor to the upstairs. Sure enough, tucked away in a corner were the Ottawa Senators.

Whoa, there's Milan Michálek! I said to myself.

Is that Zach Smith pouring shots?

That kid looks familiar. I'm pretty sure that's Erik Karlsson. He's supposed to be pretty good one day. Yep. After scoring 45 points as a sophomore, this was the beginning of Karlsson's breakout 78-point season as a third-year player.

The team had several buckets of beer up on the bar.

"Can you just take these?" I asked. I took one and nobody kicked my ass, so that meant yes. Oh yeah, no big deal, just drinking the Ottawa Senators' beer. Not since Curtis Joseph had any Leafs fan stolen from the Sens like that.

We realized we didn't have a bottle opener for any of the beer. Karlsson was looking around for one. Andrey saw this, pulled out his keys, and popped open Karlsson's beer with them.

Apparently, Karlsson had no idea you could do that, so he

pulled a few of the Sens over and told Andrey, "Show 'em!" So Andrey just stood there opening up beer for the Sens.

Then there was Kaspars Daugavins. He was a Latvian winger who rose to popularity because of a few fancy shootout moves that went viral on YouTube. He saw Andrey and me with Filatov and asked Nikita who we were. He told them, "Oh, these are just a couple of my friends. They're journalists."

Daugavins immediately got his neck up about being seen partying in front of reporters, but Filatov told him we were harmless, which is true. What's the worst that could happen? They'll write about this in a book one day?

Not long after that, Daugavins had obviously gotten over it because he was doing vodka shots with Andrey.

A couple giggling girls approached Filatov. Seeing that they were interested in Nikita, in my drunken brilliance I decided to pretend to be his Russian teammate and talk him up, as if he needed a wingman. I put on this terrible phoney baloney Russian accent and introduced him. Filatov even played along.

Unfortunately, 90 percent of the Russian I knew was just ridiculous profanity-laden phrases I had learned from Andrey.

"*Bookyet tibeeh v ladonee!*" I shouted at Filatov, with a big smile on my face. By the way, that roughly translates to "Here, take this bouquet of dicks!" It's not a common saying, but gosh is it fun.

Filatov just smiled back wide-eyed and nodded as if we were having an actual intelligent conversation. He must have been thinking, *What the hell is Andrey teaching this crazy Canadian?*

After we drank all of the Senators' beer, Andrey, Lina, and I decided to leave Filatov with his new friends and head back to our hotel.

We got into a cab. Before we got there, Andrey and I were blabbing on about something, probably hockey related. Andrey was mid-sentence in his rant when — BANG.

We jerked forward violently. Our cab has just gotten into an accident. The cabbie had tried to make it through a red so that he wouldn't get stuck in the middle of the intersection, but while he was accelerating, the car in front of him had slammed on its breaks.

Andrey just continued his rant like nothing happened.

"Andrey, can you take a breath!" I yelled. "We were just in a car accident, man! Is everyone OK?"

Our driver had already gotten out of the cab. He told us to get out and waved us toward another cab from the same company that just happened to be driving by. They rushed us into the cab and he drove us back to our hotel.

Hey, free ride! we thought. Looking back, our cab driver wasn't doing us a favour at all. We had just been in a car accident! What if one or all three of us had screwed up our neck? He were just rushing our drunk asses away from the situation before we could ask too many questions. He knew we were too wasted to care. Thank God we were OK.

We arrived back at the hotel. They went to bed while I crashed on the couch.

At some point during the middle of the night, I heard a voice and woke up. Andrey was mumbling something. I had no idea what language it was: Russian? English? Vodka?

In his mumbling stupor, I heard Andrey walking toward me.

Oh my God. If this guy does what I think he's gonna do, I'm gonna have to kick his ass.

Well, I wasn't far off.

Andrey walked over to the hotel fridge that was probably less than ten feet away from me, opened it, and just rocked a big ol' piss right in the fridge. With that, he went back to bed. Alcohol, man.

The next morning, we took some Advils but weren't up and running again until around noon.

Andrey got a message from Filatov. Apparently, one of the girls we were talking to the night before had invited him back to her place and he needed a ride back into town.

We were driving down the street, looking for Nikita, trying

to figure out which house he was in. That's when we saw him strolling down the street, kicking piles of dead leaves.

Once he noticed us, Nikita started in our direction, raised his arms above his head, and proudly screamed, "I AM SO FUCKING HUNGOVER" in Russian. And boy, was he. He looked like death warmed up. I have no idea how these NHL players do it, man. Luckily, the Senators had four days until their next game.

Filatov did his best to give me directions. "Right . . ." I didn't turn. "Right . . ." I still didn't turn. "Right, blyad!" he swore at me in Russian.

We went back to the same place we had dinner the night before and got lunch. We even saw a few of the Senators there again, looking much less hungover than us.

Stephane Da Costa was eating with his parents. Zenon Konopka was at the bar selling patrons on this little device of his that supposedly aerates wine and makes it taste better somehow. That's right, the tough guy with 195 professional hockey fights has his own wine and accessories.

Before you go judging Filatov too much, he was 21 years old. You might be thinking, *Stuff like this is why he didn't work out in the NHL.* Trust me, if you knew the partying habits of your favourite players, you would probably experience second-hand blackout.

Jared Clinton of *The Hockey News* wrote about an interview Filatov had given Alexei Schevchenko of Sports-Express.ru. Filatov talked about leaving North America due to financial issues that an AHL paycheck just couldn't cover.

Now Filatov is in his eighth straight KHL season and was even a KHL All-Star in the 2016–17 season.

After lunch, we made the long drive home.

And don't worry, we cleaned up the fridge.

STORY TIME WITH SMITTY

After the epic fail that was the summer of 2011, the 2011–12 hockey season mercifully began. Usually I would have been excited, regardless of the outlook for the Leafs, because it meant hockey was back. It also meant my videos were back, too!

That year, though, I didn't have that feeling at all.

I went to the Leafs' big home-opener party at Maple Leaf Square, but I didn't have a good time. I went into Real Sports to say hi to some friends, but that was it.

I used to work here, I said to myself. The "used to" part killed me. I wished I wasn't in such a public place because all I wanted to do was cry. I couldn't even go to Real Sports for a while after that. It just made me so upset. It was a reminder of failure.

There was one positive memory from my RealSports.ca blog and it was the first thing I wrote.

A while back, I watched comedian Patrice O'Neal talk about something that happened to him when he was younger that he called the punk test. Basically, somebody would check to see if they could bully him, and once they realized they could, they'd rob him.

In my blog post, I took that idea and applied it to the Boston Bruins, who were the reigning Stanley Cup champions. They were running away with the league in the first two months of the season. What made me make the comparison, though, was an incident involving Milan Lucic completely running over Sabres goalie Ryan Miller. Nobody on the Sabres retaliated. Why? Because it was Milan Lucic. And if you survive him, then there's Shawn Thornton, Adam McQuaid, and Zdeno Chara. The Bruins could do whatever they wanted.

The article got picked up quite a bit in Boston and started to rack up the hits. The most encouraging feedback came from Justin Bourne, a former professional and college hockey player, who had wrote about the punk test for TheScore.com.

He wrote about how I had touched on something that he as a player was never quite able to describe. To get props like that from an actual player was a huge confidence boost that I badly needed at the time.

Finally, I decided enough was enough. *No more moping, Steve. Pick your ass up. Find a job.*

My friend Tom from school was always keeping me up to date on CBC job postings. They were usually just suggestions, but one day he showed me one and said, "You have to apply for this. Do it."

Through Tom, I got an interview with his boss at CBC, a guy named Paul Burke.

This was my first actual job interview, albeit an informal one, since the disaster I had with Sportsnet, and I prepped for this thing big time. Still had to choose between the same two dress shirts, though.

The job I thought I was interviewing for was a bit outside of my comfort zone, but the bones of it had to do with hockey highlights. I figured I could at least learn the rest of it.

As we went through my job experience, Paul seemed to think so, too, but this was the CBC: they didn't need an intern for this job, they needed someone who knew what they were doing.

"What's this about YouTube videos?" he asked with a raised eyebrow.

Tap-dancing time, Steve. Let's go!

I actually got up and asked to use his computer, so I could show him what I was all about. Did I show him one of my Leafs videos I had shot on my half-decade-old webcam? Hell no! Here's me with a Canadian Olympic gold medallist driving around in a gold Cadillac.

We spoke a bit more after I showed him the video. He seemed to only be half-listening. This time it wasn't because there was a TV above my head, though. I could see the wheels turning in his head. He was thinking. The longer I talk, the longer I stay in this room, and the longer he thinks. *Keep blabbing, Steve! It's the only thing you're good at!*

"I'm not sure the job we spoke about earlier would be the greatest fit for you," he began.

My heart sank. Here we go — yet another failure. This damn business. It's the recession that ruined it. Nobody's hiring, that's why I can't get a job. Why of all times did I have to graduate now? Why couldn't it have been in the 1970s or 1980s? I'd stroll into work with a half-unbuttoned silk dress shirt and about six pounds of gold chains around my neck.

"Good morning, Steve!" I'd hear.

"Oh! Good morning, Johnny Carson," I'd reply.

"Did you get that raise you asked for, Steve?"

"They actually gave me more than I asked for, Johnny!"

"That's great news! Oh, and Steve . . ."

"Yes, Johnny?"

"You're my best friend."

But no. Because the banks don't know how to make cars anymore or whatever the hell is going on, I've put all my eggs in the hockey basket and I'm totally screwed.

That conversation took place in my head over the span of about 0.5 seconds. Apparently Paul's sentence wasn't done.

"I'm not sure the job we spoke about earlier would be the greatest fit for you," he'd begun before Johnny Carson had interrupted. "But you know what? I think we could use you somewhere else."

If I didn't think I would have been arrested, I would have sprinted down to the CBC atrium, set a table on fire, and put myself through it like a professional wrestler. Hell yes!

In reality, I probably said, "Oh, that's great."

The job, which was part-time, usually Friday and Saturday nights, was simple: make highlights for the CBC Sports website. What made this gig even cooler than Leafs TV is I was expected to voice the highlights as well. This meant I needed to write a script for them, too. With editing, that's a lot of work.

On my first night of training, I was introduced to several of my new coworkers.

"This is Smitty. He'll be your editor on most nights."

"My editor?" I asked.

"Well, yeah. Did you think you were doing that on your own?"

"I did at Leafs TV," I replied.

"Oh," they laughed. "Well, you'll like this better then."

I still had to send the editor the clips I wanted, but that was a hell of a lot easier than cutting up a highlight pack on my own.

We made somewhere between five and 10 highlight packs per night. Instead of six-minute monsters for one game, each pack was 60 to 90 seconds long. It wasn't just hockey, either. Basketball, baseball, soccer — you name it.

Not every business is like this, but sports media is definitely a field where you get to say, "Here, look what I made today." It was one thing to make a highlight pack, but to send people a link to a pack that had my voice on it gave me extra pride. It was like a personalized stamp.

Hockey and soccer were the easiest packs to make, by far. They're low-scoring sports so, for the most part, just show the goals. There are other things, but that's the meat of it.

Basketball and football were difficult and not just because I knew less about them. They're high-scoring sports, so you need to pick and choose which scoring plays you're going to show, then let your writing do the rest. For example, there might have been an amazing dunk, but if it was a relatively insignificant basket in the game, you need to throw in that it was part of a 15–2 run, or something. A football player might make an impossible catch but get tackled at the two-yard line. Well, don't show them running it in — that's boring. Show the incredible catch and just say that it led to a touchdown.

Another weird one was fights.

At Leafs TV, I usually included fights. The highlight packs needed to be six minutes long and the Leafs sucked so my choices were slim. At CBC, you could pick and choose. If the fight changed the story of the game, then of course you included it. Highlight packs are storytelling. If you omit something that explains the story of the game, you're doing your audience a disservice.

One of the older guys I regularly worked with told me to never include fights in highlight packs. He was nice enough to sit down with me after one of my first shifts to give me some tips. It was then that he told me not to include fights. I thought that was weird, but whatever. Fine.

Then one night, there was a game with a big fight that had an effect on the rest of the game. Smitty asked me why I hadn't included it and I told him it was because I was told I shouldn't.

"By who?" he asked.

I told him. Truth be told, after a month or so there, I still didn't know who my boss was or how the hierarchy worked. I just assumed that everybody who was older than me, which was everybody, had authority over me.

"Well, I don't want to piss him off," I said. "Isn't he my boss?"

Smitty gave me this look as if to say, *Oh, honey.* He just laughed and said, "He's not your boss. Show the damn fight."

Talking to Smitty every night at CBC was something you didn't even have to pay me to do. Jeff Valks, one of my other coworkers, referred to it as "Story Time with Smitty." I never knew who was going to be my editor when I arrived for my shift, and I liked them all, but when I saw Smitty, I would text my girlfriend, "Story time!!!"

Smitty read a lot of weird stuff. One extremely slow weeknight, he showed me all these conspiracy clips on YouTube. Like fun ones, I mean. Aliens and stuff.

He always had little random gems to drop during conversations. I was talking to him about trying to lose some weight. He told me to avoid eating potatoes with dinner.

"Your body knows what to do with food, like, 'Oh, OK, I like that, I'll use that, that too,' but the potatoes are pretty much useless. Your stomach's just making vodka with those things."

Another time, I was telling him about my friend's stinky cat.

"That's just a dominance thing, like a claiming thing," he explained. "You use the parking garage down the street, right? You know how it smells like piss? That's aggravating to you, right? You get aggravated. That's something ancient in you, dude. You're smelling another male's piss and something in our brain is going, 'Who the hell does that piss belong to and what are they doing here?' It's like they claimed your space and that makes that ancient thing in your brain get all bent out of shape."

I loved working with Smitty. Oh, no, it couldn't possibly be that pee smells disgusting, Smitty. It has to be ancient monkey chemistry or something.

I haven't even gotten to the best part about the job: *Hockey Night in Canada*.

My first Saturday night at CBC was a dream come true. We did all our work on the eighth floor, but we were invited up to the 10th where the "Coach's Corner" studio was. Outside of that studio, there were snacks, coffee, and something you could grab for dinner. It was usually pizza, but they sometimes had sandwiches and, for a little while, calzones.

On more than one occasion, I heard someone complain "Ah, pizza again?" I remembered when I had to beg just to get my $300 intern invoice processed, and I wanted to smush their face right into their pizza. It's amazing they feed us anything, you brat.

Every so often, I would catch a glimpse of Don Cherry. No, he wasn't constantly shouting about Russians or visors, but he was definitely shouting. There's something about his voice that just carries; it's from the diaphragm.

Working Saturday nights meant sacrificing my weekends. I didn't mind. That was the gig. And I loved the job.

My friends loved it, too. This new job meant they all had a sober friend downtown with a car. I would get out of work around 2 a.m., when the bars close. My friends would text me throughout the night and let me know if they needed to be driven back to Scarborough or Pickering. We all started referring to the Saturday night drives as the Dangle Dial.

That name would take on a new meaning in a couple years, but we'll save that for later.

Driving home at two on a Sunday morning meant driving home with people who had been out all night. Many of them had to be drunk, showing off for their friends, or both, winding and bending all over the place. The Don Valley Parkway was horrifying. It's amazing I didn't get into an accident. For the love of God, don't drink and drive.

I eventually figured out who my boss was at the CBC — a guy named John Pudy. He was awesome to work for: very friendly, very understanding, and very kind. That season, the Leafs had a strong first half and looked poised to finally make the playoffs, only to choke and miss out yet again. Luckily, Pudy had found out about my videos, and he came up with the idea of having me do daily playoff recap videos for the website. Of course I wanted to do that — and I could talk about actual playoff teams instead of the stupid Leafs.

I sat in the studio as the L.A. Kings defeated the New Jersey Devils in the 2012 Stanley Cup Final, winning their first-ever

Stanley Cup. The hockey season was over, as was my employment at CBC for the time being. I wasn't laid off, but there just wasn't enough work for the lowliest associate producer to actually do.

Overall, it was a great job, but there were definitely times when I had some doubts. At Leafs TV, my face was getting on their website and on TV on a regular basis. Here I was just doing highlights. *Is this what I want to do forever?*

You would think that asking myself questions like that would help me focus on making my LFR videos better. Nope! They were arguably the worst they'd ever been.

My editing was fine. My speed and energy weren't bad. But the Leafs had truly broken my heart. I had begun to fall out of love with them and honestly wasn't sure if I wanted to continue making LFR videos the next year. I had stopped caring about my YouTube channel, the thing that helped get me this far in the first place. I thought maybe I was pigeonholing myself, limiting myself to a losing team, with no future for the team or myself. I remember one video in particular near the end of the season, after yet another soul-sucking Leafs loss, my postgame video was barely a minute long. Rather than review the game, all I did was list the things Chicago Blackhawks captain Jonathan Toews had accomplished since the last time the Leafs made the playoffs. Zero effort, zero heart in it, and zero fun. Who the hell wants to watch that?

I didn't appreciate my toys anymore, and I was about to have them taken away.

YOU HAVE TO KNOW THE GAME

I was thrilled the zoo gave me my job back in the summer of 2012. I wasn't totally sure they would say yes, but they agreed to let me go back to doing commentary on the zoomobile. I could still remember the tour. Heck, I did that tour so many times, I could probably still do it today.

I was making some cash, most of my old zoo friends were still there, and the new folks were cool, too. It was great.

It helped that I had the security blanket of CBC returning in just a couple months; I didn't get many shifts in the summer without *Hockey Night in Canada*.

There was constant talk about a potential NHL lockout shortening or even cancelling the upcoming 2012–13 season, but I didn't think it was really going to happen. Surely the NHL owners and NHL Players' Association would come to a deal.

June turned into July and there was no deal. July turned into August and there was no deal. August to September: nothing.

Finally, on Saturday, September 15, while I was on the back of a zoomobile, the NHL lockout was announced. Let's get the obvious out of the way: I was pissed. Really pissed. My cool job at CBC was gone and my security blanket was gone. Suddenly I looked around the zoo and thought, *Well, this is it. I just work at the zoo.*

But, come on. How long could this thing possibly last? Don't panic, Steve. Just enjoy your time among the animals . . .

One stormy day, I was working on the zoomobile. The number of busses going around that day had decreased due to the rain and low attendance. That day, my job was to stay behind at the main station to wait on guests and answer questions about the schedule.

When there weren't any guests, you were supposed to clean the station. While I was sweeping, two women who worked in the office came down. We started talking about this and that, just making idle chit-chat, when one of them, wearing thick black-framed Kyle Dubas glasses, asked me what I planned on doing once I was done working at the zoo.

"I used to write for this junior hockey show," I explained with pride.

"Oh, do you know who Stan Butler is?" Kyle Dubas glasses asked.

Of course I knew who Stan Butler was. At the time, he had been the head coach of the Ontario Hockey League's Brampton Battalion for over a decade. In fact, even though the team would go on to relocate to North Bay, Stan Butler is still their head coach.

When I covered junior, the Battalion had Cody Hodgson. Some of you might scoff at that name now, but before he ran into back problems, Hodgson was one of the best, if not the best, players in all of junior hockey. He was selected 10th overall by the Vancouver Canucks in 2008, put up 92 points during the 2008–09 season, and was named the CHL Player of the Year. He even led the 2009 World Junior Hockey Championships in scoring, with 16 points in six games.

So, yes, I was very aware of who Stan Butler was, I explained. We even had him on the show to talk about Hodgson, as well as a young teammate of his named Matt Duchene, who ended up going third overall in the 2009 draft.

"How do you know him?" I asked.

"My husband and I are good friends with him," she explained.

Right away, my broke student senses started tingling. When you have no idea what the future holds and sense a potential opportunity, it's hard not to be a little selfish.

Realistically, what could this person do for me? Probably nothing. But what if she could make some kind of an in-person introduction with one of the most experienced coaches in junior hockey? What if I somehow got an exclusive interview with him and an executive at TSN or Sportsnet saw it? Like many times when I was looking for an opportunity in media, I didn't really know what I was looking for at that exact moment, but at the same time, I knew I was looking for it.

It was an opportunity to talk about hockey on a slow, boring day while, at the same time, impressing some of my older coworkers. Even if it didn't lead to some kind of opportunity in media, at least I could be in the good books of someone with a little seniority.

Then the conversation took an abrupt turn.

"Do you play hockey?" the other woman asked.

I always hated answering this question. There's only so many ways you can jazz up "No." The real answer was "No, I don't currently play hockey, but I also never have." I never used to say it like that; I would always give some wishy-washy answer, but it still always ended up at the same place: No.

"What?" the lady with the Kyle Dubas glasses asked with surprise.

Yeah, I was used to that. I would always say something along the lines of "Well, I don't really talk about X's and O's" or "It's not like I'm trying to become an analyst." Most people would just accept that answer, assume that maybe there are some things about me or my work that maybe they don't know, and move on.

Nope. Her next question really hit me.

"How do you do what you do?"

I don't know if she meant to ask it the way that she did. It could have been delivered in a curious way, like, "Oh, that's interesting. How do you talk about hockey even though you've never played?"

This wasn't that at all. Her voice said, "How do you do what you do?" but her facial expression said, "Who the hell do you think you are, kid? Where do you get the audacity to talk about a game you don't even know?"

I was taken aback. You won't often find me at a loss for words, but I didn't have a response to that.

The other lady must have seen the look on my face, because she sheepishly responded to her friend on my behalf with something to the effect of "He doesn't need to be a hockey player to talk about hockey."

At this point, a lot of people might pick up on the idea that they have created a bit of an awkward situation. Not Dubas glasses, though. She doubled down.

"You have to know the game," she said, deepening her voice while slowly nodding her head with her eyes closed.

She said, "You have to know the game," the way I imagine you tell a kid the truth about Santa Claus. She might as well have said, "I'm telling you this for your own good: drop this ridiculous little dream of yours right now, you silly child."

I don't remember the conversation continuing for long after that. I was too busy internally processing the seemingly unalienable truth that I needed to change career paths.

Soon after, both women left me alone at the station, either because their break was nearly over or they had decided to go be bored somewhere else.

When I knew they were both out of sight and after I quickly peeked into the front courtyard to make sure there were no customers around, I started to cry. I wish I could say it was a stoic single-tear type of cry, but no, I cried like a baby.

I couldn't have looked more pathetic if I tried, sweeping and crying alone in the rain. After a minute or two, I realized that one of the tour busses would be returning. I intentionally left the cover of the main station and walked into the rain to get soaked, so, hopefully, nobody would be able to tell I had been crying.

I wasn't upset because of what she'd said — she didn't say anything that I hadn't heard online for over half a decade — it was the way that she said it.

Sometimes, people can say something to you and it has no effect. Then somebody else could say the exact same thing in a different way, and it's like their words cracked open the dam that kept all of your greatest fears and insecurities from flooding into your mind.

In my mind, she was right. What the hell was I doing? I was a total fraud. I didn't know anything about hockey, and now I knew everyone could see right through me. Nobody took me seriously and nobody would ever take me seriously. What was I going to do for the rest of my life? What could I do? I wasn't good at anything else and, apparently, I wasn't even good at this media thing, either. Had I made a mistake? Was I in too deep to abruptly change career paths now? Were these past few years all for nothing? Was interning a waste of time? Was school a waste of time? How the hell was I ever going to move out of my parents' house?

I'm a loser.

It might sound a bit dramatic, and of course it was dramatic. If there's anything that a frustrated, confused, and insecure person who's trying to figure out who they are can be, it's dramatic.

A while after this incident, maybe a few months or a year later, my friend Fisher and I went to a local watering hole in east Scarborough called the Black Dog Pub. Retired Detroit Red Wings forward Kris Draper, who grew up just a few blocks away from the pub, would bring the Stanley Cup to the Black Dog whenever he got his day with it after a Red Wings championship.

A few minutes after we sat down at the bar, Fisher pointed to an older man down the bar from us.

"Do you know who that is?" he asked.

I knew exactly who it was: Stan Butler.

A couple years before, I would have been in awe to even be in his presence. I might have even gone over and introduced myself. Hell, we had already spoken on the phone before. Why not?

Instead, I couldn't help but stare daggers at him. Was that fair? Of course not, but the sight of him reminded me of that rainy moment at the zoo. The beer probably didn't help, either. Luckily, I don't think he noticed.

I've had many moments of frustration and doubt about my successes and failures in the sports media business, but that one always sticks out as one of the worst.

THE
LOCKOUT

In summer 2012, TheLeafsNation.com approached me to bring me on as a contributor. Specifically, it was Cam Charron, who now works in the Leafs analytics department, and Thomas Drance, who is now the VP of communications and PR for the Florida Panthers. At the time, though, they wrote for a collection of team-specific hockey blogs for The Nation Network.

And, then, two months later, Andrey and I were in his apartment again, with no hockey to write about because of the stupid lockout.

We usually laughed until our faces hurt whenever we would hang out, but this was different. We were two young guys trying to establish ourselves in hockey, but because of the NHL lockout, there was no hockey.

Well . . . not "no" hockey. One thing the Kontinental Hockey League, or KHL, had was a surprisingly decent YouTube channel. They uploaded highlights for almost every game, and Andrey and I would watch them.

While it was great that the KHL decided to do this, they still clearly had no idea what they were doing content-wise. The highlight packs were often nine or 10-minute monstrosities. They usually didn't even have commentary, and if they did, it was in Russian. No transitions, no flow — any first-year media student could have done better the morning the assignment was due, while wasted.

What drove us nuts about the bad video quality wasn't just that it made the videos harder to watch, but we thought the KHL was blowing a legitimate opportunity to give their league more exposure to a hockey-starved North American audience. With no NHL hockey and with so many of the NHL's brightest stars flocking overseas, the KHL should have been pulling out all the stops. They could be making a lot of money . . .

Wait a sec, make money . . .

A light bulb went off. At this point, I didn't know how to do much in this business, but I knew I could make a hockey highlight pack. I know how they flow, I know how to edit video well enough, and I know how to write scripts.

While Andrey wasn't as technically savvy, he knew the league well, knew the players, and, maybe most importantly of all, he knew Russian. When we were confused by a play, all Andrey had to do was listen to the commentary or look for a game recap and he could translate it instantly.

We hatched a plan: make our own KHL highlight packs, about 90 seconds to two-minutes long each, with English commentary. Andrey could pitch this idea to his contacts within the league, and we could essentially sell their own highlights back to them, but they'd be way better. North Americans would love it and the KHL would open itself up to a whole new market.

No fancy studio. No budget. Just me, Andrey, and my laptop.

It was a great idea in theory, but at the end of the day, who the hell are we? We were fresh-out-of-school dummies with no real reputation. Sure, we had a great idea, but we needed to prove we could execute. We decided to pick a game and make a demo.

The next day, Andrey came over to my parents' house and we got to work. We couldn't have picked a better game: Metallurg Magnitogorsk against Salavat Yulaev. NHL stars like Evgeni Malkin and Sergei Gonchar were on Metallurg while Salavat was a team with a track record of winning championships. To boot, Malkin and Gonchar were making their season debuts.

It was a barn-burner. Malkin got nailed with a big hip check in the first period. It was 3–2 for Salavat after two periods. Malkin set up the tying goal in the third. Finally, a player named Sergei Zinovyev scored his hat-trick goal, in overtime, to give Salavat the big 4–3 OT win.

The video was almost three minutes long, which is at least twice as long as it should have been, but it was solid work. Yes, it looked like it had been made on a MacBook, but that's because it was. I knew what I was doing, though; the writing flowed well with the action.

Before I go making myself sound like a tech wiz, guess how Andrey and I recorded the audio for our commentary. Microphone? No, I didn't have one of those. Our phones? That would have been smart, and we would eventually go on to do that as the season progressed, but no.

We recorded ourselves on a camera.

I'm serious. We actually recorded video of, like, our chests, and just cut out the audio and put it underneath the game footage.

As bootleg as that sounds, it was at the very least good enough to get the job done.

Andrey was an encyclopedia. He made sure to always mention if a player was drafted or had played in the NHL. It gave the North American audience something they could relate to, maybe even create some nostalgia. "Oh, yeah, I remember that guy!"

The reception was great. About 5,000 people saw the video in the first three days it was up on my YouTube channel, which was a great number for me at the time. As we predicted, over 70 percent of our audience was from North America.

We thought the KHL would love it, but guess what. The video got flagged for a copyright violation because we were using footage we had ripped off the KHL's YouTube channel.

Luckily, a bunch of our Russian "Joining the Rush" viewers messaged the folks at the KHL to tell them that they wanted to see more highlight packs from us.

Andrey sent the demo pack to a bunch of people overseas. Two of them were play-by-play guys, one of whom put Andrey in contact with a producer. The producer didn't see much use for the packs because he didn't see how they would fit on TV, but we were getting the word out, which was the most important part.

One of the people who saw it was a young media professional in Russia we called Vladdy. He was the former media manager for the KHL team CSKA Moscow (Central Red Army) and now a video editor with the KHL. He put the video into the hands of a guy named Sergei, who happened to be a managing editor with the KHL's marketing department. Andrey worked out a deal for them to pay us by the pack. If we covered games, we got paid.

Sometimes we would do it at my place and sometimes we'd do it at Andrey's, but we churned those highlight packs out like a factory. On top of that, Andrey found Russian sites to pay us for our "Joining the Rush" videos, and he even managed to get us some money to make clips for a national TV station in Russia. Those videos must have sounded horrible on television. I talk too fast for a lot of Canadians, so I can only imagine how much they struggled just to read the subtitles over there.

There was even a "Joining the Rush" fan page on a Russian social media site called VK.com. Some 15- or 16-year-old kid set it up so that other fans of the show could talk about the channel and share memes.

Years later, Andrey told me that kid was Alexandar Georgiev, a current goalie for the New York Rangers. Because the world is smaller than the tiniest Russian doll.

The first payment from the KHL came late. I was worried, but Andrey told me to sit tight. Sure enough, it finally came. Was it the right amount of money? It was hard to tell because of the exchange rate of rubles to American dollars to Canadian dollars. *You know what? It's a decent enough chunk of change. It's probably right. I'll take it.*

That happened a few times over the next few months. *Ah, that's probably right.*

Andrey and I also made our way down to Sarnia, Ontario, to cover a Team Russia versus Team OHL Subway Super Series game. Nail Yakupov, who had recently been drafted first overall by the Edmonton Oilers, was one of Russia's best players, and we had been sent to do a feature on him. We interviewed both him and his former OHL teammate Alex Galchenyuk, in Russian. Well, Andrey did. I held the camera.

When I wasn't doing KHL highlights, I was trying to broaden my horizons even more with a couple odd jobs.

I worked for a startup agency called Ambit as a junior social media strategist, and, basically, my job was to just come up with Nike tweets. It didn't really work out — it just wasn't for me.

I also gave a shot at being the in-arena host for the OHL's Mississauga Steelheads. They paid me $30 per game to help do giveaways, prizes, contests, and all that fun stuff — ignore the fact that I still lived in Scarborough and spent at least half the money getting to the games and back.

The KHL highlights kept ramping up, so thank goodness I was able to start splitting the Steelheads hosting duties with a girl named Aly Munro. She was a lifesaver, and by the end of the season, she was the full-time in-arena host. Since then, I've even seen her host for the Toronto Blue Jays.

That was the hustle until finally, blessedly, the NHL lockout ended in mid-January 2013.

I had my KHL stuff, the Steelheads, and I'm getting CBC back? Beautiful!

But I wasn't just happy to get hockey back. I got my YouTube channel and LFR videos back, too.

They say absence makes the heart grow fonder, and that was definitely the case for me when it came to the LFR videos. "You don't like this toy anymore? Well, then, I guess you won't miss it, right?"

No, actually. I missed it. A lot.

I was full of piss and vinegar and ready to bounce off the walls, not just for the videos, but because I had actually missed the Leafs. I had gotten away from that fact. Maybe I was trying to become more professional, but I decided to ditch that charade. I'm Steve Dangle, and I'm a Leafs fan. It's what I am. If you're interested, then hello and welcome, and if you're not, hey, the internet is a big place.

My first shift back at CBC was everything I wanted it to be. I remember sitting down in front of all the screens, and with five minutes to go before puck drop, my boss John Pudy walked into the room. He came straight for me, shook my hand with a smile, and said, "Welcome home."

What kind of boss does that? A great one.

With the return of the Leafs came the return of James Reimer. No more injuries like the previous season, just his slightly awkward, bulky style, winning hockey games.

Something else was bubbling over.

I remember 2013 as the real beginning of the analytics war. Hockey's new advanced stats had been around for a number of years, but they gained a heightened popularity in 2013, once hockey and all the blogs that came with it started writing again.

At the same time, the pushback increased tenfold. Older, traditional types called stuff like Corsi a bunch of meaningless blogger nonsense.

The fact that James Reimer kept bailing out the Leafs throughout the shortened 48-game season made the team even more fun to yell and scream about. I felt like Jessie Spano from *Saved by the Bell*. "I'm so excited! I'm so scared!"

To add to the fun, I thought, *Hey, you know what? How about I marry my girlfriend?*

It was time. Sarah-Louise and I had been together for six years, and I knew I wanted to spend the rest of my life with her. After thinking I wasn't going to make any money this season, I had actually made a decent chunk of change. I was saving up for a down payment on a house.

I dipped into my savings account and bought her a ring with all my rubles.

Also right around that time, March 2013, I got the bright idea to apply for yet another job. This time, it would be part-time hockey highlights at the NHL Network, which was actually in the TSN studios at the time. To my surprise, I got the job. Just a couple shifts per week, but it was something.

To recap, I had:

- CBC,
- NHL Network,
- the KHL highlights and "Joining the Rush,"
- the Mississauga Steelheads,
- Ambit, the startup agency I freelanced for, and
- the LFR videos.

I basically didn't sleep. But this squirrel was storing all his nuts in a hole, in the hopes of marrying his girlfriend and moving out of his parents' tree.

Sarah-Louise was a supply teacher. On my first night at the NHL Network, she texted me to tell me she had taken the next day off because the school she was supposed to go to was far away and there was a snowstorm.

Oh my God — she's off tomorrow and somehow I'm off from every one of my jobs. This is it. I have to propose. I told her I got us a behind-the-scenes, special access tour of the Hockey Hall of Fame. She wasn't a hockey fan at all when I met her, but it had grown on her over the years, and she had wanted to check out the Hockey Hall of Fame. I made up the behind-the-scenes part because I wanted to go straight to the Stanley Cup room, which is at the end, and I needed an excuse to bypass the rest of the exhibits to go straight there. As soon as the place opened, we went to the Cup room and into the vault where they keep the old nameplates from the Cup. She always told me her only condition for a proposal was privacy. Can't get much more private than a vault.

She said yes.

One day, after the engagement, I was going through my finances. It was hard to keep track of everything. I was trying to figure out if the KHL had given me everything I was owed. I came up with a number.

"What?" I blurted out.

"What is it?" Sarah-Louise asked.

"It's OK," I told her. "I must have made a mistake."

But I didn't. I calculated it two, three, four, five times, and all five times I came to the same conclusion: the KHL owed me money.

How much money?

$11,635.

I had just turned 25 and we were trying to move out and get married. That's a life-changing amount of money. I alerted them to the issue . . . save that thought.

The Leafs made the playoffs for the first time since I had started making videos. Six. Long. Years.

With a combination of excitement for hockey being back after a long lockout and the Leafs being playoff bound, my viewership boomed. Maybe people were just happy to watch upbeat Leafs coverage for a change, but I know I was having more fun with my videos than I had ever had before.

We know how that ended . . .

I was in Maple Leaf Square for Game 7. With Phil Kessel's 3–1 goal, the crowd roared. With Kadri's 4–1 goal, everyone verged on spontaneous combustion. I was jumping and screaming along with everybody else. The world was the happiest blue-and-white blur.

I remember thinking about how the Leafs would get the New York Rangers in round two. *Dude, they can beat them! I* thought. *Hell, they just beat the Bruins!*

Shortly after . . . I can still hear the chants.

"Nah nah. Nah nah nah nah. Hey hey hey. Goodbye."

"Shut up!" I screamed internally. Actually, it might have even been out loud.

4–2. Oh God.

4–3. This isn't happening.

4–4. It happened. I literally buckled at the knees and collapsed. If there's footage of Maple Leaf Square at the moment that goal was scored, there's no way you couldn't pick me out of the crowd. I hit the deck like I had been shot. And I had been shot, right in my feelings.

It was the least enthusiastic Game 7 overtime atmosphere in Stanley Cup playoffs history. It's like we were all waiting for it. When the Bruins, Patrice Bergeron specifically, scored to win the game, the crowd's reaction wasn't even a fraction of what it was when the Bruins tied it. I didn't even react. I just looked down at my wife-to-be, she looked back at me, and we waddled off to the train for the quiet ride home.

I had finally converted Sarah-Louise into a Leafs fan, and this was her first real heartbreak with the team. She handled it pretty well, though. I think she was just glad I could finally shave my playoff beard.

MRS.
DANGLE

I remember the day I decided to marry her.

I was extremely pissed off about something. Like day-ruined mad. I don't even remember what it was. Something to do with Andrey and the KHL videos we did.

She called while I was having a private pity party for myself. Within about 45 seconds, she made me laugh. I don't even remember what she said, all I know is that in less than one minute, all the frustration I had felt over absolutely nothing just melted away.

She didn't know it at the time, but that was the moment I decided I wanted to spend the rest of my life with her.

I asked Sarah-Louise's dad for permission to ask her to marry me on February 28, 2013. I know this because there was a Leafs game on. We met at Magwyer's in Ajax under the guise of asking for "tax advice."

I showed up early. The Leafs were playing the Islanders that night, so I sat down, ordered a drink, and watched the game. By the end of the first, it was a 1–1 tie.

Finally, her dad sat down with me while I beat around the bush with agonizing small talk. Thankfully, he cut me off and asked, "What can I help you with, Steve?" Word salad poured out of my mouth as I said basically everything other than "Can I marry your daughter?" I also got distracted because the Leafs had a great second period: James van Riemsdyk put them in front, and Nazem Kadri scored his second of the night to put them up 4–2 by the end of the period.

After I finally asked and he agreed, and after I yammered on because in my nervousness I ended up getting pretty drunk, my future father-in-law drove me home. By the time I got back to my house — sorry, my parents' house — the Islanders had tied it 4–4 and it was heading to overtime.

Luckily, I got dropped off just in time to watch Mikhail Grabovski set up Dion Phaneuf for the overtime snipe on Evgeni Nabokov, for the 5–4 Leafs win.

That wasn't exactly one of the most important Leafs wins of all time, or even of that season, but I will never forget it.

Sarah-Louise bought me my first webcam. She made me a cake when I got 89.7 percent in a university class because that was the closest I was ever going to get to a 90. She also made a cake when I got my internship at the Fan 590. She put up with my tired cranky ass when I would drive us to our job at the zoo after a night of interning. She puts up with me yelling and screaming about a hockey team for a living. She's been to all kinds of events I've spoken at, including the tailgate parties at Maple Leaf Square, when I was so nervous I could've passed out.

Likewise, I'm always there for her. When I'm working from home, I try to keep the house nice so that she can just come home and relax. When she was in school, I supported her and cheered her on while she wrote about 20 essays in one month, trying to get into teacher's college.

We make each other better. At least, I know she makes me better.

If you meet someone who brings out the best in you, wants to make you happy, and wants to help you succeed, and you want to do the same for them, you're going to win more often than you lose.

SIDNEY CROSBY'S PANTS

Let me take you back in time about nine years. Remember that grade 11 math class I told you about? The one all the way back in 2004? A teenaged Adam Wylde said to me, "I think one day, you and I will have our own sports show together."

A few years later, I started up my own YouTube channel, but I was a long way away from having my own show.

Adam, on the other hand, was killing it. At age 19, he worked at a radio station in Barrie, Ontario, doing overnights. Shortly after, he got a job as an evening DJ on a radio station in Halifax, Nova Scotia, which he dropped out of school to pursue.

One day, he called me in a panic.

"Hey Adam, what's —"

"Steve!" he interrupted. "Turn on Jack FM!"

"Why would I —"

"Just turn on Jack FM!"

I had no idea why he was asking me to do this. People our age didn't really listen to Jack FM because its reputation, bluntly, was that it was music for old people. It had previously been a relatively popular and hip station called KiSS 92.5, but it had rebranded years prior.

"What's playing?" he asked.

"Nickelback," I told him.

"OK. Just wait until the next commercial break."

Because I'm a really good friend, I waited until the end of the song when a radio promo began with music and an unfamiliar voice. To my surprise, it wasn't Jack FM anymore.

"It said KiSS 92.5," I told him.

"Yes!" Adam yelled. "Buddy, I'm coming home!"

He had only learned about the station's rebrand back to KiSS five seconds ago. Granted, as a guy in his early 20s, he was a lot more likely to get a job at cool, young KiSS than Jack, but he was talking like he had already gotten a job he hadn't even applied for yet. That's Adam, though. Supremely confident in his abilities.

To the surprise of no one who knew him, Adam got the job and was back in Toronto, working evenings on KiSS 92.5. When I was in Vancouver for the 2010 Olympics, he threw me a bone by letting me call in to his station to be his Olympic correspondent. Shortly after, he took an evening gig at Virgin Radio in Toronto, which led to a job as a morning radio host for Virgin radio in Calgary. Just like that, Adam was gone again.

After a few years in Calgary, Adam returned home to KiSS 92.5 in Toronto, but this time for an afternoon show. Which brings us to spring 2013.

Before he had left for Calgary, Adam introduced me to his friend Chris Shapcotte, a Vancouverite who was the imaging producer for CHFI, a massive Rogers radio station in Toronto. Chris had listened to my campus radio show on Fusion Radio and sent in a show intro because he thought the show could use better production value to spice it up.

Unbeknownst to me, Adam and Chris had actually talked to each other about doing a show with me years ago. Adam said he thought I should have been on the radio a long time ago, but his job in Calgary had put that idea on hold.

With Adam back in Toronto for what finally looked like a while, they brought up the idea again.

We arranged to meet for a couple drinks at the big Jack Astor's at Front and University.

The idea was never really even discussed as a podcast. It was just this "thing." Adam felt I needed a clear setup guy to keep me on track, so I could "crank home runs," as he said. Adam would obviously be perfect at that. Chris, on the other hand, wanted to be the behind-the-scenes guy, looking at the nuts and bolts of the show and taking care of production.

There was already built-in chemistry between Adam and me, but, admittedly, I didn't know him that well at that point. Adam had lots of other friends and he was always going off to different cities. Still, we stayed in touch. To me, Adam was a good example that staying friends with people after school can be a bit of work, but if the effort is mutual, your friendship is meant to last. Chris, on the other hand, was this bubbly guy who disarmed you with his friendly demeanor and goofy giggle. And once he disarmed you, he would slice you in half with a brutal joke you weren't expecting.

We were honestly just talking random nonsense. I remember talking about something I read about Sidney Crosby needing custom-made pants because of his giant hockey ass.

After a few minutes, I realized I had been the only person talking for a while. That's not exactly uncommon, especially in hockey talk. What struck me, though, is that Adam and Chris kept looking at me and then looking at each other with a smirk. At first I thought they were making fun of me, but after a moment, I got the impression that it had been a test, almost like I was being air-checked to see how well I could hold a conversation.

We made the decision to start the podcast shortly after. Working with the KHL and the NHL Network delayed things, but once the KHL season wrapped up at the end of April and the NHL Network laid me off, my scheduled freed right up.

Because Adam and Chris worked for Rogers, we could book one of the Fan 590's studios, now rebranded Sportsnet 590 the Fan, and record there. Nice microphones with a full board setup, a soundproof studio, and even phones if we wanted to have guests. It was a huge advantage.

At the end of May 2013, we completed our first show. It was a bit awkward: Adam's voice and my voice had all the chemistry of me trying to talk to girls at my grade six dance. All the while, Chris was just sitting there in the corner. Every now and then he let out a barely audible giggle, but he still didn't say anything. I remember thinking, *It's dumb that there's another person in here and they're not talking.* I'm a goldfish. If he makes a sound or a face, I can't not react to it.

To Chris's credit, he agreed to start talking on the mic. I'll always respect that about him because many behind-the-scenes folks would rather be caught dead than on the mic. Chris was willing to give it a shot.

The first five shows we recorded were ridiculous. After all, we began in the middle of the conference finals so there weren't many games to talk about. So what did we talk about? The same stuff anyone talks about when they're trying to get to know each other . . .

In one particular episode — and I don't even know how we got to the subject — we started talking about strip club experiences. It might have been because I had recently been to a bachelor party for the first time. I talked about how I hated strip clubs and that they were so awkward. I was talking to a friend when a stripper got my attention by grabbing my no-no place. It's not the most polite way to say hello, if I'm honest. Upon hearing this, Adam gave birth to our show's first hashtag: #StevesPeePee.

In one of his first on-mic stories, Chris shared his own terrible strip club experience. He was trying to make awkward conversation with the dancer. "So, do you like your job?" It was cringe-worthy, hilarious, and, most importantly, vulnerable. One of us would lay out a deeply embarrassing story, and the rest of us felt like we had to rise to that level. It's one hell of a way to get to know each other.

After our second show, we looked at the first shows' listens: over 1,000 on SoundCloud. Adam and Chris were surprised. I'd had a feeling it might happen, though. After all, it's not like we were starting from scratch. By that point, I had an audience on YouTube that I had been building for six years. I figured a couple of them would check out the show.

Our second episode blew up in part because of Tumblr. If you don't know what Tumblr is, it's difficult to describe. It's a trip, to say the least. To severely over-simplify it, there are a lot of pictures, rants, and memes, like most social media sites. We talked about Sidney Crosby a lot that episode, and when we tagged "Sidney Crosby" or "Pittsburgh Penguins," a lot of people on Tumblr checking out those topics gave us a click.

Chris had very few Twitter followers, but his social blew up out of nowhere. Adam did have some followers, but they were mostly looking for Justin Bieber tickets. All of a sudden, they're getting people telling them their sports opinions suck.

It stressed them out a bit, Chris in particular. Because we were always ripping on each other on the show, people did the same to us online. Sometimes it got confusing. "Why is this person yelling at me? Are they playing along or do they actually hate my guts?"

Our listeners were rabid. We weren't really sure why, but we were definitely striking a nerve.

Spring 2013 was actually the perfect jumping-off point for the show.

The Leafs, a team whose fan base had only known suffering for the past half-century, had just suffered one of their most humiliating losses ever. It was 4–1 . . .

On top of that, the Leafs were ignoring all the warning signs from advanced stats that bloggers had been pointing out to them for at least a year. For Chris, our show's resident Canucks fan, it was also great because this was the beginning of the end for the Canucks. After years of dominance, their window to win wasn't just closing, it was slamming shut. If we didn't go with the name *The Steve Dangle Podcast*, we could have just as easily gone with *The Hockey-Related Anxiety Podcast*. For the record, it wasn't my idea to call it *The Steve Dangle Podcast*. We tried to come up with some sort of hockey play on words like *The Puck-Head Podcast*, but Adam insisted *The Steve Dangle Podcast* was the way to go.

We tried to cover the rest of the league, but we couldn't help but rant about the moves our teams were making. The Leafs bought out Mikhail Grabovski, let Nikolay Kulemin and Clarke MacArthur walk for nothing, acquired Dave Bolland and Jonathan Bernier, and signed David Clarkson. *The Pension Plan Puppets* blog famously wrote an article called, "Who Had a Better Free Agency Day: Dave Nonis or a Potato?" The potato won in a landslide, which pretty much sums everything up.

Meanwhile, the Canucks goalie controversy ended, or so we thought, with Cory Schneider getting dealt to New Jersey in exchange for the pick that was used to draft Bo Horvat.

In many ways, the show was therapy for us. I think our listeners felt the same way. Whether we were helping fans laugh away the pain or people were just laughing, everyone was having a good time.

Despite launching our hockey podcast with just two weeks left in the playoffs, our listenership grew and the show gained momentum over the summer. It was all very fast and unexpected, but we loved it. It was so fun watching Adam and Chris, two guys who were like, "Sure, I like hockey," discover the depths of the online hockey world.

The deepest parts of the online hockey world were discovering us, too.

HOME
ICE

Part of the podcast's early success had to do with how unhappy I was at CBC. During my first season there, I was so happy I could have spun around in circles singing *The Mary Tyler Moore Show* theme in the lobby: "You're gonna make it after all!"

In summer 2013, the mood in that building wasn't exactly *I've made it*.

Pudy's fantastic "Welcome home" moment lasted for most of the rest of the hockey season, but I could tell something had changed. By the summer, people were dropping like flies.

Concessions had to be made, certain things had to be cut, and people had to be let go. Money was being put into the new studios for the upcoming 2014 Sochi Winter Olympics, but day-to-day stuff was very different. People around me were getting dumped on with more and more work, meaning there were a lot of unhappy campers.

The YouTube videos I had made for CBC during the 2012 playoffs never made their way back either, which annoyed me. They had paid me to make them, but that just wasn't in the budget anymore. What drove me nuts is I would have gladly done them for free, something I should have pushed them harder on.

Late in November 2013, it was announced that Rogers would be taking over the NHL broadcasting rights beginning in the

2014–15 season. It was devastating. I still remember being on a conference call the next day with a bunch of other CBC employees. They tried to explain that Rogers had agreed to partner with CBC, that they would be using our studios, and so on.

This really upped my passion for my YouTube channel and podcast and made me redouble my efforts. I even bought a new camera for the first time in over half a decade. That season was hilarious, too.

The Leafs made all these offseason changes that basically every blog hated. The Clarkson contract began with a 10-game suspension and didn't improve much from there. The Leafs' success only made the so-called mainstream media versus bloggers debate even more vicious. The old guard would cry, "Where's the Leafs' big downfall you were talking about?" while all the bloggers would say, "Give it time, idiots."

The gong show surrounding the Leafs that season was great for my videos and great for the podcast. It also helped that on the Canucks side of things, this was the infamous and disastrous coach John Tortorella season, when he went berserk and tried to get into the Calgary Flames locker room to fight Bob Hartley. I was at CBC the night it happened.

Working in a sports newsroom when something crazy happens is the best, especially when nobody online knows about it yet. The slow burn of everybody realizing what just happened or what is happening is priceless.

"Um, so John Tortorella just tried to get in the Flames locker room."

"What?"

"Yeah, he tried to fight the whole team."

"Are you serious?"

"It might have just been Bob Hartley, I can't tell."

"Is there footage?"

"Yeah, throw the TV on Blue 2."

Then someone else would walk into the room.

"Hey, did you see —"

"Yeah, I was just showing it."

It's especially fun when it happens during a commercial break, as this incident did. I would rush to open Twitter and realize, *Oh my God, nobody knows yet. This is going to be amazing.* Then the bomb drops and everyone goes bananas. It's a popcorn-grabber.

It wasn't always the most fun, though. Before the 2013–14 season, I would lament to my wife-to-be that certain people at CBC didn't seem to appreciate their job, how cool it was, and they complained too much. But during that season, I had absolutely become one of those people. I thought I was going to be laid off at any time, and it didn't feel like there was a future for me there. There was pretty much no joy left in the job.

Yet another reason to focus more on the podcast, which I loved, but I did have bills to pay.

After a few months of the show, we just started straight up asking on the podcast itself: "Hey, if any of you work at a company or something, we could really use a sponsor."

We did that for a short while, and then we got an email.

It was a listener of ours from Vancouver. He worked with Panago Pizza, a West Coast pizza chain that was expanding eastward. He had pitched the idea of a partnership with us to his bosses. He basically told us, "Hey, if Panago reaches out, don't get weirded out by it."

We all huddled around the phone in Chris's studio for the phone call. We basically let Adam take the reins because he actually knows how to talk business. They would ask a question and we would have a quick, silent conversation with our eyes to agree or disagree.

After the phone call, we were pretty sure they were interested. Adam put together prices for two packages: a one-month sponsorship and a three-month sponsorship. They talked for what felt like months, trying to figure out what was best for both parties.

Finally, Adam called me. As always, I was in my bedroom.

"Are you sitting down?" he asked.

"Yes," I told him truthfully, sitting in my boxers on the blue yoga ball I used as a computer chair because I'm a professional adult person.

"They offered us a year."

I thought Adam was pulling the meanest prank ever. I was like, "OK, if you're joking about this I'm gonna chokeslam you."

But he was serious, and, evidently, so was Panago.

"They had only one request," he added. "Can we change the hashtag to something other than #StevesPeePee?"

I was more than happy to get rid of that, since it was Adam's stupid idea in the first place.

The agreement began in November, and just like that, our podcast had a title sponsor. Others followed. J.P. Wiser's Whisky arranged a whisky tasting event and we got to meet our listeners for the first time. We were amazed by how far some people had come from, and it was a great experience to put so many faces to Twitter handles.

CBC was an income source, though not a huge one, and YouTube money basically covered a tank of gas or two each month, so the podcast sponsorship was a huge boost. Still, the prospect of Sarah-Louise and I finding a house before our wedding looked bleak. It would look better if the KHL paid the $11,635 they owed me.

After months of emails with confusing instructions — there was something about forms I had to fill out, even though they had been paying me prior to me signing anything — I finally signed a contract, scanned it, and sent them the form. Oh, I know. Don't even get me started.

"What happens now?" I asked in an email on September 24.

"Well, I guess nothing . . ." they responded, meaning I didn't need to do anything else.

"That's great!" I responded on the same day. "Do you have any guess for when the money will arrive?"

No answer.

"Hey, Vladdy!" I sent on October 2. "I'm still waiting on the money. Do you know how much longer it will take?"

No answer.

"Hey, Vladdy," I said again on October 7 (notice the passive aggressive punctuation change). "I am still waiting on the money. Do you know how much longer? I hope you are well."

Again, no answer. I sent one more email the next day.

"Answer me."

I had basically given up. *Well, I've been scammed out of over 11 grand*, I thought. I tried to rationalize it in my head that at least I had made *some* money off the experience, but, damn, I was so screwed.

On Halloween 2013, I was in my parents' kitchen, checking my online banking. I sat in stunned silence and might have even touched the screen to make sure I wasn't hallucinating. The money had finally come. Every. Single. Dime.

Trick or effing treat, eh? I jumped out of my chair. I nearly cried. Sarah-Louise was teaching that day, so I texted her: "Let's go look for a house."

We looked at a few houses in the Durham region. Our budget wasn't very big, but thanks to our recent rubles, we had a respectable down payment. Finally, we settled on a house in Oshawa that we would move into in March. It was a lot farther east than I wanted to live, but if the trade-off was actually having a house, then we'd make it work.

Before we could move in, there was the Sochi Winter Olympics.

Most of my coworkers were assigned to upload all our online content and videos and type in all the boring metadata, which was my worst nightmare. It looked like theirs, too. They had tried to teach me how to use the brand-new back-end of the Olympic page that none of us had ever worked on before, and I struggled mightily. Maybe they were throwing me a bone or maybe they just wanted to actually have stuff uploaded properly and on time, but my boss at CBC assigned me a role where

I would be prepping graphics and transitions for our update and fill-in shows. I was so thankful. Every time I walked by my friends, they looked like Leonardo DiCaprio in *The Revenant*, post-bear. I'm sure they would have liked to scream like him, too.

We moved into our house right after the Olympics, I worked five more shifts at CBC, then I got laid off. Good start, good start.

That made money super tight leading up to the wedding, but between the podcast sponsorship and the little bit I got from TheLeafsNation.com and YouTube, I thought we could at least scrape by, and I could find another job once the hockey season began again. Sarah-Louise was teaching at the time, working four long-term occasional (LTO) contracts at the same time. She drove to four different schools each day. She busted her ass and I wanted to pull my weight. Finding a new job was a daunting prospect, and with a mortgage now, I couldn't afford to sit back and wait.

Could I get a job at Leafs TV? Well, they had laid me off, and now that some time has passed they've laid off half the people I used to work with, too, so that's bad.

Could I get a job at CBC? Wait, no, they *just* laid me off.

Can I get a job at The Score? I had spoken to them once, but it didn't go anywhere. They're downsizing every day, so that's looking bleak, too.

I could try NHL Network again, but if they needed me, wouldn't they have just hired me back?

I tried TSN, which turned out to be one of the most frustrating and fruitless experiences ever. When I was at the NHL Network, I was a Bell employee and I had access to their database of emails. On one of my final shifts, I wrote down as many emails addresses as I could. The higher they were on the food chain, the better.

I just went for it and emailed Ken Volden, a vice president and executive producer at TSN. Hey, shoot your shot. To my shock, he actually answered and we arranged a meeting. It was around 20 minutes long, and it went so well that we had another 20-minute meeting a while later.

He said he liked me, but I would have to start at the bottom and work my way up. "No problem!" I said truthfully; I just wanted to be in.

He arranged a meeting between myself and a guy in charge of the people in the newsroom who edit all the highlights you see in the background on TSN. That went well, too! I thought I had a job for sure.

The guy brought me in again.

"So, we had to hire internally before we could look at external candidates. We *might* be able to bring you in to do highlights once a month, if that. But you're not gonna touch hockey for about a year. You'll be doing, like, basketball and tennis.".

I honestly considered sending them an invoice for the gas I spent to get there that day. Needless to say, I didn't get that golden opportunity, either.

The biggest and seemingly only option I had left was Rogers Sportsnet, the company that had just bought all the NHL rights in Canada. Every person in the country hoping to work in sports broadcasting would be applying there and they were definitely not about to hire me, a mediocre video blogger who had more lay-offs under his belt than years out of school.

So, for the first month or so in our new house, when I wasn't making a new podcast or video, I was playing *South Park's Stick of Truth*. On the podcast, Adam and Chris used to make fun of how I worked *so hard*. It was a funny bit, but no, I was literally just playing *Stick of Truth*. One time, I left our front door unlocked, and my mother-in-law burst in while I was playing the infamous Underpants Gnomes level. Don't google it at work.

When we moved into our new house, our internet provider was a company called TekSavvy. We were having difficulty getting it set up because something was wrong with the phone lines the previous owners had left.

While on the phone, I was just making idle chit-chat. I mentioned that I needed the internet for work, and I explained about my videos.

The Leafs, who looked playoff bound for sure, suffered yet another epic collapse and missed the playoffs again. With the new freedom of living in a house with no parents to bother and the fact that my wife-to-be was off at work while I made most of my videos, I could be as loud and as crazy as I wanted. And because of how the Leafs were doing, I wanted to be pretty loud and crazy.

To my shock, tech support patched me through to their advertising and marketing department and we started talking about YouTube sponsorships.

I told them I would get back to them and called Adam right away.

Adam is talented and has a sharp, gifted mind. His brilliance shines brightest when he's motivated, and he wanted to help me succeed like it was his duty. Maybe it's because he saw my potential to be part of a new wave in media. Maybe it's just because he's a great pal.

Adam negotiated a deal for me: a few thousand dollars for 40 videos in about 40 or 50 days with a TekSavvy logo in the corner. It would involve the end of the Leafs' season, as well as almost daily videos throughout the playoffs.

The day Sarah-Louise and I got married, we had about $900 to our name. What would we have done without this deal? Sold stuff? Cancelled the honeymoon? I'm not sure. Thanks to Adam and TekSavvy's tech support, we'll never know.

We made it to the wedding. Maybe a little like Indiana Jones barely sliding underneath the closing door, but we made it.

The deal ended up expiring, but I was encouraged. There had to be other deals out there, right? And you know what? Screw it! If I can get someone to sponsor the podcast and I can get someone to sponsor the videos, then I don't need anybody else. I'll make it on my own.

Never mind all that now. I got some marrying to do.

TOGA
PARTY

Despite the nervous anticipation, the day before my wedding was just like any other. It was a nice, relaxed, and sunny summer day. My wife-to-be had a couple of last minute errands, but I was off scot-free. All I had to do was hang out and try not to freak.

Out of my childhood friends, I was the first to be getting married. In fact, out of my seven groomsmen — I know, that's a lot — only one of them had been in a wedding party before.

My best man, Derek (not my fake lawyer, another Derek), decided, *Hey — I'm the best man. Why don't I take the day off and help my buddy take it easy?* At least that's what I thought he was thinking.

We went to the local bar that we basically kept open for about half a decade as soon as it was socially acceptable to start drinking, right around lunchtime.

We had some beers and talked about the wedding. Good stuff.

We got some more beers and then some lunch. Still good.

Lunch is done. Hey, another beer? Another beer! Great.

I was thinking less about the big day ahead and more about how gosh darn nice it was outside. I'm feeling pretty good. How many pitchers is this now?

After a while, one of my other groomsmen, Matt, got off work early. Hey, Matt! Great to see you! Hey, let's get some beer.

A little later, Matt's brother Andy, another one of my

groomsmen, showed up. Andy, great to see you, man. Hey, let's get a beer. Oh, you're driving? Alright, I'll have yours, too. I love you guys. I have the best friends *ever*.

I know what you're thinking: *My goodness, Steve. Weren't you worried about being hungover on your wedding day?*

Nonsense! I'm 26 years old and it's what? Five in the afternoon? Relax! I'll have a nice big dinner, go home, drink a bunch of water, and have a deep, peaceful sleep. I'll be awake and fully refreshed by 7 a.m., ready for pictures.

"Hey," my best man said, "I have an idea."

"Alright now, guys," I warned. "I'm not going to do anything crazy the night before my wedding."

"No, no," he responded. "Look, you know my carousel?"

Whether Derek invited us or we just invited ourselves, we were always up at his cottage.

On the kitchen counter, there was a little liquor carousel. It's this thing you put bottles of booze in, spin it, and pour shots out of it. Anybody who was ever lucky enough to be invited to the cottage was well aware of the carousel.

Derek's plan was simple: Let's go up to the cottage, which was about two hours away, and take a picture standing next to the carousel to send to the bridesmaids, just to freak them out a bit. After that, we'd come home, no problem.

"We'll be home by 11 p.m., at the latest."

When I woke up that morning, there's a good chance I would have said no. In this state, however, you know, that doesn't sound like such a bad idea. I'm getting married tomorrow, it'll be fun; no harm, no foul.

"Alright. Let's do it!"

Andy took us to my parents' house. I had to tell them about the plan since I was sleeping there that night. They weren't too keen on the idea, but it didn't matter much at that point.

We stayed for a little bit, sang a particularly boisterous rendition of "Happy Birthday" to my sister, and left for Derek's house after some cake.

Just as we got to Derek's house, we bumped into his dad, who had just arrived *back* from the cottage.

We told him our plan. I could have sworn the other guys told him a couple other things when I was out of earshot. His dad senses started going off.

New plan: Andy would drive us to the cottage and Derek's dad would come with us (read: babysit) and drive us home.

"No problem!"

So off we go to Ontario cottage country — Severn, Ontario, if you've ever heard of it. The farther we drove, however, the more I sobered up.

We were going really far away from home. I had to get up at 7 a.m. I was getting *married. This is risky.*

Sensing my heightening desire to bail, the guys made an announcement.

"Hey, Steve, uh . . . we heard there's gonna be a toga party in Gravenhurst tonight."

No. No way. Absolutely not.

Forget the fact that Gravenhurst is nowhere near where we're going and even farther away from home, there's absolutely no way I'm going to a toga party the night before my wedding. Are you nuts?

These guys love to mess with me, I'm so gullible. They've gotta be messing with me.

"Come on, man," they pleaded. "It'll be fun!"

"Shut up, there's no toga party," I said dismissively.

After talk of togas died down, I drifted off to sleep in the back of the car.

When I woke up, it was mostly dark. We had arrived at the cottage a little bit behind schedule.

At this rate, I wouldn't be getting home until almost midnight. Whatever. That's still enough time to get about seven hours of sleep. That'll be plenty.

We went into the cottage and strolled over to the infamous liquor carousel. With Derek's dad assuming idiot-sitting duties, my three friends and I grabbed shot glasses and picked our poison.

"Alright," I told them, "let's drink these and go home."

But they were ignoring me. While one of them started pouring the shots, the other two were grabbing bed sheets out of drawers.

"What are those for?" I asked.

"Togas," they said, nonchalantly.

Ha, ha. Very funny, guys. I'm not an idiot. I appreciated their commitment to the prank, but I wasn't going to fall for it. I know I can be gullible but I'm not *that* gullible.

With shots in hand and our stylish bed sheet togas, we smiled for the camera.

We took the picture and drank our shots.

"Alright, Steve, it's time to go to Gravenhurst."

"No, we're not."

"Come on, man. There's a toga party."

"Shut up. No, there isn't. Let's go home."

"We can't go home yet."

"Why?"

"Steve, we've been over this, man. Gravenhurst. Toga party."

I just started to ignore them as we all loaded back in the car, still wearing our togas. Derek's designated driver dad was behind the wheel now. There's no way this responsible adult, this retired man who has already spent at least five hours in a car today, is going to drive us even farther away, especially for a stupid toga party.

It was dark as we drove off. I squinted out of the window to see where we actually were.

For 15 minutes, I kept my eyes on the road like a hawk, looking for any street signs or landmarks I recognized.

Pff, these guys aren't fooling anyone. I recognize all of this.

A few minutes pass.

I think this is . . . yep. I know where we are. Great. We're heading home.

A few minutes later.

Hm . . . I don't think I recognize this.

Next turn.

It's just dark out, that's all.

Next turn.

"We're going to a friggin' toga party in Gravenhurst, aren't we?"

"Man, we told you."

Bunch of jerks.

As I came to grips with what was about to happen, my mind started going through the unending list of ways this could go horribly, unforgivably wrong. Forget showing up to my wedding hungover — what if I didn't show up to the wedding at all?

As Matt claims to have said to the other guys while they were coming up with this evil scheme, we were one flat tire away from ruining a wedding. What would have happened if we couldn't find a way back? My fiancée had family fly from overseas to be here. There would have been a bunch of severely pissed-off Scottish people riding around cottage country hunting me down with the little knives they all kept in their socks, ready to caber toss me into an early grave. And deservedly so!

The texts started flooding in. Evidently, the girls had seen the picture. The remaining four guys in my wedding party who weren't there, Adam included, started messaging me, too.

Suffice it to say, most of their texts said something to the effect of "You guys are idiots."

Like me, they all thought the guys were kidding about the toga party. I took a screenshot of where we were on Google Maps to prove that, no, we are in fact that stupid.

My wife-to-be — hopefully, anyway — took it pretty well, actually.

"Just be there for 3 p.m.," she told me. "My dad will find you."

Ah, that's nice. Do you feel the love?

After about 45 minutes, we finally arrived at our destination. I could see a bonfire through the trees. This is it. We're at a toga party halfway into the wilderness the night before my wedding.

Why am I here? I thought. *I'm an adult. I could have just told my friends no, I'm not coming, I'm going to bed. Sure, they'd make fun of me forever, but at least my future in-laws wouldn't murder me.*

We walked down to the beach where people were gathered around the fire, and I noticed something.

"Guys, we're the only ones wearing togas."

"Ha. Yeah," my friends responded.

So not only am I taking a huge risk by even being here, but I also look like a total goof.

We knew a bunch of the people there. They were joined by about two dozen others who were renting the neighbouring cottages. We explained what we were doing there and our stupid togas. Even then, they didn't quite understand the true depth of our stupidity.

"So when are you getting married?" someone asked.

"Tomorrow," I laughed nervously.

A few of the people around the fire gasped. They originally thought we were having a bachelor party or something, a few weeks or even months away from the actually wedding date. I wished that were true, but here I am.

"What time do you need to be up?" someone asked.

"Oh," I checked my phone. "About seven hours."

Most of the men there seemed to think it was hysterical. The women, however, had faces that seemed to say, "You poor, stupid child."

My hopes that we would have a quick drink then leave were quickly doused. Before I could even speak, someone shoved a beer in my hand.

There was a beer pong table set up. Or maybe it was flip cup? We could have been reading the Bible together, and it still would have been stupid for me to be there.

They were American. Don't ask where from. Pittsburgh? Maybe. I don't remember.

There was one guy there I distinctly remember named Corey. Everything about him screamed America. I think he was wearing clothes with an American flag or bald eagle on them and his yinzer accent was off the hook. Americans have a lot of nerve goofing on Canadian accents. Whatever they speak in Pittsburgh, it's not English. I kept calling this guy AAF Corey, which stood for "American as fuck" Corey.

Looking back on it, these guys were younger, and none of them were married. What if they thought it was normal to essentially abduct the groom the night before he's supposed to get married?

Ah, that's their problem. I have my own problems to solve, like why is my cup empty? Wooo!

Time until wedding-day wake-up call: six hours.

One of the last knucklehead things I remember from that night was "playing" one-inch punch with our friend Dave. Dave is about ten years older than us, but he has the energy of an eight-year-old who has just shotgunned a Red Bull.

One-inch punch is basically when you hold your hand out, with your fingertips touching your friend's arm. Then you punch them from that distance. If you're still confused, go watch *Kill Bill*.

"Steve!" he'd yell. "I got this great game."

"I —"

"Alright, look, here's how it works."

Bang — he punched me.

"Aw, come on, Steve! You moved! Here, it's like this."

Bang!

"Ow!" I yelled. "You wound up for that!"

"Shut up, no I didn't. Stop moving!"

Bang!

"Alright, Jesus, it's my turn now!" I winced.

Time until wedding-day wake-up call: five hours.

A short while later, almost everybody who was there when we had arrived had gone to bed. It was time to go. Or, at least we tried to leave. Remember Matt? Yeah, we lost him and didn't find him until our third lap around the fire.

Finally, mercifully, Derek's dad fulfilled his designated driver duties and started driving us home.

"Wait, no," Andy said. "We need to stop for coffees."

Time until wedding-day wake-up call: four hours.

The last thing I remember before falling asleep is Derek's dad serenely sipping his coffee in the driver's seat and Andy passed out in the passenger seat, somehow still clutching his own coffee.

When I finally arrived at my parents' place, it was about five in the morning. My mom, seriously not amused, answered the door.

Whatever, Mom. You're not even the woman who's most mad at me right now.

Two hours later, after basically closing my eyes and opening them, I got up and was able to get ready and in my suit to take photos with my parents and sister, no problem. Something about the ridiculousness, the impossible stupidity of it all, combined with the fact I survived it, made it all seem funny.

Now, this is always the asterisk I throw out when I tell this story: I was 26.

If you've already lived through your late 20s, you know what I'm talking about. If you're not there yet, that is right around the time where your liver starts to go, "Alright, that's it. Knock it off," and your hangovers triple in power.

Late in the morning, my groomsmen, both guilty and innocent parties, arrived, and we relived the idiocy from the night before, each of us remembering something that the others couldn't, our collective hangovers growing together.

At some point, the phone rang.

Brian, my longtime neighbour and friend who I grew up playing driveway hockey and basketball with, was on the other end.

He couldn't come to the wedding because his first child had just been born mere days before. He still wanted to give me a pre-wedding pep talk: it was 20 minutes of wisdom I badly needed, and any nausea I was feeling melted away.

He told me to remember that this day was all about my wife and me. It sounds so simple, but if you've ever been to weddings, you know there are many distractions. What if something goes wrong? It doesn't matter. The whole point of your wedding day, or any couple's wedding day, is to celebrate the union of two people in love. Everything else is secondary.

Our wedding cake? Yeah, half of it had collapsed by the time we got there. We didn't care. I had spent so much time finding hockey cards to put under random chairs to see who would win the centerpieces. At the end of the night, people were like, "Hey, how come there's a hockey card here?" because we forgot. Again, who cares?

Brian's pep talk and copious amounts of water were exactly what I needed at that moment. One of my oldest friends, who couldn't even be there, had made a huge impact.

The story of the rest of my wedding day? Well, you just had to be there. Luckily, she said, "I do."

But I remember I left wearing a toga again.

WHERE DO YOU SEE YOURSELF IN FIVE YEARS?

Hockey season was fast approaching. I still didn't have a job, but I had basically made up my mind that I was going to try to work for myself, even if it meant struggling financially.

Over the past few years, I had had dozens of coffee conversations with people as I desperately tried to find a job or, at the very least, get some advice. One of those people finally called me back one day.

Remember Dave Cadeau, the producer at the Fan 590 who told me to get a job at Future Shop? He was now the assistant program director of the station.

Dave and I had stayed in touch since my days as an intern, even if it was only once in a blue moon. He was one of the first people at the Fan who knew about my videos even when I was afraid people would judge me.

For some reason, Dave always seemed to support what I was doing. I don't know if he necessarily thought it was good stuff, but I think he always saw the potential in it or appreciated my enthusiasm.

One day in September 2014, he called with a neat little idea.

Basically, Rogers had just bought all the NHL rights in Canada, meaning they had all the hockey games. Rogers also owns a lot of radio stations around Canada. They wanted everybody on every station to mention hockey on the air from time to time, even if it was in passing. The issue was that a bunch of them weren't sports radio stations. It's not exactly fair to ask a DJ at a pop station who doesn't even watch hockey to talk about it and know what they're talking about.

And that's where I was supposed to come in.

Every morning, they wanted me to make a two- or three-page clickable PDF full of hockey info, linking to stories, tweets, videos, and more that I could send to radio stations around the country.

Dave knew I basically lived on Twitter and read about hockey all day. I was tapped into the blogosphere as well as the mainstream. I was always up to date on what was going on. Dave saw me as the perfect candidate.

There was only one catch: we had to convince his boss.

I still remember the meeting: it was Dave; the other assistant program director, Jason Rozon; and their boss, Don Kollins, the program director of Sportsnet 590 the Fan.

As a relatively anxious person, I'm always amazed when I have unexpected moments of calm. Like, dude, this is it. If you don't get into Sportsnet, you're totally screwed, aren't you? But something about the whole situation and how unlikely it all seemed kind of put me at ease. The worst they could tell me was no, and I'd heard no plenty of times and it hadn't killed me yet, so screw it, bring it on.

Dave re-explained the idea and why he thought I would be a good fit for it. I talked a little bit about my experience, my YouTube story, resume, and so on. After a while, Don started throwing lots of questions at me. It was a position of importance with a lot of influence on radio stations around the entire country. If he could find a reason not to hire me, he wasn't going to hire me.

Finally, he asked my least favourite question: "Where do you see yourself in five years?"

I hate that question with a fiery passion. We work in media, man. After my stints at Leafs TV, NHL Network, and CBC, I wanted to answer, "I dunno. Laid off again?"

Whenever members of today's Leafs organization get asked about the state of the team, they always say something that I think is just a great way of thinking for anybody, no matter what field you're in: they have a five-year plan that changes every day.

It was my interview to get into university all over again. Do I make something up or just be honest? Screw it, give him the truth.

Here's a rough version of what I said:

"You know, in 2009, I was getting on a plane to go to the World Juniors in Regina, because of a YouTube channel I had started. Five years before that, it was 2004 and YouTube was just coming into existence. Facebook was still in its infancy. Twitter didn't even exist. Most of the tools I use every day for my job didn't exist. So, in 2004, I could've given you a wonderful, thoughtful answer as to where I see myself in five years, but it would have been completely wrong. Right now, all I see myself doing is growing my skillset and trying to become better at as many things as possible. So where do I see myself in five years? I have no idea, but I can make something up if you like."

I don't know what smartass demon possessed my tongue in that moment, but I couldn't even believe the words as I was saying them. What was I thinking?

Out of the corner of my eye, I saw Dave and Jason look over at Don. I was looking right back at him, refusing to break eye contact. He just smiled for what felt like an hour before giving a little chuckle and looking at Dave like, *Who is this guy?*

But I had been laid off before. I had been hired before. I'm not an idiot. I know what I'm doing. I'm a grown-ass man now. I have a house now and bills to pay. Do you want me or not?

A few days later, I got the job.

I would basically be working seven days a week until the Stanley Cup was awarded in June, with the understanding that as soon as the season was over, I was off for the summer.

Screw the details: I work at Sportsnet.

The place I told myself I shouldn't even apply to because it was so unrealistic had just hired me.

My wife was at work at the time, so I drove to Scarborough to tell my parents. I wanted to tell them in person. When I got there, my phone rang. It was Chris.

"Hey, man!" I said.

"Hey, I have something to tell you," he said, sounding sombre.

"I have something to tell you, too!" I said with oblivious excitement. "You first."

"I'm leaving the show."

It was like somebody took a dump in the middle of a birthday party.

Adam and Chris had been having their differences for a while. I always thought they'd work it out, though. I still don't have the greatest idea of what exactly it was, and, frankly, it's none of my business. It's certainly not my story to tell, either.

On top of the stress of losing our producer, I was struggling during my first couple weeks at the new job. I would cry when I got home, which eventually evolved to me crying in the car on the way home, which turned into barely even holding it together at work. Why? I wasn't sad or anything. The job was challenging, but I wasn't overly anxious about it.

After a couple of weeks or so, these "episodes," as I called them, stopped. It was just like what happened when I started working at the zoo — something that came and went every now and then. They were gone for now, but they would drop in to say hello a couple of years later.

For two weeks before the NHL's regular season began, I went into Sportsnet to make mock versions of the prep sheet. I thought I was doing an OK job.

Finally, we had a meeting to go over one of my drafts. Don Kollins was one of the people there, as well as Julie Adam. At the time, she was the vice president of programming at Rogers Radio.

She asked me to explain one of my stories. It was something about a Claude Giroux injury.

"I don't really care," she said matter-of-factly. She wasn't being mean, she was just telling the truth: she didn't care.

It was brilliant advice. Hockey fans care that Claude Giroux is hurt but what about someone like my mom? She likes hockey, but she pretty much watches only Leafs games. What does she care about the captain of the Flyers?

Instead, there was one story out of Newfoundland about a man named Patrick O'Brien. He was a goaltender who was also a paramedic. One day, a spectator had a heart attack during a game. O'Brien leaped into the stands, most of his equipment still on, and saved the man's life.

There was another story about Washington Capitals defenceman Mike Green. They stopped making his favourite brand of hockey stick a few years ago, and he spoke about it in an interview. The Capitals blog *Russian Machine Never Breaks* wrote about it, and their readers started offering to give back sticks Green had signed for them years ago. He ended up getting a bunch of sticks, used them in NHL games, and even put up some points.

They wanted stories that everybody would be interested in, not just hardcore hockey fans. Human interest. Even if it meant going outside of the NHL — that's what they wanted, so that's what I gave them.

Driving into Toronto from Oshawa seven days a week was taxing. I noticed that as I got better at it, I was able to get the prep sheet done earlier each night. Finally, I took a risk and went home once the sheet was mostly done, added in final scores from my house, and sent out the prep sheet to over 1,000 people throughout the country from home. It didn't take long for me to just say, *Why don't I just do it from home?*

One day, there was an event I really wanted to go to, but I still had to finish the sheet. I knew I could do it from home,

I just wanted permission. I carefully asked Dave for his blessing. Luckily, he said yes.

"Great!" I said. "Because I've already been doing that for two weeks."

"OK . . ." he said. "Really wish you had told me that, but the sheet has been improving, so go ahead. You can work from home. If the quality dips, though, you have to come in. Deal?

Hell of a deal. Saving about two hours round trip every night was incentive enough.

On the podcast side of things, fans missed Chris and constantly asked for him for months. I was worried we would lose all the momentum our show had gained.

Enter: Jesse Blake.

Adam thought Jesse was underutilized at KiSS 92.5, where he worked on Adam's show. In the same way Adam thought I should be on the radio, he thought Jesse had the potential to do a lot more. Adam worked with him and already knew he was great. He was technically masterful, but he was also funny.

We met for breakfast, and I agreed to bring Jesse on board. It was going to be an interesting experiment. After all, I barely knew him. It was great that he was even younger than us, though. It changed the energy and perspective of the show.

Not everyone was happy right away. "The show sounds different!" some listeners would yell.

Well, yeah. The chemistry had changed. Adam and I went back and forth more because Jesse barely spoke. He still had to find his voice. Talking to him off mic, however, I knew the potential was there.

After a couple of months at Sportsnet, I was contacted by Dan Tavares. I had previously worked under him at CBC, and he was now at Sportsnet, too. He was one of the people who got the sheet every day, and he knew about my YouTube channel and podcast. He basically thought, *Hey, we have this guy, why not use his videos?*

They started posting my videos and podcasts to the website and also asked me to write articles and make separate videos for Sportsnet's YouTube channel. I wasn't about to pass up that opportunity.

Then November 18, 2014, happened.

The Leafs, my beloved Leafs, got thumped 9–2 by the Nashville Predators. I didn't even watch the whole game. I didn't bother going into in-depth analysis. They just sucked.

I absolutely blew a gasket in the video. The blue room in my basement still bears scars from that video, including a black mark on my door because I threw my phone at it.

"Nashville just scored!" Sarah-Louise yelled down the stairs.

"Again?" I yelled back.

"Yeah, they've got nine goals now!"

That only caused me to go more berserk. I uploaded the video that night and went back to the sheet.

Before I went to bed, I checked to see how the video was doing. Right away, I knew I had struck a nerve. In three hours, that video already had about as many views as most videos got in a week.

When I woke up the next morning, I had tweets that they had used clips from that video on the radio. I got a few emails from Rogers people around the country as well.

I had to go into Sportsnet for something that day. As soon as I walked in, Sid Seixeiro, a sportscaster known for ranting and blowing his lid, stopped what he was doing, stood up at his desk, and started clapping. "Steve Dangle, ladies and gentlemen! Steve Dangle!"

At the time, the most views my channel had received in one day was 18,874. The day after that game, I had 47,221. Right now, the video is pushing 200,000 views. I still get tweets about it.

Now everyone at Sportsnet, and, really, everyone who worked at Rogers, had a frothing face to put to the name that emailed them each morning.

Soon enough, I got the chance to hit the airwaves, too.

Don Kollins came up with an idea: it was a little rapid-fire segment where I would call in to the Jeff Blair show to rant about hockey and essentially bother him for about a minute. When Don pitched the idea to me, he was struggling to think of a name.

"The Dangle Dial?" I asked.

And just like that, the name of my designated driver service was now the name of a radio segment.

Because Jeff's show was in the morning and I was staying up until 2 or 3 a.m. every night to do the prep sheet, we would prerecord the segments at night and Jeff would dub over them live on-air, usually without even listening to them.

The gag was that I was annoying Jeff, but I'm pretty sure I was just annoying most of his listeners.

I met a longtime viewer of my videos that year. They said how much they loved my YouTube channel, the podcast, and even the stuff I had written.

"What do you think of the Dangle Dial?" I asked.

"Oh, it's just awful, Steve."

They said it like it was an intervention.

Whether it was a flop or not, after a while, Panago began sponsoring the segment so it continued. The radio station actually made money off that thing. I was grateful for the opportunity, but it wasn't my best work, and after a few months, it mercifully ran its course.

At the end of the season, Sportsnet asked if I was interested in working on segments for playoff shows. Hell yes.

I'd be working with a producer I knew from Leafs TV named Amanda and Sophia Jurksztowicz, the on-camera talent and someone I spent four years at Ryerson with. Once again, the world is about the size of a hamster cage.

We made cool segments. Sophia and Amanda did most of the work, and I helped with research and scouring Twitter. We did this one segment that explored the science behind a hit where Dustin Byfuglien laid out Ryan Kesler. I contacted a guy on Twitter named Stephen Burtch, a Leafs blogger by night and physics teacher by day, to understand it. Using speed and the size of the players involved, we figured out that if you could harness the energy generated by that hit, it could power a light bulb for about 17 seconds.

What was even cooler about that gig is we got to work behind the scenes with the entire *Hockey Night in Canada* panel, mostly George Stroumboulopoulos, Nick Kypreos, Kelly Hrudey, and Elliotte Friedman. I told Kelly Hrudey I still had his autograph from when he thought I was John Tavares at the 2007 NHL Awards.

I was a bit nervous to meet Kypreos, though.

A producer from Sportsnet saw a video I had made about why tanking was a good thing. After all, it was the Horachek-era Leafs and they stunk, so I had nothing else to talk about. I made a ridiculous video where I put on an army helmet and got out a toy tank.

Kypreos wasn't amused. They showed my clip live on Sportsnet and then came out of it with Kypreos saying I came across as a big loser.

My phone basically didn't stop buzzing for half an hour. My friends saw the clip, my uncle wanted to fight him. It was a very bizarre moment.

But Kypreos couldn't have been nicer to me when I met him, and we even took a picture of him grabbing me by the collar for Twitter.

The night the Blackhawks won the 2015 Stanley Cup, we all gathered in the big Sportsnet studio to celebrate the end of the season. Elliotte Friedman popped a bottle of champagne and gave a really nice speech thanking everybody behind the scenes for their hard work.

Strombo echoed more of the same, telling everyone they did a great job in year one. He was surprisingly shy about it and didn't want to make it a big proclamation or anything. He was getting a lot of criticism and he knew it, but he took it all in stride.

I had worked my first full season at Sportsnet and managed to not get laid off in the process. Jesse had found his voice and became an integral part of the podcast, adding a new structure to the show as well as a personality. The YouTube channel was reaching heights it had never reached before. In short . . . everything was coming up Milhouse.

For the record, about five years after my job interview at Sportsnet, this book was published. You just never know.

USE
YOUR
HEAD

You might have noticed that on a few occasions throughout the book, I've cited anxiety attacks or something like them.

Up until a couple years ago, I would have just referred to it as me being ridiculous. And why not? After all, I would feel horrible for two weeks or so, but after a while it would go away. I was just being silly, as usual.

The real bad stuff began around May 2016, the end of my second season with Sportsnet. It got way worse in the summer, despite having every reason to be happy. What's the problem? I've finally got the job I've always wanted, I'm doing well, and I've gone two years without getting laid off, which feels like a world record. My wife, family, and friends are amazing. The Leafs have the first overall pick and are about to draft Auston Matthews. Life is good. Isn't it?

I would start to relax a bit and I would think it was gone, but the feeling would just come back again. Unlike the previous times, it wouldn't go away.

My lowest point was my TEDx Talk. For whatever reason, I was asked to take part in a TEDx Talk at Laurier University in Waterloo, Ontario. They wanted me to talk about my journey through media and whatnot, and I thought I would give it a shot. My wife came with me and, luckily, Sportsnet's Faizal Khamisa was asked to speak as well, so I had somebody else to talk to.

I got there at 10 a.m. and realized there were over a dozen speakers. I was scheduled to be second last.

Faizal told his incredible story about how he beat the odds, kicked cancer in the ass, and became a successful sportscaster. Another talk was from a photojournalist who had been to war-torn countries. Yet another was about how women are underrepresented in certain fields, particularly tech and how that led to, among other things, the poor development of virtual reality technology.

I get up there and I'm like, "I have a YouTube channel."

Besides the fact that I probably shouldn't have been there in the first place, the idea of getting on stage and talking about myself to a crowd of people was nauseating. How am I going to tell my story to these people? I don't even like my own story because I hate myself right now. Almost every day, I would privately tell myself I was my own least favourite person. No pity party; I meant every word of it.

It lasted throughout the fall until my wife put her foot down and begged me to seek help. That broke my heart, but she was right. She's the person I confide in the most, and although she wanted to help, she's not a therapist.

I've learned a lot of things in my life, and I wish some things didn't take me as long to learn as they did. Some of them were just issues of growing up, maturing, and regular little bumps and bruises that help you grow. This is one lesson that shouldn't have taken over half a year — and in some ways more than a decade — to learn the hard way.

I've hurt my back, I've hurt both shoulders, I've accidentally sliced my finger open. What did I do every time something like that happened? I saw a doctor. I used treatment. I worked toward making those body parts better. For some reason, there was a reluctance to go get my head fixed. I wanted to toughen up; I didn't want to be weak. See? When people talk about the stigma around mental illness, that's the sort of thing they are referring to.

I finally went to a therapist, and it's one of the best decisions I've ever made.

It's not like, "Poof! It's fixed! You'll never feel sad again!" But now I know how to handle it better. When I'm losing the battle, I go for a check-up.

Therapy isn't always cheap, which can be an issue. If you call your local mental health clinic, many of them have less expensive options for therapy as well. There are a growing number of online options, too.

I've said this many times on the podcast and on social media: if you think you might need help, go get some damn help. You deserve it.

JUST
ASK

Sometimes the answer is so simple you miss it.

In the 2015–16 season, the Florida Panthers made the play-offs, finished with the best record in the Atlantic Division, and their 103 points in the standings was tied for fifth in the entire NHL. All this earned head coach Gerard Gallant a nomination for the Jack Adams Award for coach of the year.

The next season began, and their results were mediocre out of the gate. The team wasn't recapturing the magic of the year before and had run into injury trouble as well.

In late November 2016, barely two months into the season, the Panthers fired Gallant. It was an extremely controversial decision at the time. Gallant was fired after a road game in Carolina and pictures had leaked of him out on the curb, in the middle of the night, waiting for a cab to take him to the airport.

Hockey talk on all platforms was on fire. Old school pundits and bloggers were butting heads on Twitter, with some of the older crowd referring to the Panthers as "The Computer Boys" because of their more analytically inclined staff members. Sportsnet analyst and former Panthers coach Doug MacLean was also going at it on Twitter with Doug Cifu, the Panthers vice chairman, partner, and alternate governor. Don Cherry got on "Coach's Corner" and called the firing the worst in the history of the NHL live on *Hockey Night in Canada*.

One thing many people did was ask the question: "What on earth are the Panthers thinking?" There's absolutely nothing wrong with that question, but it bothered me that nobody seemed to be asking the Panthers themselves. I'm not talking about the players, I'm talking about the decision-makers, the guys in charge, the owners.

One afternoon, a silly little idea came to me. I mean, thanks to Doug MacLean, we know Doug Cifu has Twitter, right? Why don't I send him a tweet and see if he could come on the podcast?

On December 1, 2016, I sent this tweet to Doug Cifu's handle, @Dougielarge: "Hello, good sir! What are the odds you would call into my podcast to talk hockey sometime? We usually record Tuesday / Thursday."

The whole thing was basically a gag to get a laugh on Twitter. Hence the "Hello, good sir!" It was just so silly. He's a co-owner of an NHL team and a company CEO. This guy's not gonna answer me.

He responded in less than 20 minutes.

"Our computer boys (tm pending) are calculating the odds . . . looks good . . . DM with details . . . no hockey expert but will try . . ."

Doug Cifu had no idea who I was, let alone anything about my podcast. Maybe he just wanted a platform to vent after Panthers management had been getting torn to shreds all week. I definitely know he did his research and asked around about us, I guess to make sure we weren't going to be total jackasses to him and not let him talk. After a few DMs and some schedule squishing, Doug agreed to be on our show.

December 5, 2016 — that episode is one of my favourites. We had Sportsnet's Chris Johnston on, always one of our favourite guys to talk to, and then Doug called in. Despite his busy schedule, he stayed on the phone with us for 46 minutes.

We started light, poking fun at the fiasco of a week he was having. Adam, of course, was asking about his lengthy career in business because he's always prepared and is just naturally more interested in boring stock talk. But then we really got into the hockey, and what made this story such a controversial one: the human element.

"Did you learn from this, do you think?" I began to ask. "The obvious solution to me: this does not blow up nearly as big as it does without that picture. Without Gerard Gallant outside the arena in Carolina. Was that a learning experience?"

Not a lot of well-established CEOs would be willing to take questions from some shmuck with a podcast about whether or not they learned a lesson from something. To Doug's credit, he answered thoughtfully.

"Absolutely. It was not the way we wanted this to go down, obviously. It looked like we were a dysfunctional organization when quite the opposite is the case. We're very unified and we collaborate, and we talk. There's no politics, and we try to be very collaborative in our decision-making. I felt awful that it embarrassed Gerard. He's an unbelievably talented and very, very decent man. So, look, it was frankly an embarrassment and we have apologized to Gerard, and he, because he's such a mensch, on his own contacted [Elliotte] Friedman and said the whole taxi thing didn't go down that way, it was one hundred percent his decision. Had I been there, would I have managed it differently? Absolutely. I'm more experienced with dealing with crises I guess than other folks are . . . but at the end of the day, it looked terrible, it didn't reflect well on the Florida Panthers, and for that we apologize."

It was a bloody gem of a soundbite. It was so good, in fact, that Jeff Marek and company used it on Sportsnet's *Hockey Central* that night. Elliotte Friedman later cited us in his weekly phenomenon "30 Thoughts" (now "31 Thoughts" because of the Vegas Golden Knights), one of the most popular features in all of hockey. In many ways, having Doug Cifu on our show completely changed the perception of the podcast for a lot of people.

All because we asked.

Now, it's all well and good for me to say, "Ah, just ask people and they'll definitely join your podcast, YouTube channel, or campus radio show," when I've been doing this for over a decade and have some followers. You know what, though? *Just ask* worked earlier in my career, too.

When I wanted to get an internship at the Fan 590, I just asked. When I interviewed the mayor of Oshawa for *Junior Hockey Mag*? I just asked. When Jordan Eberle made that first video with me on my YouTube channel? I just asked. You know when I started getting more subscribers? At some point, I started asking people to subscribe at the end of my videos. Just ask.

The saying "the worst they can say is no" really is true, and I've been told no plenty of times. The whole reason I called the mayor of Oshawa was because nobody else answered their phone that day. Mark Messier has turned me down for different social media posts twice. Man, Sportsnet told me no, and then a few years later, they were the ones who called me.

On a different day, Doug Cifu might have been like, "I'm CEO. I can't be wasting my time with these dumbasses," and just blocked us. But that day maybe he was in a silly mood and thought, *Eh, why not?*

If someone tells you no, put your hand on your chest. Feel that? You're not dead! Congratulations, you've survived. Now you're free to explore all kinds of other possibilities.

One thing I will say, though: at least have some tact when you ask. Allow me to have a "kids these days" moment: a lot of students are pushy as hell on Twitter, and sometimes even email, demanding my time like I owe it to them. How about I'll give you my time when I have time to give, as long as you don't act like you're sticking up a convenience store? What's the saying? You catch more flies with honey.

You'll get what you're looking for or you won't. You'll never know unless you ask.

LOUD
NOISES

A few years ago, an old friend of mine who is now a teacher asked me to talk to her high school class about being a YouTuber. I tried to tell her students what I know, but I ended up learning something from them. I speak there once a year and always play the same game.

"Who here is on Snapchat?"

Almost everybody raises their hand.

"Who here is on Instagram?"

Again, almost everybody put up their hand.

"Alright. Who here remembers MSN Messenger?"

Most faces look confused, except for a few kids who say, *"Oh, yeah."*

One time I asked, "Who here knows what Napster is?"

For those of you who are literally too young to know, Napster is an ancient file-sharing software people used to illegally download music. For the first couple of years that I asked that question, a fair chunk of the class seemed to at least be aware of its existence. Finally, one year I got stone silence except for one student who raised their hand.

"Is that the thing from the Facebook movie?" they asked.

In that moment, I grew a giant grey beard and hundreds of liver spots before fossilizing and turning to dust on the spot.

And guess what? *The Social Network* is nine years old now, so if you saw it in theatres, you're old, too.

In the ancient time of six years ago, kids wanted to be pop stars, movie stars, or TV stars. Now, millions of kids will tell you, "I want to be a YouTuber."

Whether you're talking about YouTubers who discuss science or politics, who stream *Fortnite*, or post makeup tutorials, they all share a common denominator: they're people.

This is something a lot of people forget. Sometimes, pockets of social media can seem like a hellhole, but outside of the anonymity it can provide, I think it's like all other aspects of life: some people are cool and some people suck. Sometimes cool people do sucky things and sometimes sucky people do cool things. Like the real world, whatever that means anymore, people are complex and nuanced.

Take trolls for example.

If you want to talk about using social media to make a living, or, hell, even if you just want to exist as a human being on social media, you're going to have to deal with trolls. I'm on social media pretty much all day, every day, especially during hockey season. I pay more attention to how people act than I'm proud to admit.

Similarly, I make loud and obnoxious videos about the Toronto Maple Leafs, considered by many — hello, Alberta — to be a loud and obnoxious team. It used to be that if you didn't want to see my videos or even know who I was, you didn't have to. Now that I work at Sportsnet, my content gets promoted into Twitter timelines, Facebook newsfeeds, and even TV screens of people who wouldn't mind seeing me take a crosscheck to the teeth.

As someone who gets a lot of flak online, I've noticed that it primarily comes from three distinct groups of people:

People who post anonymously without their picture and/or name.

Dudes who, at an alarmingly high rate, take selfies from a low angle.

Pleasant-looking people with their young children in their photo.

The anonymous jerks are the easiest to dismiss. They're either bored or just straight up crappy people, or both. This is the only way they feel any kind of power. If you ignore them, their power evaporates.

Here's all you need to know about the stoic-looking, low-angle selfie folks: directors shoot characters from a low angle when they want them to look bigger and more imposing. Cat's out of the bag, Brad! Again, it's more of the same. They want to feel better about themselves.

The parents: I've found that the younger the kid in the photo, the nastier the comment. Know why? They have kids. You know what kids do? Cry, scream, and poop their pants. Zero hyperbole. Intermittently, without warning, and often in the middle of the night. They're sleep deprived and pissed off, so they take it out on you. There's a reason angry comments spike on Mondays. Just let them blow off steam, man. Don't sweat it.

And then there's you.

You have stuff to do, like not being a garbage person to strangers. Your life is dope and you do dope shit. Focus on that instead.

"But, Steve, I want to block them."

Ah! I'm glad you brought that up. Generally speaking, you should never block people on Twitter. If you want to create content for a living, then you should *definitely* never block anybody on Twitter.

First of all, a lot of people get off on it. Some people literally write who they're blocked by on their bio. It's like a badge of honour. They hang you on the wall like a stuffed deer head. In a way, you acknowledged them. They got to you, which is what they wanted.

I used to do that — block people who got on my nerves — but I've stopped. Mute jerks instead, so you won't have to see them but they can see you. In fact, I even went back and unblocked a lot of the people I had previously blocked. Why would you deprive someone of seeing you do well? I know, I'm Max Pacio–petty.

Besides, if they cool off, which they often do, they might still click on some of your stuff. And if they still hate your guts — who cares? Have fun yelling at nothing. I'm busy.

Trust me, I know it's easier said than done. I'm trying to get better, too.

Another quick word of Twitter advice: don't lob grenades from bed. Don't try to make a big point or go hard at people while you're lying in bed. Whether you've just woken up or you're trying to go to sleep, don't go blasting your dumbass zombie thoughts to the entire internet when you're in that state. I've made that mistake enough times that I think you can trust me on this one. Try putting the phone down at least 15 minutes before you go to bed and don't pick it up for 15 minutes after you wake up. It's better for your brain, anyway.

But focusing on the bad is easy. Most people online are cool, they just don't get as much attention. If you give it a chance, you can find some fun and interesting things on social media, have enriching conversations, and maybe even make some friends.

While it's often fun and games, there's a certain responsibility that comes with talking online. When you gain a larger platform with some followers, it's tenfold.

One time at a podcast event in London, Ontario, we had hundreds of people show up. Most of the audience were somewhere between 10 years younger than us and 10 years older. But there was one kid who was, well, a kid. His dad brought him.

The moment I met him, I thought, *Man, we swear too much on the podcast.*

Now, we obviously mark the show as explicit for a reason, but kids are going to find the show anyway. That's the reason why I rarely ever curse on my own channel. It used to be because I thought it would hurt my employability. Now it's because I'm worried kids will hear it.

Forget swearing. No matter what you're saying, your words carry weight. Having over 100,000 Twitter followers and thousands of people watching you and listening to you is something that can be used the wrong way. I want to be careful about it.

Sometimes it's hard to even have a hockey conversation on Twitter with this many followers. For example, someone could tweet at me about why they think a certain player isn't great. I'll respond to them with my opinion. Even if I keep it civil, people see I've responded to this in their timeline and then just start ambushing the person I was originally responding to. I'm used to people calling me an idiot, but now this person's freaking out — I was just trying to talk to them about how Josh Leivo deserves a spot in the lineup!

The responsibility that comes with having a large platform wasn't something I considered very much until the past couple of years. Now I'm starting to feel the weight of it. I want to be on the side of the Jedi, not the Sith. It's a work in progress, but I'm trying.

Every time you get on your platform of choice, you can use your powers for good or bad. Choose wisely.

JAKIN

The tale of Jakin Smallwood is one of my favourite things that has ever happened with our podcast. It was also an eerie reminder.

In 2015, Adam Herman of the New York Rangers site *Blueshirt Banter* wrote a list of all the first names from the WHL draft and a lot of them were strange "new" names. For example, there were four kids named Chase.

The next year, another list came out, and we saw Jakin. We were just ripping on the strange new-age first names we hadn't heard of before. Once we released the episode, our listeners tweeted us, asking if we noticed the player's last name. Now that they mentioned it, we had hardly paid attention to the last name. Then I saw it.

I couldn't wait for the next show.

"His name is . . . Jakin Smallwood," I practically yelled.

"His name is *one* letter away from 'Jackin' Smallwood.'"

"I'm surprised you came out and said it," Adam laughed. "I thought you were just going to imply."

"Jackin' Smallwood, Adam!" I screamed back.

A few days later, a girl on Twitter posted a video of this teenager, probably in early high school, eating salad while that very clip from the show played in the background. She was laughing at him, and he was just, you know, eating salad. I looked at her name. Her last name: Smallwood.

Oh my God. The kid in the video is Jakin Smallwood.

We ended up having him on the show and he was a great sport. He even called us between classes. He almost accidentally gave out his phone number before we stopped him.

He told us about his hockey dreams and how he was a draft pick of the WHL's Moose Jaw Warriors. Later, in December 2017, he was traded to the Kootenay Ice. I'll have you know that in the 2017–18 season, he led the Triple A Leduc Oil Kings in scoring, with 43 points in 33 games, thank you very much. The Ice eventually called him up for a game, too. I shot him a text after his first call-up to the WHL to congratulate him.

Luckily, everything turned out fine. Everybody laughed and no feelings were hurt. That was an excellent reminder, though: you never know who's listening, and if you talk about somebody, they might hear it.

I'll promise this right now: if he makes it to the Show, I'm getting a Smallwood jersey.

INFILTRATING SUIT COUNTRY

The second game I went to with my mom was on October 28, 2002: the Leafs were hosting the Anaheim Mighty Ducks. Again, we were given the tickets. Somebody couldn't go, so we got the spoils.

The price on each ticket: $210. Our jaws dropped. The only time I had ever held over $200 in my hand was after my first communion. At this point, I had just started high school and was crazy into rap music. Sure, 50 Cent had fancy cars and enough jewelry to open up a store with Russell Oliver, but to me, this was the most baller experience ever.

We sat fifth row. I never saw people sitting in the fifth row. Whenever I watched the games on TV, the platinum section would be empty. I was always hating on "The Suits." *They're not real fans — not like me.*

Tonight, I was sitting with them.

A uniformed worker from the Air Canada Centre started walking into our section. *Uh oh,* I thought. *They found the riff-raff. Well, Mom, it was a good try, but they have to kick us out now.*

It turns out that it wasn't ACC security but rather ACC seat service. They actually walked over to you, took your order in your seat, then brought it to you. My mom and I were blown away.

These two guys sitting a few seats down from us couldn't

have been a bigger stereotype of a typical "suit" if they tried. Fast-talking, suit-wearing, but no tie because, you know, we're off work now and this is our idea of letting loose.

One of the guys gave one of the servers his credit card and my mom heard him tell her to bring them each a beer every half hour. I never knew her to have a passion for math, but she turned into a certified accountant.

"Wow," she started, before muttering out some mental math. "Two beers, so that's about what? Twenty dollars? How long is the game? Three hours? So that's — oh my God! So this is how the other half lives," she laughed.

To make the experience better, the game was a banger, too. It was definitely worth the price of admission that we didn't even have to pay in the first place.

Alyn McCauley scored on Ducks goalie Martin Gerber just 1:56 into the game, assisted by Robert Reichel and Tie Domi. 1–0, Leafs.

Four seconds after the next faceoff, Domi dropped the gloves with Kevin Sawyer right at centre ice. Pandemonium!

"Oh!" my mom exclaimed at the sight of violence, like a mom.

While they were throwing punches, they slowly drifted over to our side of the ice, right by the blue line. Domi got knocked off balance but managed to get up again before getting the final takedown.

I screamed myself hoarse. I look up at the clock on the Jumbotron, which I could barely see from the fifth row, and there was still 18 minutes left in the first. Just two minutes in and already a goal and a fight!

I couldn't help but notice that the platinums were still kind of empty. You snooze, you lose, suckers! I felt like a secret agent in those seats.

Matt Cullen tied it up for the Ducks before the end of the first, but the Leafs exploded in the second. *Bang!* Nik Antropov bagged his fourth of the season. *Bang!* Alexander Mogilny got his fifth of the season. *Bang!* Captain Mats Sundin scored his sixth of the season, and just like that, it was 4–1, Leafs. You see, kids, back in those days, you usually felt good about the Leafs having a 4–1 lead.

For the first time ever, I saw a goalie get yanked. Head coach Bryan Murray gave Gerber the hook and put in a goalie I was fairly certain I had heard of before, named Jean-Sébastien Giguère.

Steve Ruchhin scored for the Ducks in the third, but Robert Reichel added a shorty for the Leafs with about five minutes left.

"How you like us now, Giguère?" shouted one of the now-thoroughly wasted suits in a bad French accent.

Of course, I was happy the Leafs had won, but I'll always remember how happy my mom was. She had a huge smile on her face.

Moments like that are irreplaceable. Mom sacrificed a lot for my sister and me, as well as my dad. One of those sacrifices was her social life. My dad would go to his band practices, but my mom didn't get out nearly as much. Her thing was just being an amazing mom.

Plus, the Leafs were now undefeated in two games with my mom there. That helped, too.

MY FIRST GAME

Ken Reid is one of my favourite guests we've ever had on the podcast. He's an anchor on Sportsnet and an East Coaster through and through. When he came on the podcast, he spoke about his high school in Pictou, Nova Scotia, and specifically his gym teacher Mr. Jankov, who would shout, "Outta here, boy!" whenever he kicked a student out of his class.

Ken was promoting his book *One Night Only* about players who managed to play only a single NHL game. Because Ken was such a riot, I think he sold a lot of books that day. In many ways, Ken is responsible for putting me on the radar of ECW Press, the publisher of this book.

Ken is also responsible for the first full-equipment hockey game I ever played.

One day, Ken texted me and asked if I wanted to join his hockey team for the Celebrity Hockey Classic Series, a series of charity hockey tournaments. Different NHL alumni were in charge of different tournaments, and it just so happened that the one Ken wanted me to play in was led by none other than Eric Lindros.

There's just one small problem: I can't play hockey. At least, I had never played before. I could barely skate and I definitely didn't know how to stop.

"So?" Ken replied.

He explained that at least one other member of our team was just learning how to skate himself. The point of the tournament wasn't to turn heads in the scouting department, it was to raise money for charity. Not just any charity, either. It was for Easter Seals, a charity for children with physical disabilities.

Not only is Easter Seals a great cause, but it's one that helped my family directly. It was difficult for all four of us — both of my parents, my sister, and I — to get out of the house together at the same time. Usually just the park and McDonald's. Easter Seals holds summer camps designed to enrich the lives of kids with physical disabilities, like my sister, and their families. They provided a fun experience that we all still remember and look back on fondly. Easter Seals also provided funding for leg braces and a walker for my sister.

Not to mention, the tournament was scheduled to be in Whitby, just a 15-minute drive away for me.

Steve, what's the issue here? You can't play hockey? Well, Ken said you don't have to know how. Plus, it's down the street and it's for charity. You've always wanted to finally play a game. What are you waiting for?

Had it not been for Easter Seals, I might have chickened out. But it was finally time. At 29 years old, after a decade of talking hockey for a living, I was finally going to play in my first full-equipment hockey game.

In the week before the big day, we got our schedules. Our team was scheduled to play at eight, 11, and one. Now, I've only played shinny a couple of times, and from those experiences, I know that sometimes ice is only available really late. *Wow, we have a 1 a.m. game?* I thought. *Ah, whatever. It's for charity!*

The night before the tournament, there was a draft party not far from my home, in Oshawa. Every team in the tournament was there and there were about two dozen NHL alumni in attendance, as well.

Ken introduced me to some of our teammates, including Dennis Maruk. If you've never heard of Dennis, that's part of the reason why Ken helped him write the book *Dennis Maruk: The Unforgettable Story of Hockey's Forgotten 60-Goal Man*. Maruk is one of just 20 players to ever score 60 goals in a season. The only problem is that he accomplished this feat during the 1981–82 NHL season, the year Wayne Gretzky scored 92, the still-standing record. In fact, Maruk finished *third* in goal-scoring that season because Mike Bossy scored 64.

Each team got to pick one NHL alumni to play on their team with them. The draft party was set up so that whichever team raised the most money got the first pick, the second-place team got the second pick, and so on. We had already made up our mind that we were picking Dennis, no matter what.

At one point, Eric Lindros was invited to say a few words to everybody. The more he spoke about Easter Seals, the amount of money we raised, and how much kids are going to benefit as a result, the more you could tell how much the tournament's success meant to him. He was genuine. Anybody can smile and take a few pictures, but a true superstar uses their platform and takes action with pride.

I snapped out of my Eric Lindros love fog when I overheard my teammates talking about the next morning. I wanted to hear what their plans were; maybe there was a team breakfast I hadn't heard about or something.

They thought I was kidding at first until one of them asked, "Wait, do you think all our games are tomorrow night?"

As it turns out, they don't hold hockey tournaments for children's charities at one in the morning. What was I thinking? That meant our first game was at 8 a.m., in about 10 hours.

It was hilarious but now my whole work schedule was shot. The Leafs were playing in L.A. that night, a 10 p.m. eastern start. I also had an article to write and was supposed to submit a short video to use on TV the next night.

I rushed home and told my wife. She just laughed because, believe it or not, this isn't the first time she's had to help me out because I'm an idiot.

The plan was to turn on the game, write the article at the same time, and make the LFR video afterward. The TV hit just wasn't going to happen.

The Leafs got slaughtered that night. They beat the Ducks 3–1 the night before, but on the second half of a back-to-back, poor Curtis McElhinney was getting shelled in net and the Kings were up 3–0 after one. At one point in the second period, they were up 5–0. You might remember that as the night Auston Matthews was awarded two penalty shots in the same game. The Leafs made it interesting at the end, but they still lost.

There was one other problem. I took a look at the equipment my friend had loaned me for the game. I realized that since I had never worn equipment before, I wasn't even sure how to put it on properly. Mrs. Dangle came through with the clutch YouTube tutorials. Hey, gotta start somewhere, right?

I finished my work around 4 a.m., slept for maybe two hours, then got up for the big day.

When I entered our team's locker room, there was a name-plate with "Steve Glynn" on it. They gave me a green jersey with white and black stripes and it even had my number 10 on the back. I tried to hide how much I was geeking out, but I failed miserably. I had been waiting for this moment for years.

I sat near Brendan Dunlop, a friend and Sportsnet anchor, who was basically my hockey dad for the day. I told him about my equipment tutorials from the night before. The tip he gave me: bottoms first.

We suited up and got on the ice for warm-up. As I skated around, I could already tell how much better everyone on the team was, but I gave them a heads-up of the grocery stick Ken had recruited for their team.

"No cage?" someone asked. Maybe it was because I didn't want to look like even more of a rookie than I already was, but my helmet didn't have a cage or visor.

"Dude, the face," they said. "You're on television."

I thought they were just joking until someone took a high

wrist shot that whizzed by my head. As soon I could, I rushed out and got a cage screwed on. Nick Kypreos can wear a hockey scar with pride because he earned it for being a tough guy, whereas I would've gotten mine because I'm a stooge.

It was for the best, too. Our first opponent's alumnus player was Al Iafrate.

In our first game, the other team quickly realized I was a bum and took it easy on me. That didn't stop me from being a minus two on my first shift, falling twice, then tripping over the bench. We got caved in 8–2 in our first game. It was awesome.

"Stumpy" Steve Thomas was our next team's alumnus. Maybe he rubbed off on them because they were a bit rougher. One of the other team's guys was clearly playing for a contract and beaking at our bench. Conveniently, one of our guys showed up in a bad mood because he missed the first game. One thing led to another and there was almost a full-on line brawl.

I'm watching from the bench like, *Please have mercy; I'm just a brittle, little child.*

To recap, our designated enforcer missed the first game, got kicked out of the second game, and was banned from the third game. At a charity hockey tournament. If you wrote that into the script for *Goon 3*, they'd be like, "Come on. No one's *that* crazy."

Game two was an improvement for me. Not only did I manage to not fall down, but I also completed a pass to Dennis Maruk . . . 's skates. We lost that one, too.

The third game was a lot more even. On one shift, I shadowed former Leafs captain Rick Vaive, meaning I briefly casted a shadow on him while he blew by me. The guys even insisted I take a few faceoffs. I even managed to win a few. Thank goodness, because if I had lost them, it's not like I could get the puck back.

After the third game, we all went back to the locker room. Compared to the rest of my teammates, I was fresh as a daisy. You don't sweat that much when you barely know how to move around on skates. We stunk, but we had had fun and raised a lot of money, which was the reason we were there in the first place.

Someone from Easter Seals walked in the room.

"Is there a Steve Glynn here?"

She handed me a big white wooden stick with Eric Lindros's autograph on it. Apparently I was my team's top fundraiser, which meant I got to play in the all-star game. Good thing I'm still fresh!

Instead of one alumnus per side, the teams were divided evenly between alumni and regular Joes. Now I could humiliate myself in front of even more of the people I grew up watching!

As soon as I walked into the locker room, there he was: Eric Lindros. The Big E. The guy from the cover of *NHL 99*.

There were some other guys on our team: Lindros's "Legion of Doom" linemate from the Flyers John LeClair, Wayne Primeau, and Ric Nattress, just to name a few. Dennis Maruk was even on my team again. He must have been excited to see me, too, a walking, talking minus sign.

I told everybody who would listen that this was my first day playing hockey. They couldn't have cared less. Their days of playing for a deal are over. They just want to have some fun and help out the kids.

When we got on the ice for warm-up, it was obvious that things were different for this game. There were spectators watching in the stands and there was a red carpet on the ice. All the alumni were wearing the jersey of the NHL team they had played for the most. I looked over at the other team: Leafs jersey, Leafs jersey, there's another Leafs jersey, and another. Oh my God, we're just playing against Leafs alumni.

So on my first day ever playing hockey, I got to play with Eric Lindros against the Leafs.

We all lined up on the blue lines for the anthem. Lindros said a few words. Players wheeled kids from Easter Seals onto the ice for the ceremonial puck drop. They weren't messing around.

The alumni pretty much let common scum like me do whatever we wanted, but they turned on the jets when they were one-on-one with other alumni. I couldn't help but stare in awe at what these guys could do. Months after the tournament, I found a picture on the Easter Seals Ontario website, and if you look closely enough in the background, you can see me picking my nose on the bench. That was the biggest contribution I made to my team.

Lindros and LeClair got a clear two-man breakaway. LeClair, over to Lindros, who buried it. The Legion of Doom hadn't even lost a step. When they got back to the bench, Lindros leaned over and yelled to LeClair, "I missed you!"

My biggest on-ice contribution was a blocked shot, I think it was by Gary Leeman, and I even kind of meant to do it! He even congratulated me. Nik Antropov wasn't trying to make friends, though; he dangled my jock off.

At one point, I got the puck in the offensive zone. Everyone backed off and told me to shoot. I looked around and ended up passing it. They were all just being nice, but I had never scored a goal before, and I didn't want my first one handed to me. I don't care who I'm playing with or against, I want to get better and actually earn my first goal. Is that dumb? Am I nuts?

After the game, we lined up, shook hands, and hit the showers.

Like I've said, I didn't grow up playing hockey. That means I never really grew up in locker rooms, either. To this day, they make me kind of uncomfortable. I don't even like public bathrooms because *blech*.

NHL players are the polar opposite of that.

These guys throw off their clothes with a single flick of the wrist. They've been doing this their entire life. Practice? Locker room before and after. Morning skate? Locker room before and after. Game day? Locker room before and after, not to mention guys like Patrick Marleau who dive into an ice bath at intermission. Professional hockey players spend half their life just getting changed.

I don't know when it happens but at some point, older dudes just stay naked. I think it starts after your 48th birthday, but that's just a guess. *Who's got time for a towel? Not me, I'm old, get out of the way.*

So now I'm in a room with my idols, who are naked, and I'm trying my best to cope. There's just a lot going on. Eyes to the floor. Eyes to the ceiling. *Please, Lord, I need to see zero percent of this.* At the same time, these guys I grew up watching are trying to make friendly banter and I'm trying to listen. I just played hockey with them for like 45 minutes.

The locker room started to clear out. It took me longer than everyone else to get my equipment off and shove it into the bag because I had no idea what I was doing. Plus screw showering here, dude. I live 15 minutes away; I'll shower at home. I know a lot of you are judging me right now and I don't care because shut up, my bathroom has a lock on it.

I realized that one of the half-dozen or so people left in the room is Lindros. Throughout the festivities of the tournament, I still hadn't introduced myself or anything. I didn't want to bother him or ask him for something like an interview or podcast appearance. I just wanted to let him know I thought what he did with this tournament was awesome, I could tell it meant a lot to him, and thank him for helping to organize such a great event.

Only problem is, for some reason, this guy's still stark naked. No towel, nothing. But it's OK, that's fine, he's going to get dressed eventually, right? I just made small talk with a few of the other guys on the team. Dennis Maruk was still there and I spoke with Ric Nattress, too.

After like five minutes, this guy was still naked.

Alright. I don't want to just stand here like a creep. I gotta leave. But I also want my little moment with Lindros. The scenario I came up with in my head is that I would walk over to him to introduce myself, he would realize he had no clothes on, quickly grab a towel, and we'd shake hands.

I walk over to him. There he is. We make eye contact. I extend my hand for a handshake. He grabbed my hand back.

And just stood up.

Now I'm shaking hands with a butt-naked Eric Lindros. This, uh . . . was not a moment that I saw coming in my life.

I told him how much I appreciated the tournament and how much he helped with the charity. He thanked me for coming out. I'm just staring him dead in the face because there's no way I'm looking anywhere else right now.

Then we said our polite goodbyes, and I left.

I'm walking out of the arena like, *Did that seriously just happen?* Then I drove home and had a shower. I know, shut up.

I stunk on ice that day — literally — but it was for a good cause. Between all the teams at the tournament, we helped raise over $325,000 for Easter Seals. That was the whole point of it all. It felt amazing to help pay back a charity that did right by my family all those years ago.

And that's the story of my first hockey game.

I should mention that the next fall, in 2018, I played in the tournament again. This time, Ken made me captain because I was the top fundraiser my first time around. I wrangled a bunch of the players we had previously and I also recruited over a dozen of my friends and family. We ended up signing up 30 players, enough for two full teams.

We called ourselves Rachel's Raiders, in honour of my sister. Our alumni were Steve Thomas, the player I saw fight Darcy Tucker in my last ever game at Maple Leaf Gardens, and cantankerous Hockey Hall of Fame goalie Billy Smith.

I still stunk on ice but I had learned how to stop on both my left and right, and I could pull off something that resembled a crossover. I'm not quite Mitch Marner level, but I'm working on it.

Between our two teams, we raised over $55,000 for Easter Seals, while every team in the tournament combined to raise nearly half a million. We did a tremendous amount of good for people who need it, and to me that feels much better than scoring a goal. At least, I assume so, I still haven't scored.

Oh, and the next time I met Lindros, he had his clothes on.

INTERMISSION

When I got back from summer break in 2015, I found out they were going to discontinue the sheet. I thought I might get laid off again, but thankfully, things were different this time.

Dan kept me under the digital budget instead of the radio side. The plan was for me to keep making videos and doing my podcast, which remained independently owned. Added to that, however, I wrote articles for Sportsnet.ca, made videos for the Sportsnet YouTube channel, and there were TV hits once or twice per week.

At long last, my sole job was to be a hockey blogger. Full time. This is what I had dreamed about when I decided to make a video after every Leafs game. I'm literally living the dream. As Sportsnet's own Chris Johnston puts it, we work at the toy store.

It's difficult to write about Sportsnet because I still work there and don't really have much hindsight. I do have some favourite memories already, though.

Someone who has had a strong influence on me is Mike Cormack, the managing editor of all things digital on Sportsnet. He's one of the smartest, most creative people I've ever worked with. He has the unique ability to mask criticism as ideas to get better. With Mike, it's never about how it's "bad," it's about how it could be better.

If you create content of any kind, whether it's for a living or a hobby, it's easy to become protective of it. I'm always excited to tell Mike about an idea I have because if he likes it, then it's good and if he doesn't like it, he knows how to make it better.

Mike has helped me develop several written series that have done extremely well, including my "Trade Tree" articles. It began with an article where I traced back the ripple effect of the trade where the Leafs sent defender Anton Stralman to the Calgary Flames. That article did so well that we made "Trade Trees" a regular feature.

Rather than just take clips from videos I had already made, the powers that be at Sportsnet gave me the opportunity to make 90-second videos for TV, specifically *Hockey Central*, and sometimes Leafs pregame shows. My favourite one to date was after the Leafs traded Peter Holland to Arizona about a week before he came to town with the Coyotes. My video was about my Leafs paranoia, wondering how Holland was going to find a way to beat the Leafs in his return. Sure enough, Holland scored the shootout winner. They talked about the video again after the game. Like, come on. What are the odds? Well, any Leaf fans will tell you, voodoo, wizardry, and bullshit are always possibilities when it comes to the blue and white.

The Leafs trading Phil Kessel to Pittsburgh was another big day. I made a nine-minute rant about how the Leafs completely pissed away Kessel, who, in his prime, was one of the best goal scorers they've ever had. On top of losing my mind, I also spoke about how the Pittsburgh Penguins' window to win was now and that they're "on the frickin' clock." They followed that up with back-to-back Cups and now Phil Kessel is a two-time Stanley Cup champion.

Speaking of which, I met Sidney Crosby and got him to say that on camera. Also, I've met Sidney freaking Crosby. I was at G Camp, a camp put on by Gatorade for young hockey players who have been through a lot and have amazing stories. Max Pacioretty was there, Johnny Gaudreau, noted Toronto Maple Leaf John

Tavares, Marie-Philip Poulin, Hayley Wickenheiser, P.K. Subban, Dominic Moore, Brent Burns — everybody. But Sid is Sid.

When the day began, I asked for time with Crosby and was given no promises. Around midday, I was told I could have three minutes. I told them I needed 30 seconds.

I went up to Sid and asked him to say, "Phil Kessel is a Stanley Cup champion." That was it. They didn't believe me when I told them 30 seconds; it was actually less. As a result, my Sportsnet coworker, reporter Luke Fox, who was taking the video on my phone, got a one-on-one sit-down with Sid for the remaining two-and-a-half minutes.

One of the first videos I ever made with Sportsnet was with Luke. We went to the ACC, now Scotiabank Arena, to try all their new fancy concession food. Luke came up with the brilliant grading system of Shana-hams.

Speaking of Brendan Shanahan, I got to go to Leafs media day for a feature in 2016. While I was getting my close-up with all the fancy cameras they had, I heard someone yell, "Dangle!" It was Brendan Shanahan.

"You want to get in on this?" I yelled back.

"Yeah, uh, no, I'm busy," he said sarcastically, without even looking or breaking stride.

Someone who knew me all the way back from when I worked at Leafs TV must have been keeping me in mind because when the Leafs unexpectedly made the 2017 playoffs, they asked me to co-host the tailgate parties in Maple Leaf Square for the home games. It was awesome getting on stage in front of all those screaming Leafs fans. I remembered when I wanted to cry in Maple Leaf Square after getting let go by Leafs TV, and now there I was, a lot closer to fainting than crying. And the DJ on stage? None other than DJ Dockta, the DJ I had spent many nights with in the Real Sports DJ booth while hosting the MapleLeafs.com chats. Have I mentioned the world is small?

Speaking of the Leafs unexpectedly making the playoffs, I was in the CBC building when the Leafs won the 2016 NHL draft lottery and, therefore, Auston Matthews. "The Leafs won a thing!" I even got to pose with the number one card that Shanahan held.

Brendan Shanahan played at the alumni game at the Centennial Classic in 2017. While he was unfortunately on the Detroit Red Wings alumni team, somebody else was not: Felix Potvin.

After the alumni game, I got to go into the locker room to interview him. It was a very surreal moment. The interview wasn't long or in-depth. I wasn't going to be winning an Edward R. Murrow award, that's for sure. But there he was: Felix Potvin. He was one of the reasons I fell in love with hockey in the first place, and here I was covering hockey for a living and talking to him.

Speaking of goalies I adore, I got to speak with James Reimer over the phone after his rookie season and after his first AHL game. But, finally, during the 2016–17 season, I got to formally meet him. He was fully aware of my unhealthy obsession with him, but for some reason he didn't run. Unfortunately, he was now on the Florida Panthers. Still, we had a great talk and he was a good sport. He even wore the little plastic Optimus Prime mask I brought in for him as a prop.

As for the podcast, it is everything I could ever hope for and more. Every time we do the show, I step in there with two of my brothers. Shut up, I know it's corny, just let me be emotional, alright!

Adam and Jesse have the ability to make me gut laugh until my invisible abs hurt. They're witty, they're insightful, they're original, and they're creative. People always tell us that the show just sounds like three friends talking. That's because it is.

Some of my favourite podcast guests include former Leafs goalie Ben Scrivens, who talked about his wacky 2015–16 season with the Oilers and Canadiens; Ken Reid, who is one of the best storytellers in the country, but then again so are the likes of Elliotte Friedman and Jeff Marek; everyone we've had from Sportsnet has been great; Sasky Stewart, the first lady of Australian Ice Hockey, who can spin a good yarn; Steve Simmons, who was one of our first guests and, while we often disagree, I'll always respect him for even coming on — in Adam's mom's basement, no less. Honestly, I could list every guest we've ever had.

But how do you top Ron MacLean? I mean, come on.

He held court for one hour and 41 minutes. The conversation went from hockey, to obscure professional wrestling, to music, politics, shirtless air guitar, and opening packs of hockey cards.

And lastly, we have had the true privilege and good fortune of meeting so many listeners, whether they were locals, had driven in from Ottawa or Pennsylvania, or flown in from Florida or Texas. We had a simple idea: get together, eat pizza, watch hockey. A lot of Canadians just call that Saturday, but we christened it Hockey Night in Cinema. Our podcast listeners would pack into a theatre, free of charge, Panago would provide free deliciousness, and we would watch *Hockey Night in Canada* up on the big screen.

Listeners of the podcast packed the house four times: twice in Toronto, once in Ottawa, and once in London, Ontario. We got to witness Mitch Marner score his first career NHL goal, saw Frederik Andersen pick up his first ever Leafs win, and watched the legend of Curtis McElhinney come to life.

One day on the podcast, Adam and Jesse were talking about what fans of certain celebrities call themselves. For example, fans of Beyoncé are called the Beyhive. Jesse discovered that fans of Rihanna called themselves the Rihanna Navy because she was in the movie *Battleship*. I said that was the dumbest thing ever, so, naturally, Adam and Jesse loved it and suggested listeners of the podcast be called the Dangle Navy.

For whatever reason, listeners loved it and immediately started using it and hashtagging it. Once, at a Marlies game, we dedicated a section of the stands for our listeners. Several people showed up with Dangle Navy signs and one person even came in a full sailor's outfit. I'm sure my grandpa is proud.

My life has been a whirlwind, and I'm more than grateful

for it. Hell, I was at a Leafs playoff game in 2018 and Auston Matthews's parents came up to *me* and asked for a picture. These two were acting like they weren't the two blessed godsends who gave birth to the saviour of a franchise. How does one even process that?

A few months into the 2018–19 NHL season, and my role at Sportsnet has evolved. I'm still making videos and I'm working the social media desk for Sportsnet's "Ice Surfing" broadcasts. The broadcasts are live-streamed on Twitter once a week, from a studio in the CBC building. We flip from game to game around the NHL, talking about all the action. Who's we? Stan Nieradka is our stats man. Jason York, who played in 757 NHL games, is our analyst. And our host? None other than Jeff Marek. Doesn't get much more full circle than that; I even run a knockoff version of the "iDesk."

All this, thanks to a girl who got me a $77 webcam for $23.

As I write this chapter, I'm 30 years old. I don't know what will happen next. I also know that I'm not done yet. Just don't ask me where I see myself in five years.

Hopefully my story can convince you to try something you've been afraid to try for too long — maybe learn a new skill, change career paths, or win a Stanley Cup ring.

Listen, I've believed in the Toronto Maple Leafs for my entire life. The least you could do is believe in yourself.

ACKNOWLEDGEMENTS

Let me start by saying that writing a book is really hard. So thank you for choosing to read this book, because if nobody did after all the effort it took, I'd be pretty sad.

Thank you to the incredible team at ECW Press, not to be confused with the former wrestling company of a similar name that was famous for barbed wire and tables on fire. Thank you to Michael Holmes, who held my hand throughout this process and made writing this book possible, and to my editor, Laura Pastore, for making it seem like I know English. Thanks to Jessica Albert and Jen Squires for making a beautiful cover, despite the use of my picture. Thank you to Devon Shea and the team for making the audiobook a reality without crosschecking me in the teeth. Thank you to Susannah Ames, Emily Ferko, David Caron, and the ECW marketing team for helping me hock this book. And thank you to Brian Wood, my and Ken Reid's literary agent — and everyone else's, I think.

Speaking of Ken, this book wouldn't have happened without him. He came on the podcast, told some stories about his teacher Mr. Jankov, and rambled on about one of his many books. I told him I'd love to write a book of my own one day, and with typical Nova Scotian generosity, he set the wheels in motion.

Thank you to Jeff Marek for writing the foreword, with an assist from Colby Armstrong. In Grade 10, when I called in to your show after another Leafs playoff heartbreak, I couldn't have imagined being your co-worker, never mind you waxing poetically about me in a book. You've come a long way, iDesk guy.

Thank you to Dave Cadeau, Don Kollins, and Jason Rozon for giving me a shot at Sportsnet, and to Dan Tavares, Mike Cormack, and the entire Sportsnet team. Thanks for tolerating my nonsense, late night emails, and occasional screaming fits on national television.

Thank you to the Toronto Maple Leafs. Special shout out to Felix Potvin and James Reimer for getting me through the bad times and to Brendan Shanahan for helping to usher in new good times with the Shanaplan. Shut up — it's my book and I'll thank whoever I want! Also, John Tavares is a Leaf.

Thank you to the incredible men and women who taught me throughout my schooling. Thanks for making my education a fun and diverse one. I consider myself lucky to have been your student. Sorry for being a little shit.

Thank you to the Dangle Navy, who, for whatever reason, embrace that name because you're weird. I'm glad we can be weird together. Thank you for embracing the silly idea that sports should be fun. Your support throughout the years never ceases to amaze me. Adam, Jesse, and I know how lucky we are to be a part of your life.

Thank you to all my friends. Surprisingly, there are too many to name. Thanks for taking me under your wing. I promise to shut up about the book now (if you bought one).

A special thank you is owed to Adam Wylde, Jesse Blake, and Chris Shapcotte. The podcast is an important outlet for me and less expensive than therapy. I'd be lost without it. I'm proud of what we've built and are continuing to build. And thank you to Panago Pizza for believing in us, as well as stuffing our faces with deliciousness.

To my extended family: thank you for your love and support and for helping to instill a love of hockey in me. It takes a village, and I'm fortunate to be in yours.

Thank you to my parents, Tina and Gary. You've given me such a great life. Thanks for reading to me when I was a kid and not kicking me out of the house when I told you I wanted to become a professional video blogger. Thank you to my sister, Rachel, for all the laughter and music and the constant reminder that many problems can be solved with a hug.

Thanks to our Victory Puppies, Iggy and Charlie, for the company. *Good boys*.

And lastly, thank you to my unbelievable wife, Sarah-Louise. There's nothing I could say that would even come close to thanking you enough. Whether you're holding my hand through a challenge or dragging me kicking and screaming, you're always there. With you, nothing is impossible. I love you.

Steve "Dangle" Glynn is a lifelong Leafs fan who began making YouTube videos about his favourite team when he was still a teen. Now he gets to work at Sportsnet for a living. Steve and his wife have two wonderful dogs; they live together in Oshawa, Ontario.